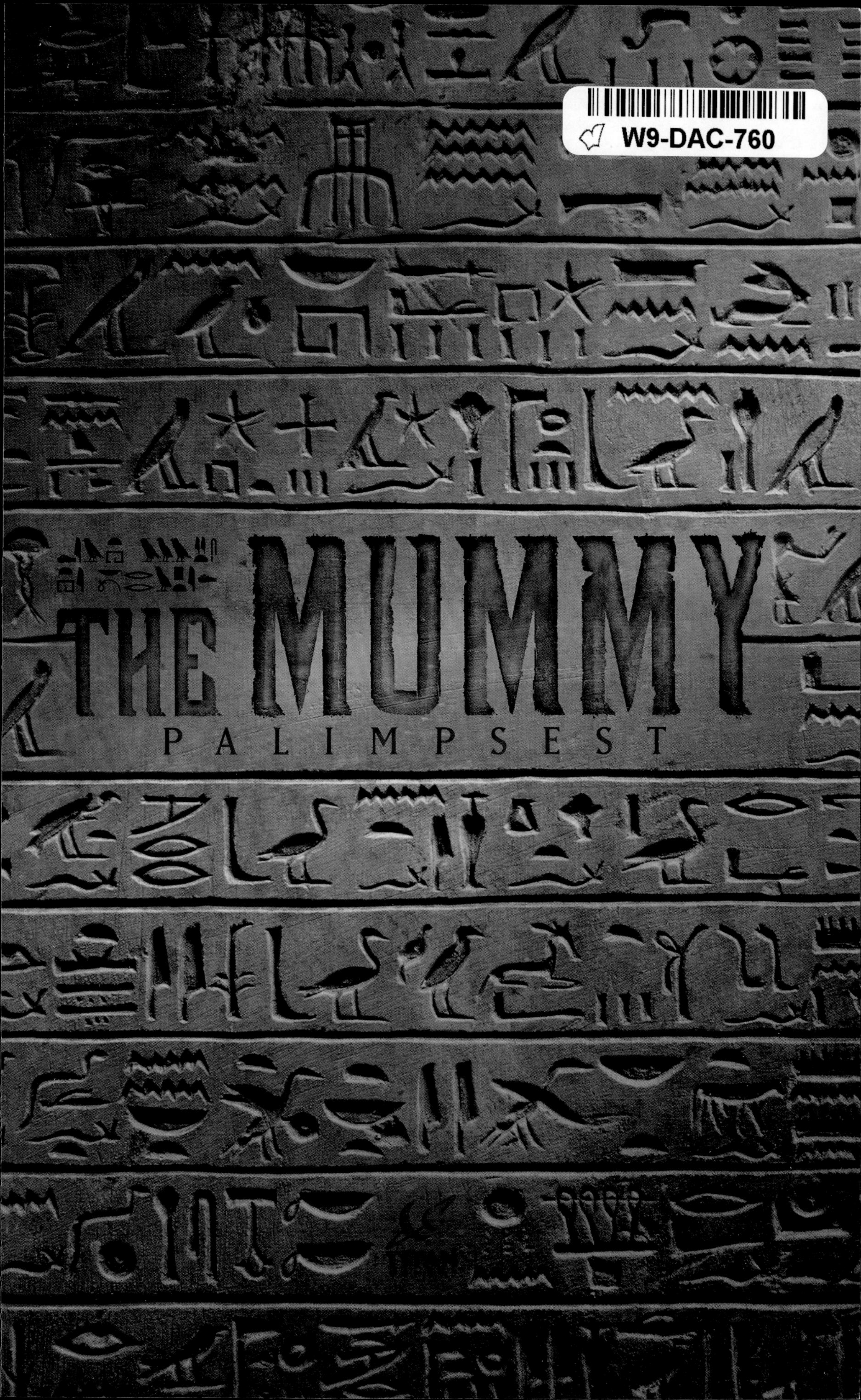
W9-DAC-760
THE MUMMY
PALIMPSEST

THE MUMMY: PALIMPSEST

TITAN COMICS
Editor David Leach
Senior Designer Andrew Leung

Senior Editor Martin Eden
Art Director Oz Browne
Senior Production Controller Jackie Flook
Production Controller Peter James
Production Supervisor Maria Pearson
Senior Sales Manager Steve Tothill
Press Officer Will O'mullane
Brand Manager Chris Thompson
Marketing Manager Ricky Claydon
Advertising Manager Michelle Fairlamb
Head Of Rights Jenny Boyce
Publishing Manager Darryl Tothill
Publishing Director Chris Teather
Operations Director Leigh Baulch
Executive Director Vivian Cheung
Publisher Nick Landau

HAMMER COMICS
Joint Chief Executive Officer Simon Oakes
Joint Chief Executive Officer Marc Schipper
Head Of Development Aliza James
Creative Executive Shanna Martens
Comic Editor David Girvan

ISBN: 9781785859786

Published by Titan Comics
A division of Titan Publishing Group Ltd.
144 Southwark St.
London, SE1 0UP

A CIP catalogue record for this title is available from the British Library

First edition: August 2017

10 9 8 7 6 5 4 3 2 1

Printed in China.

Special Thanks to
Andre Siregar, Paulo Teles and the folks at Hammer

WWW.TITAN-COMICS.COM

Become a fan on Facebook.com/comicstitan Follow us on Twitter @comicstitan
For information on advertising, contact adinfo@titanemail.com or call +44 20 7620 0200
For rights information, contact jenny.boyce@titanemail.com

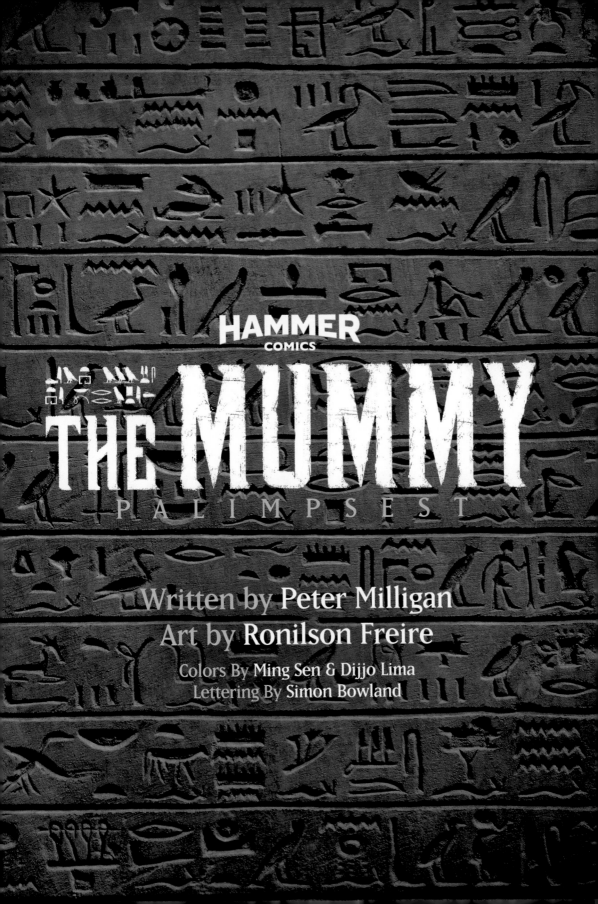

HAMMER COMICS

THE MUMMY
PALIMPSEST

Written by **Peter Milligan**
Art by **Ronilson Freire**

Colors By Ming Sen & Dijjo Lima
Lettering By Simon Bowland

PART I

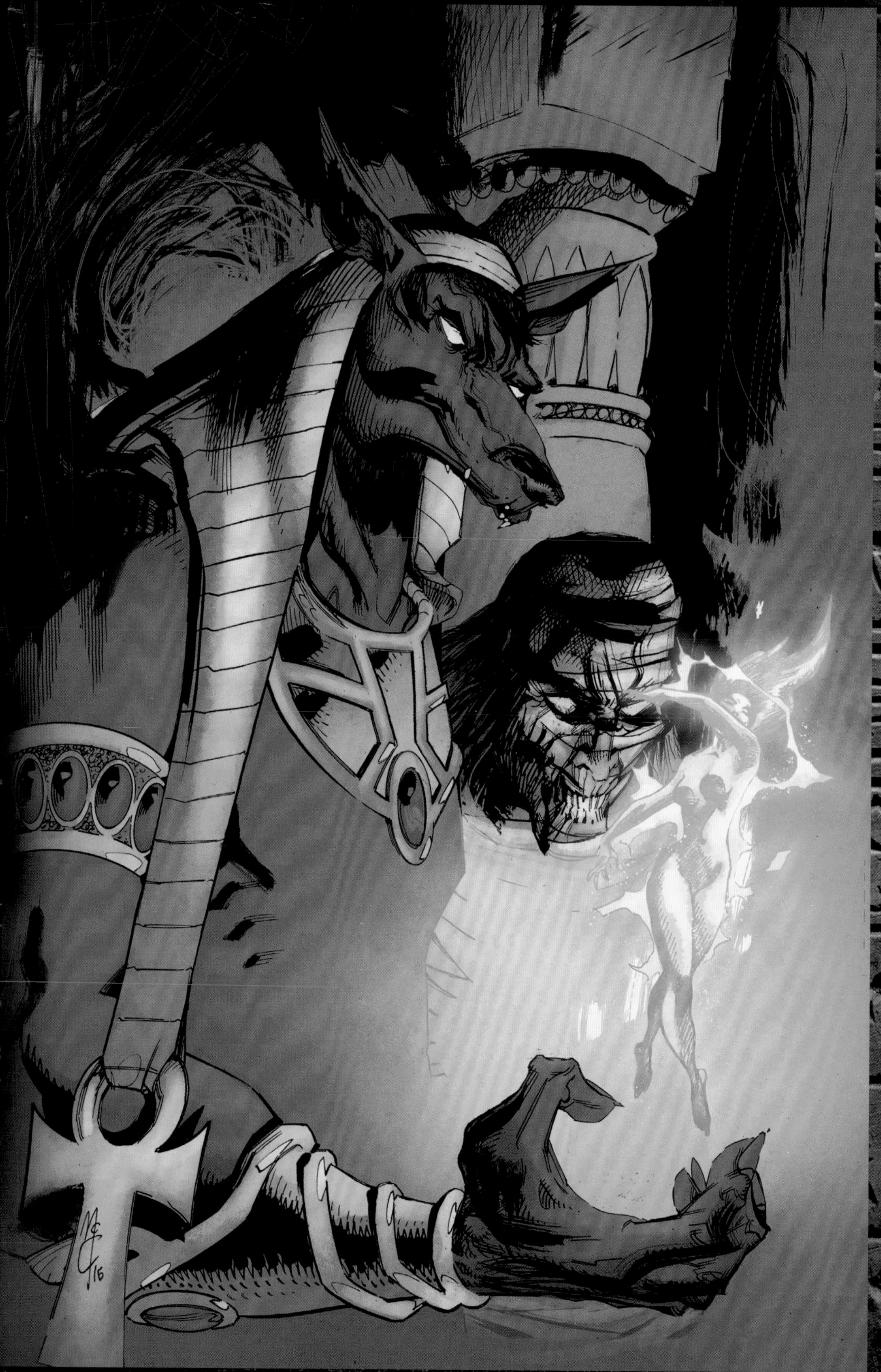

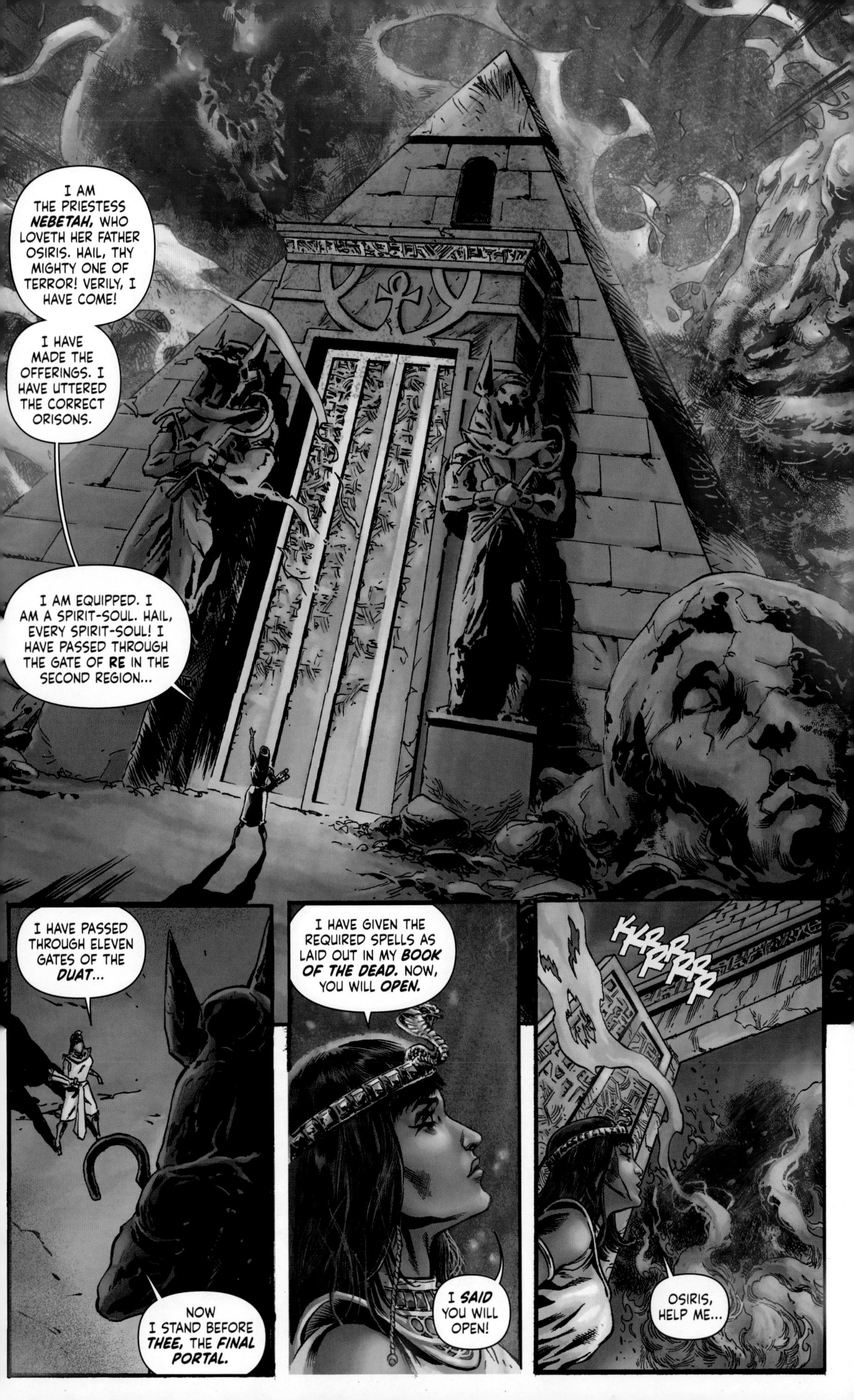

I AM THE PRIESTESS NEBETAH, WHO LOVETH HER FATHER OSIRIS. HAIL, THY MIGHTY ONE OF TERROR! VERILY, I HAVE COME!
I HAVE MADE THE OFFERINGS. I HAVE UTTERED THE CORRECT ORISONS.
I AM EQUIPPED. I AM A SPIRIT-SOUL. HAIL, EVERY SPIRIT-SOUL! I HAVE PASSED THROUGH THE GATE OF RE IN THE SECOND REGION...
I HAVE PASSED THROUGH ELEVEN GATES OF THE DUAT...
NOW I STAND BEFORE THEE, THE FINAL PORTAL.
I HAVE GIVEN THE REQUIRED SPELLS AS LAID OUT IN MY BOOK OF THE DEAD. NOW, YOU WILL OPEN.
I SAID YOU WILL OPEN!
KKRRRRRRR
OSIRIS, HELP ME...

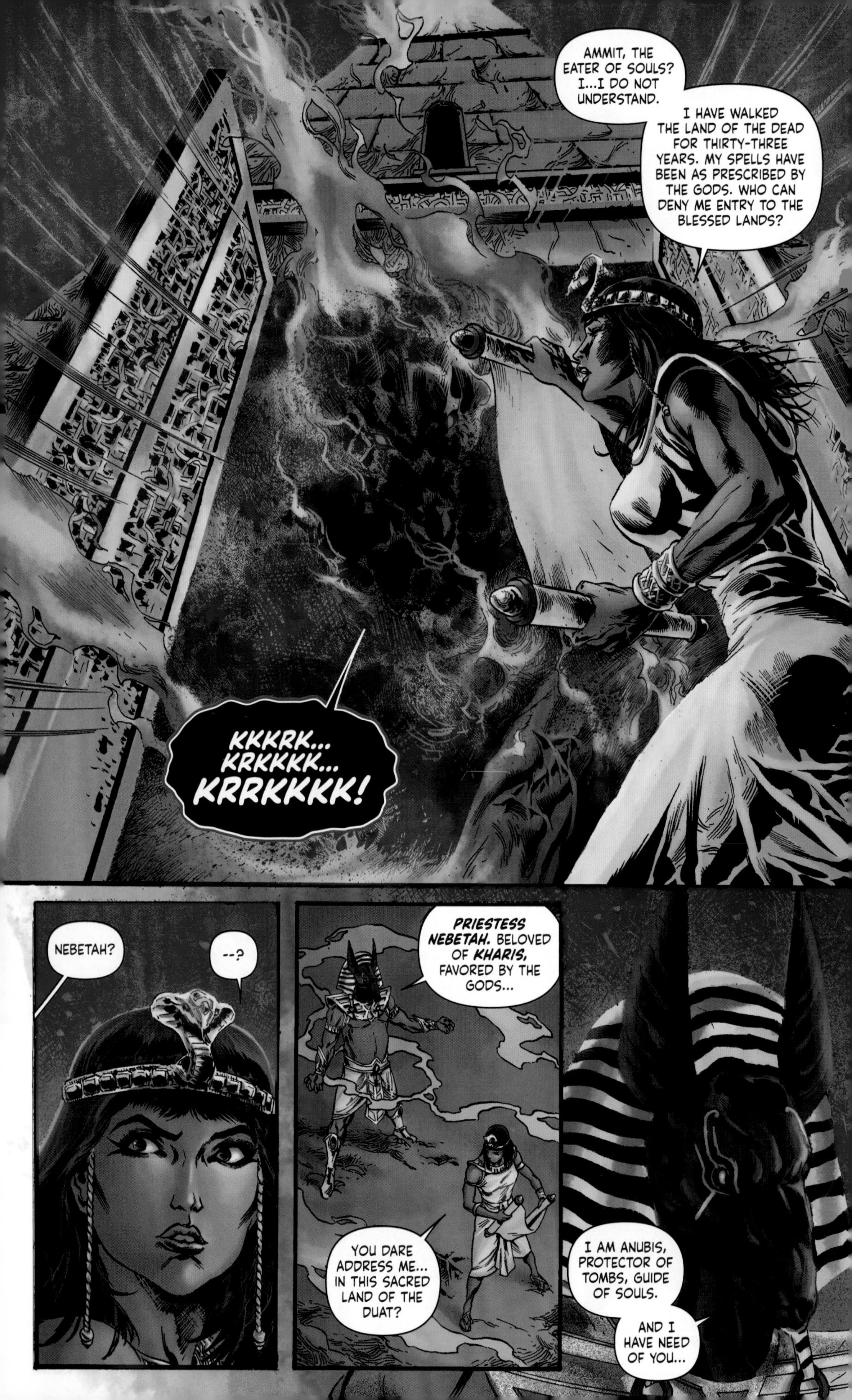

AMMIT, THE EATER OF SOULS? I...I DO NOT UNDERSTAND.
I HAVE WALKED THE LAND OF THE DEAD FOR THIRTY-THREE YEARS. MY SPELLS HAVE BEEN AS PRESCRIBED BY THE GODS. WHO CAN DENY ME ENTRY TO THE BLESSED LANDS?
KKKRK... KRKKKK... KRRKKKK!
NEBETAH?
--?
PRIESTESS NEBETAH. BELOVED OF KHARIS, FAVORED BY THE GODS...
YOU DARE ADDRESS ME... IN THIS SACRED LAND OF THE DUAT?
I AM ANUBIS, PROTECTOR OF TOMBS, GUIDE OF SOULS.
AND I HAVE NEED OF YOU...

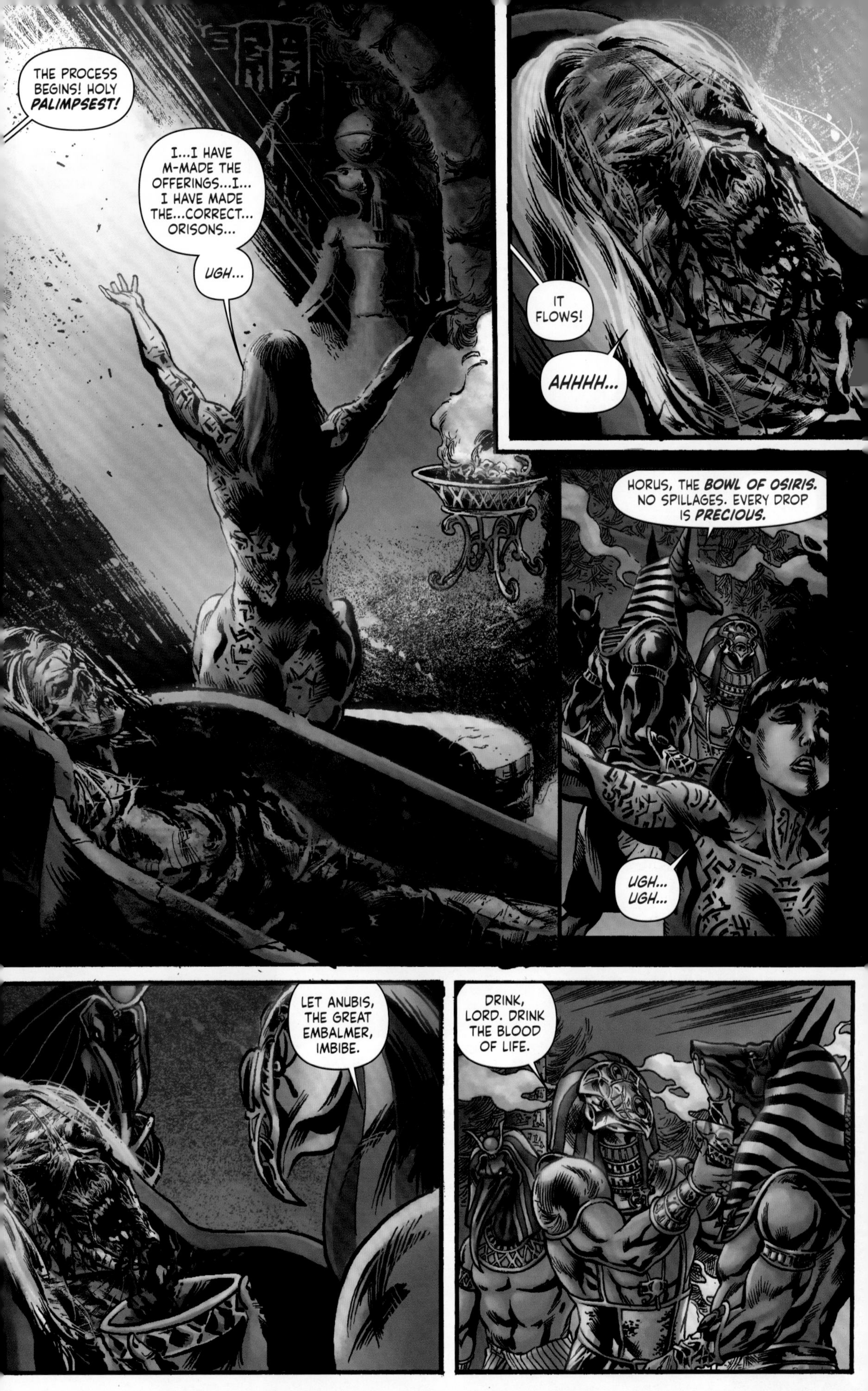

THE PROCESS BEGINS! HOLY *PALIMPSEST!*
I...I HAVE M-MADE THE OFFERINGS...I... I HAVE MADE THE...CORRECT... ORISONS...
UGH...
IT FLOWS!
AHHHH...
HORUS, THE *BOWL OF OSIRIS.* NO SPILLAGES. EVERY DROP IS *PRECIOUS.*
UGH... UGH...
LET ANUBIS, THE GREAT EMBALMER, IMBIBE.
DRINK, LORD. DRINK THE BLOOD OF LIFE.

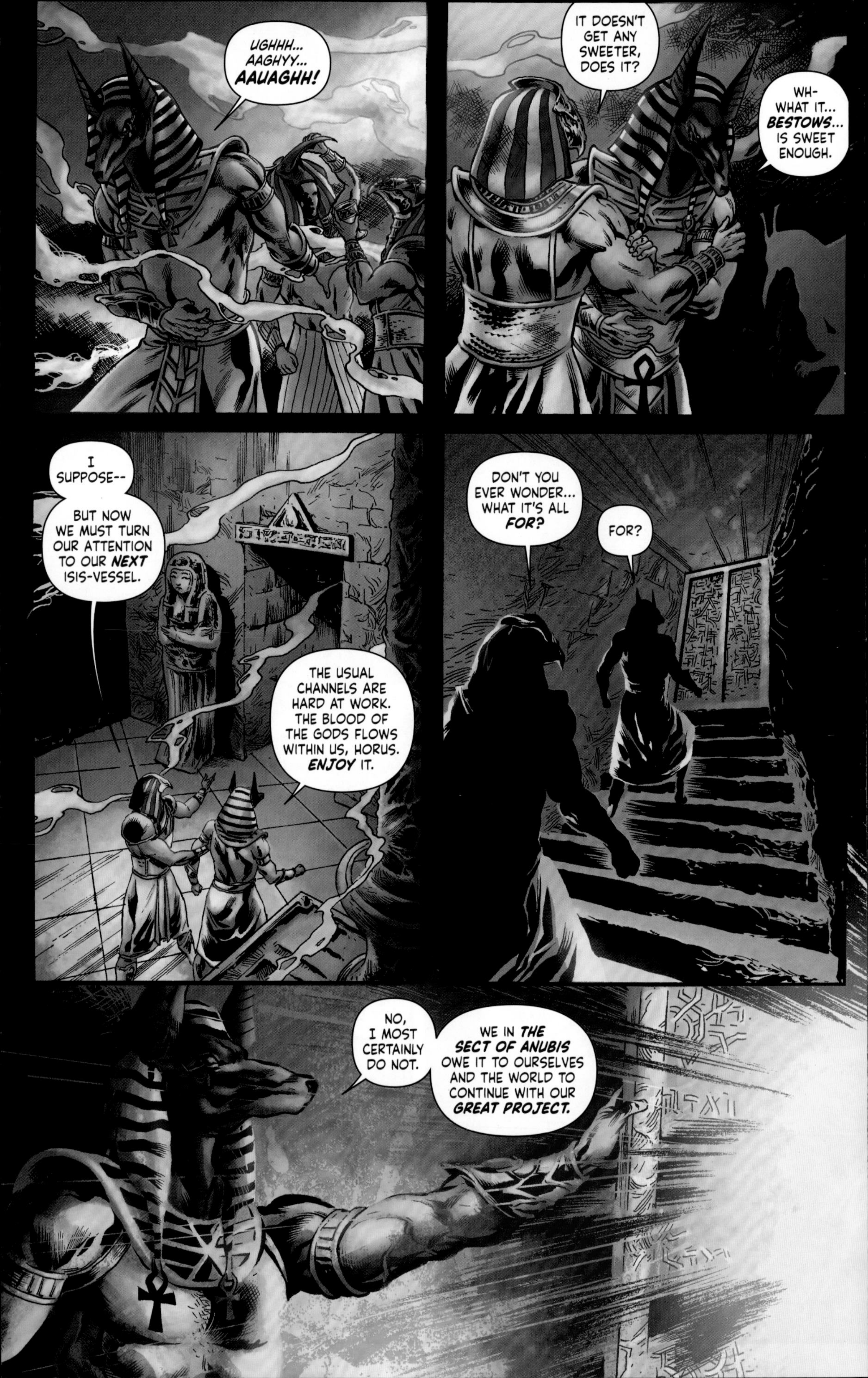

UGHHH... AAGHYY... AAUAGHH!
IT DOESN'T GET ANY SWEETER, DOES IT?
WH- WHAT IT... BESTOWS... IS SWEET ENOUGH.
I SUPPOSE--
BUT NOW WE MUST TURN OUR ATTENTION TO OUR NEXT ISIS-VESSEL.
THE USUAL CHANNELS ARE HARD AT WORK. THE BLOOD OF THE GODS FLOWS WITHIN US, HORUS. ENJOY IT.
DON'T YOU EVER WONDER... WHAT IT'S ALL FOR?
FOR?
NO, I MOST CERTAINLY DO NOT.
WE IN THE SECT OF ANUBIS OWE IT TO OURSELVES AND THE WORLD TO CONTINUE WITH OUR GREAT PROJECT.

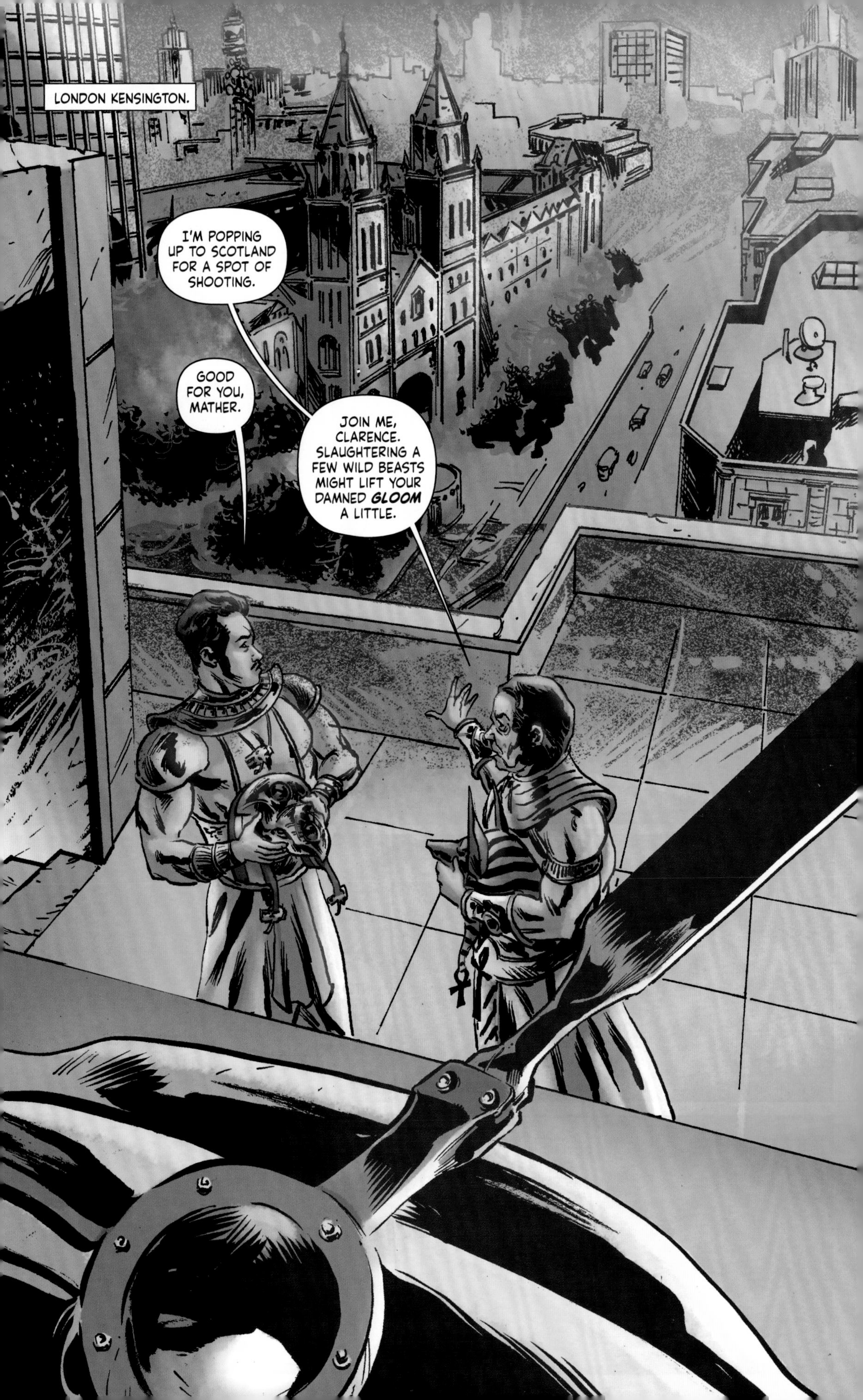
LONDON KENSINGTON.
I'M POPPING UP TO SCOTLAND FOR A SPOT OF SHOOTING.
GOOD FOR YOU, MATHER.
JOIN ME, CLARENCE. SLAUGHTERING A FEW WILD BEASTS MIGHT LIFT YOUR DAMNED GLOOM A LITTLE.

DAMNED PITY.

THIRTY-THREE YEARS LATER.

SHE SEEMED TO BE SUCH A SPLENDID *VESSEL*.

AND YOU ASSURED ME SHE WAS *MEDICALLY FIT*, DOCTOR FINLAY.

AYE. I RAN THE USUAL TESTS.

BUT THE INTENSE PRESSURE SHE WAS UNDER TRIGGERED A SUDDEN COARCTATION OF THE AORTA. IT COULDN'T BE FORESEEN, POOR GIRL.

POOR GIRL? WHAT ROT! WE ALL KNOW THAT A SWIFT HEART ATTACK WAS PREFERABLE TO THE *HORRORS* THAT LAY IN STORE FOR HER.

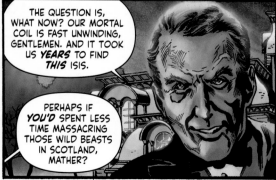

THE QUESTION IS, WHAT NOW? OUR MORTAL COIL IS FAST UNWINDING, GENTLEMEN. AND IT TOOK US *YEARS* TO FIND *THIS* ISIS.

PERHAPS IF *YOU'D* SPENT LESS TIME MASSACRING THOSE WILD BEASTS IN SCOTLAND, MATHER?

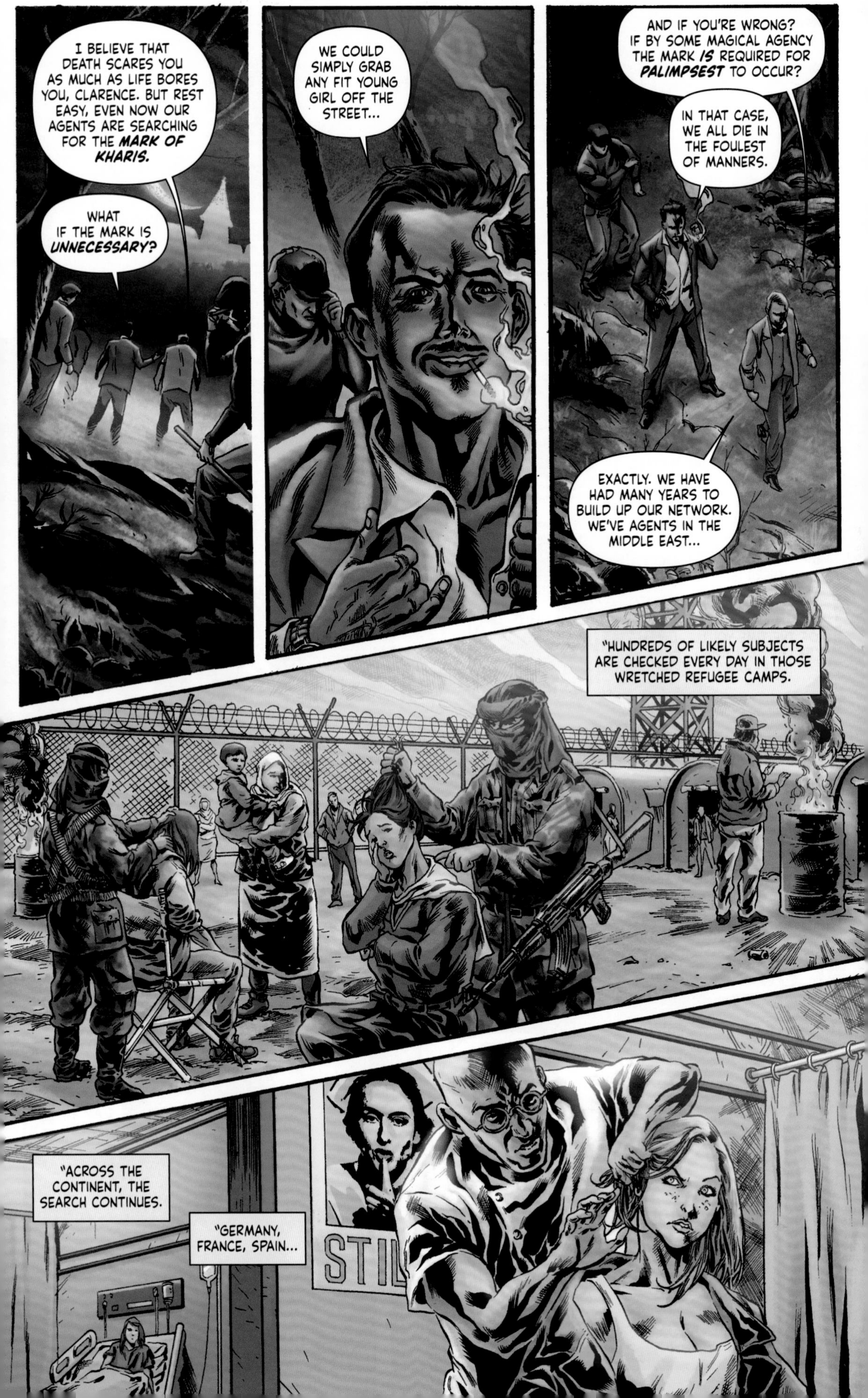
I BELIEVE THAT DEATH SCARES YOU AS MUCH AS LIFE BORES YOU, CLARENCE. BUT REST EASY, EVEN NOW OUR AGENTS ARE SEARCHING FOR THE ***MARK OF KHARIS.***
WHAT IF THE MARK IS ***UNNECESSARY?***
WE COULD SIMPLY GRAB ANY FIT YOUNG GIRL OFF THE STREET...
AND IF YOU'RE WRONG? IF BY SOME MAGICAL AGENCY THE MARK ***IS*** REQUIRED FOR ***PALIMPSEST*** TO OCCUR?
IN THAT CASE, WE ALL DIE IN THE FOULEST OF MANNERS.
EXACTLY. WE HAVE HAD MANY YEARS TO BUILD UP OUR NETWORK. WE'VE AGENTS IN THE MIDDLE EAST...
"HUNDREDS OF LIKELY SUBJECTS ARE CHECKED EVERY DAY IN THOSE WRETCHED REFUGEE CAMPS.
"ACROSS THE CONTINENT, THE SEARCH CONTINUES.
"GERMANY, FRANCE, SPAIN...
STIL

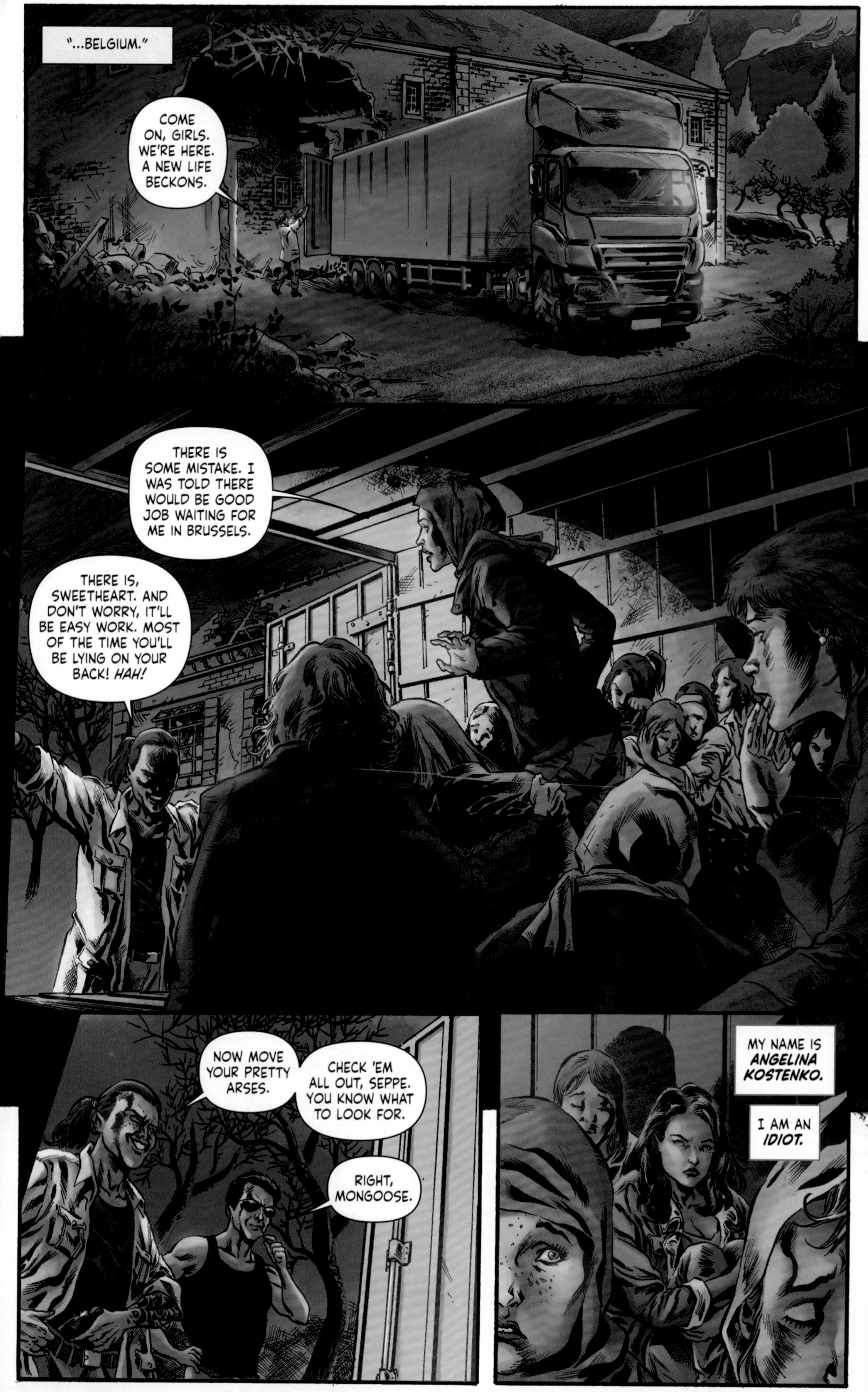
"...BELGIUM."
COME ON, GIRLS. WE'RE HERE. A NEW LIFE BECKONS.
THERE IS SOME MISTAKE. I WAS TOLD THERE WOULD BE GOOD JOB WAITING FOR ME IN BRUSSELS.
THERE IS, SWEETHEART. AND DON'T WORRY, IT'LL BE EASY WORK. MOST OF THE TIME YOU'LL BE LYING ON YOUR BACK! *HAH!*
NOW MOVE YOUR PRETTY ARSES.
CHECK 'EM ALL OUT, SEPPE. YOU KNOW WHAT TO LOOK FOR.
RIGHT, MONGOOSE.
MY NAME IS ***ANGELINA KOSTENKO.***
I AM AN ***IDIOT.***

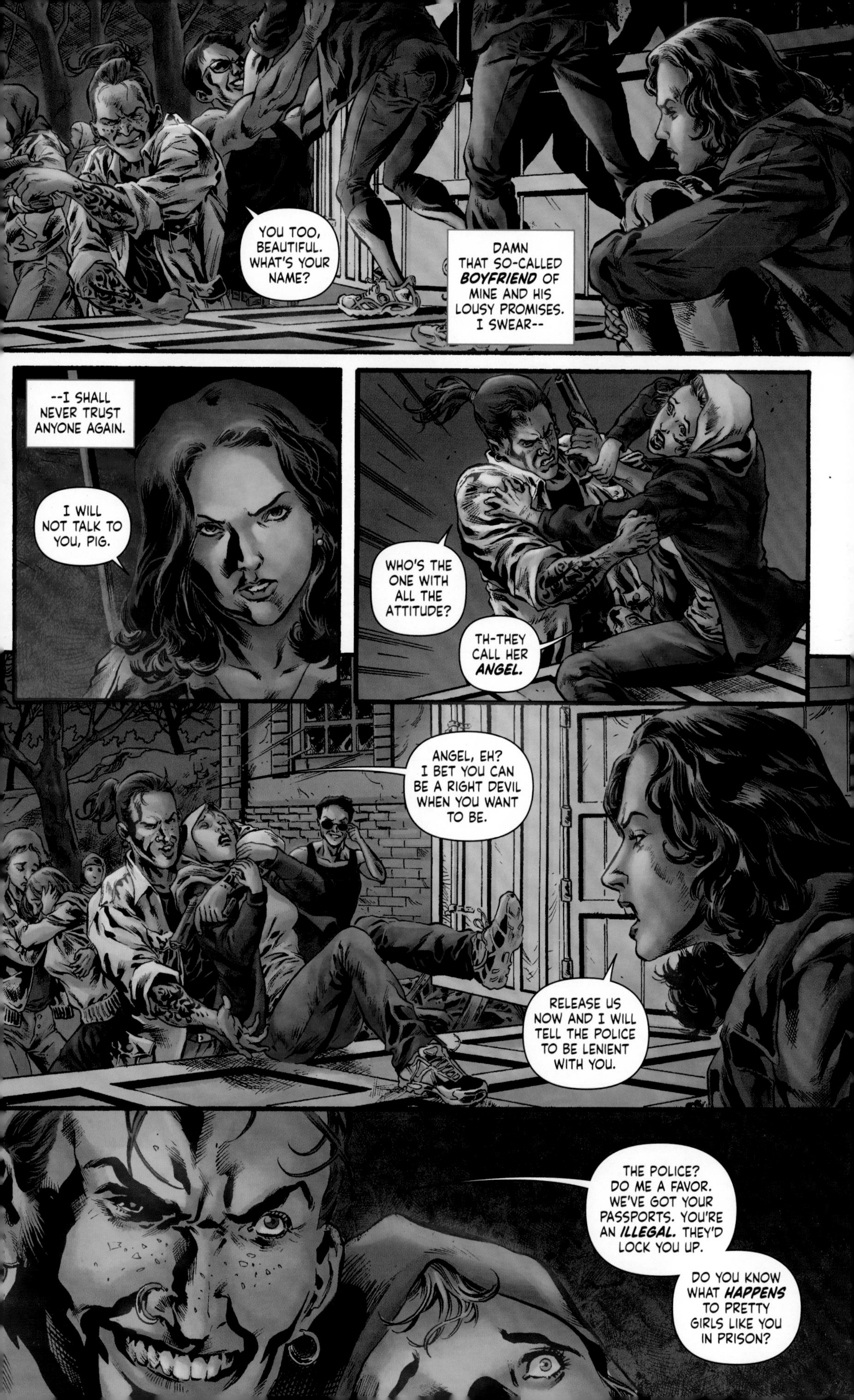

YOU TOO, BEAUTIFUL. WHAT'S YOUR NAME?
DAMN THAT SO-CALLED **BOYFRIEND** OF MINE AND HIS LOUSY PROMISES. I SWEAR--
--I SHALL NEVER TRUST ANYONE AGAIN.
I WILL NOT TALK TO YOU, PIG.
WHO'S THE ONE WITH ALL THE ATTITUDE?
TH-THEY CALL HER **ANGEL.**
ANGEL, EH? I BET YOU CAN BE A RIGHT DEVIL WHEN YOU WANT TO BE.
RELEASE US NOW AND I WILL TELL THE POLICE TO BE LENIENT WITH YOU.
THE POLICE? DO ME A FAVOR. WE'VE GOT YOUR PASSPORTS. YOU'RE AN **ILLEGAL.** THEY'D LOCK YOU UP.
DO YOU KNOW WHAT **HAPPENS** TO PRETTY GIRLS LIKE YOU IN PRISON?

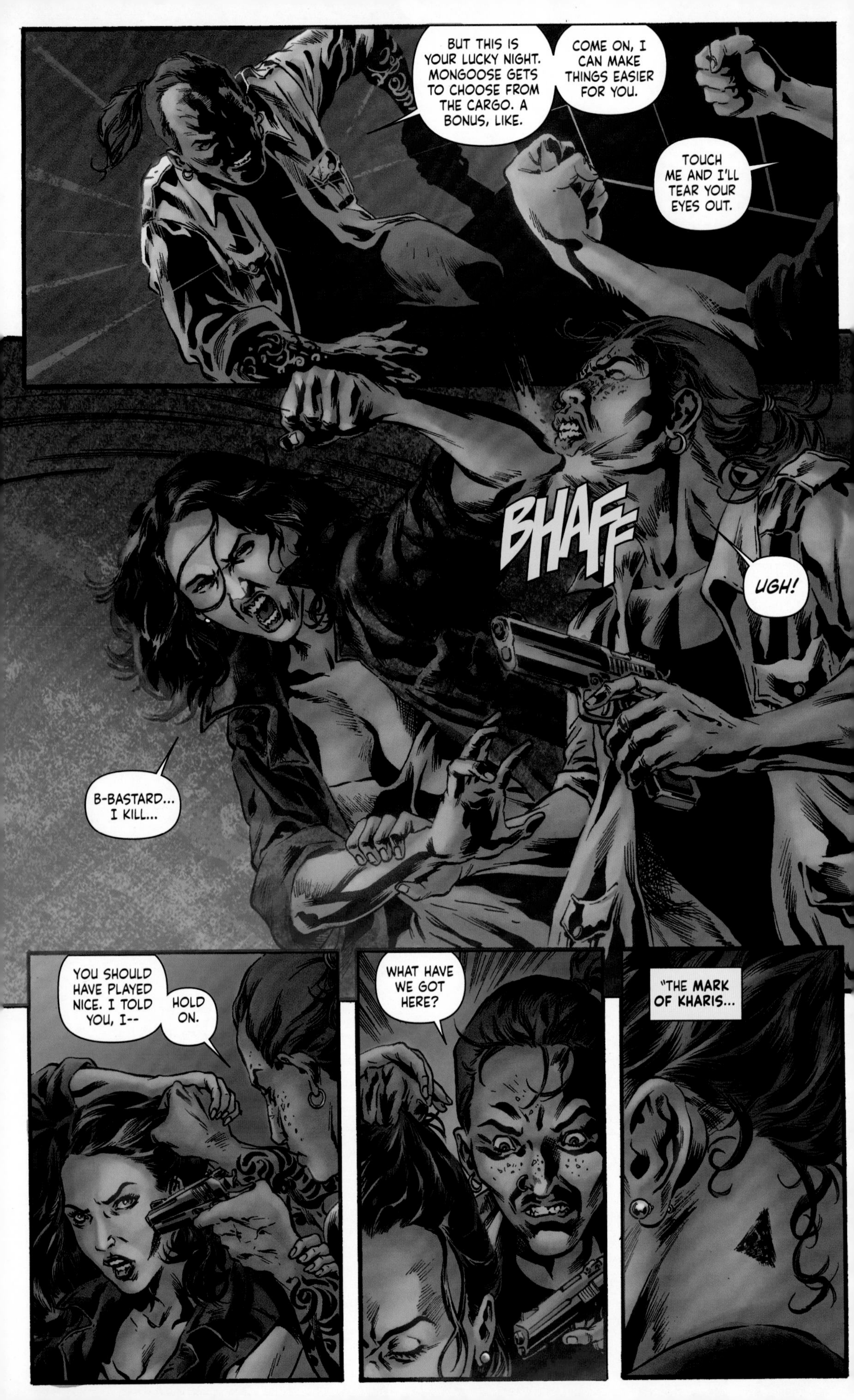
BUT THIS IS YOUR LUCKY NIGHT. MONGOOSE GETS TO CHOOSE FROM THE CARGO. A BONUS, LIKE.
COME ON, I CAN MAKE THINGS EASIER FOR YOU.
TOUCH ME AND I'LL TEAR YOUR EYES OUT.
BHAFF
UGH!
B-BASTARD... I KILL...
YOU SHOULD HAVE PLAYED NICE. I TOLD YOU, I--
HOLD ON.
WHAT HAVE WE GOT HERE?
"THE MARK OF KHARIS...

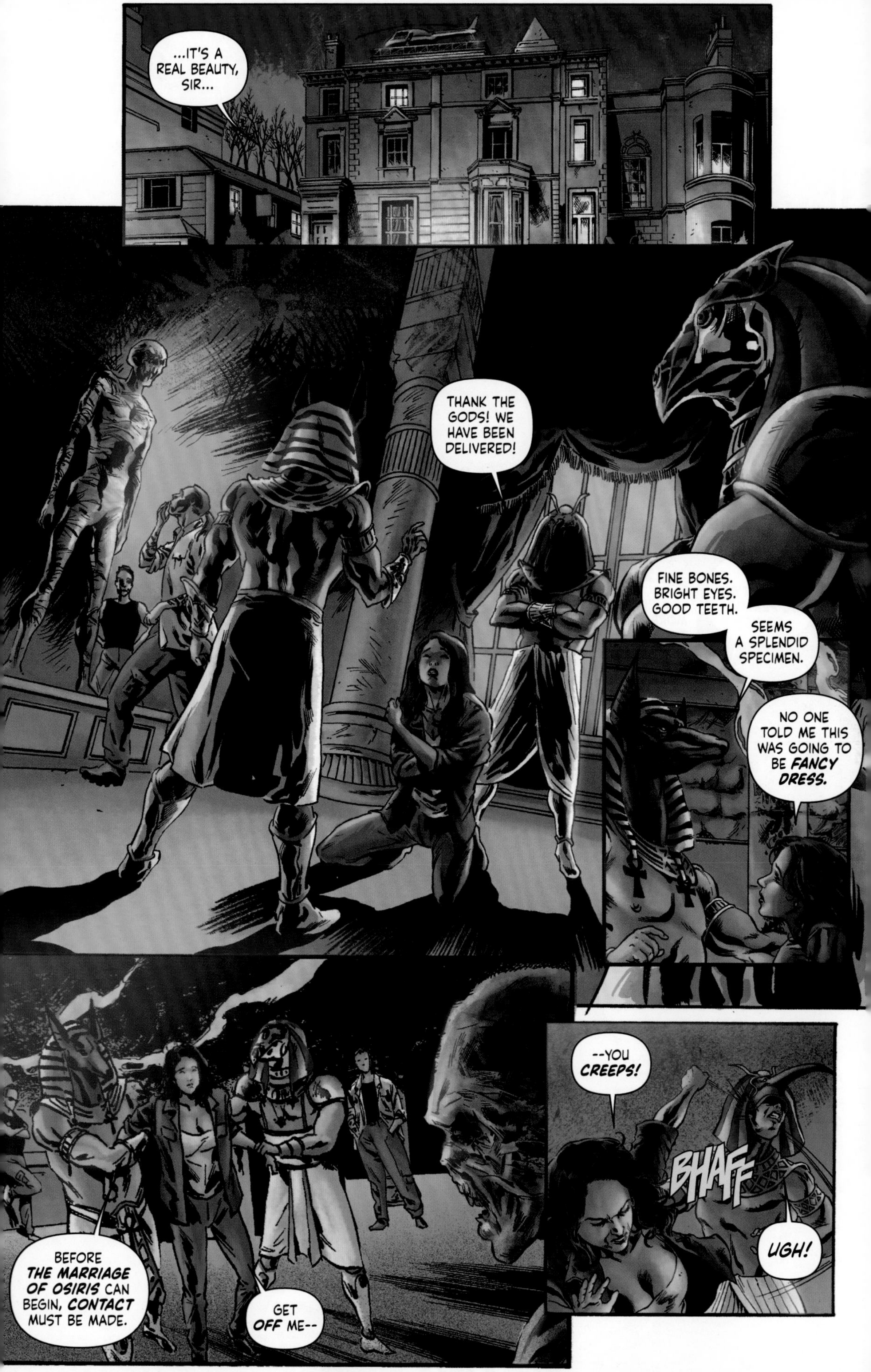
...IT'S A REAL BEAUTY, SIR...
THANK THE GODS! WE HAVE BEEN DELIVERED!
FINE BONES. BRIGHT EYES. GOOD TEETH.
SEEMS A SPLENDID SPECIMEN.
NO ONE TOLD ME THIS WAS GOING TO BE **FANCY DRESS.**
BEFORE **THE MARRIAGE OF OSIRIS** CAN BEGIN, **CONTACT** MUST BE MADE.
GET **OFF ME**--
--YOU **CREEPS!**
BHAFF
UGH!

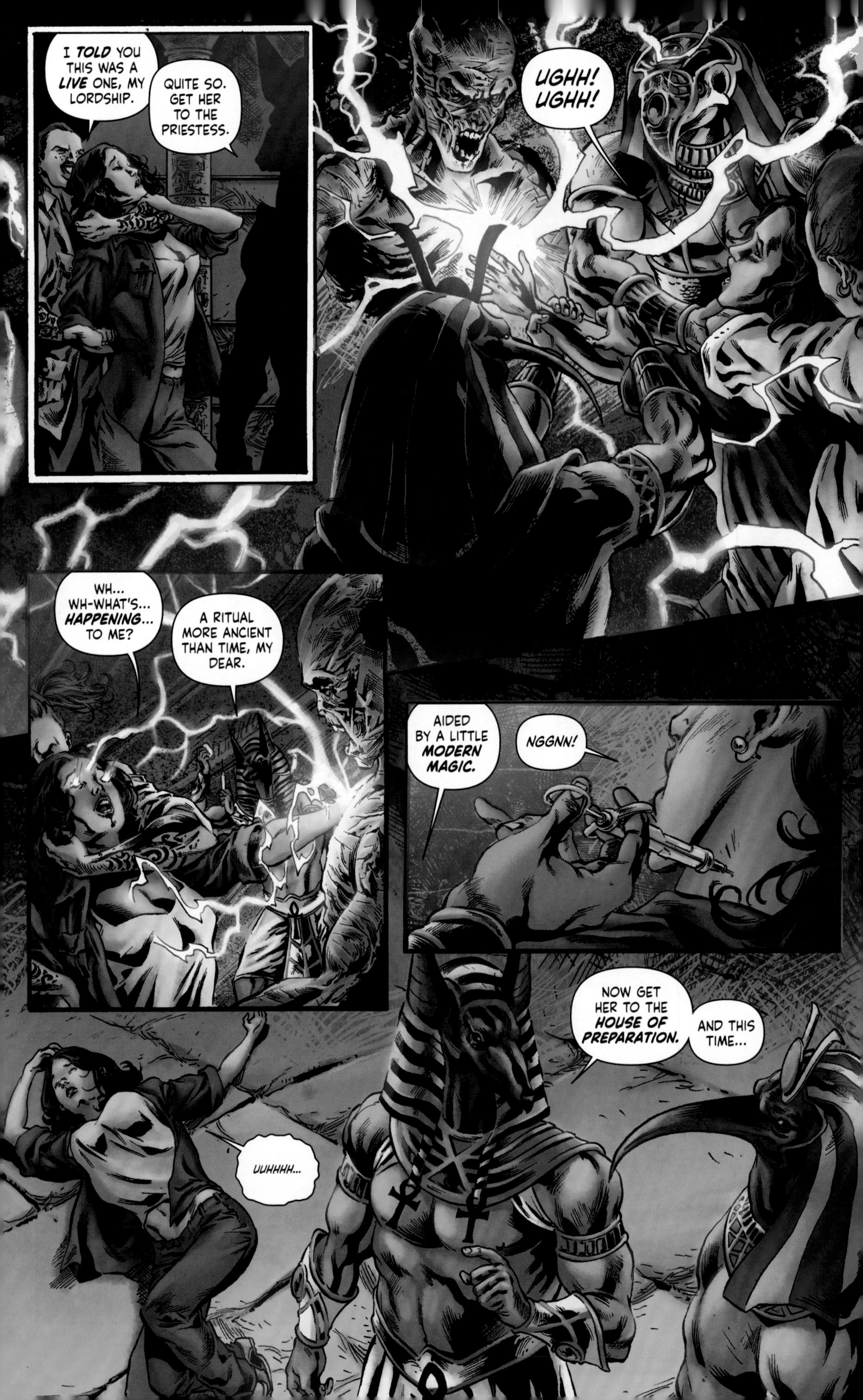
I TOLD YOU THIS WAS A LIVE ONE, MY LORDSHIP.
QUITE SO. GET HER TO THE PRIESTESS.
UGHH! UGHH!
WH... WH-WHAT'S... HAPPENING... TO ME?
A RITUAL MORE ANCIENT THAN TIME, MY DEAR.
AIDED BY A LITTLE MODERN MAGIC.
NGGNN!
NOW GET HER TO THE HOUSE OF PREPARATION.
AND THIS TIME...
UUHHHH...

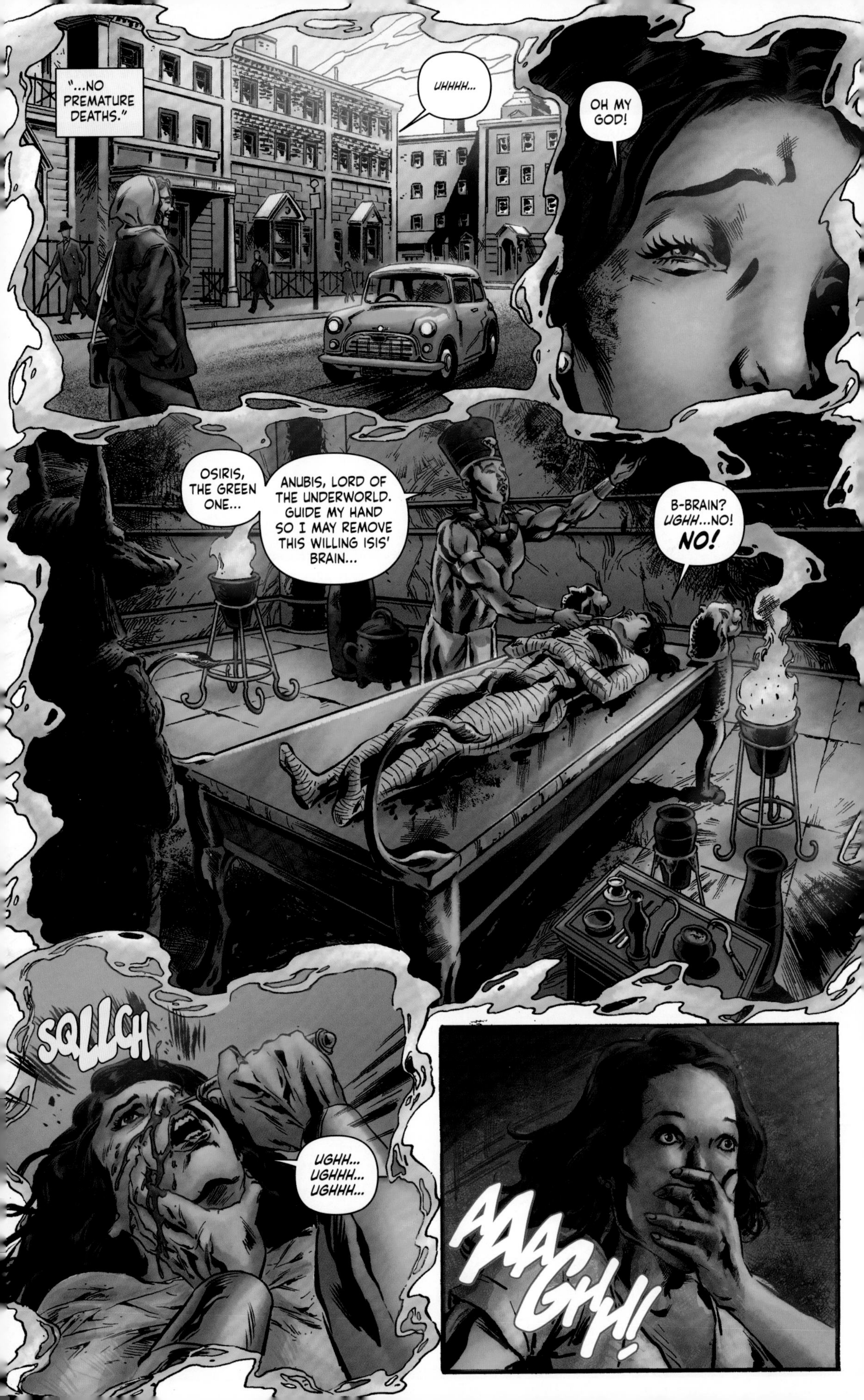
"...NO PREMATURE DEATHS."
UHHHH...
OH MY GOD!
OSIRIS, THE GREEN ONE...
ANUBIS, LORD OF THE UNDERWORLD. GUIDE MY HAND SO I MAY REMOVE THIS WILLING ISIS' BRAIN...
B-BRAIN? UGHH...NO! NO!
SQLLCH
UGHH... UGHHH... UGHHH...
AAAGHH!!

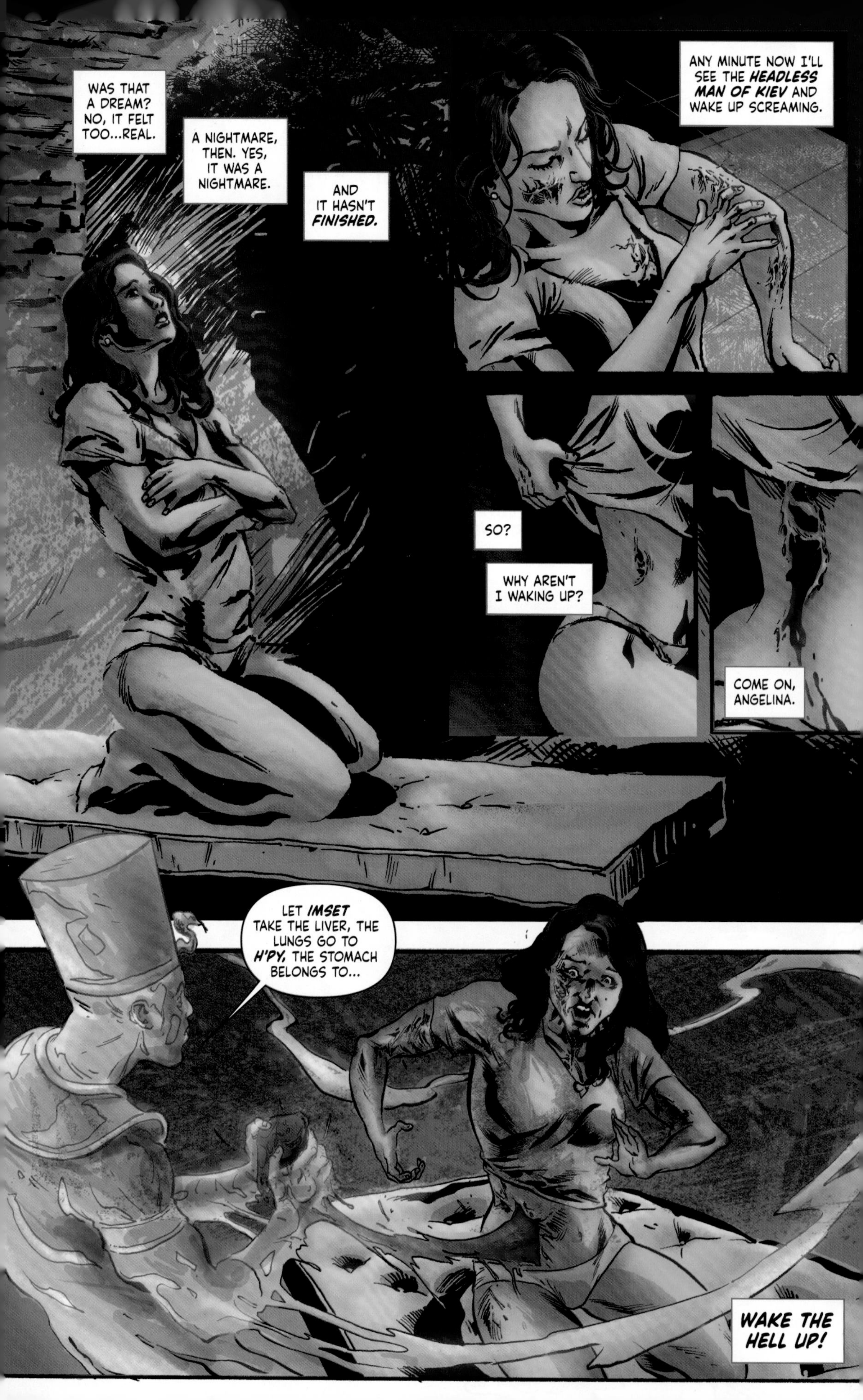
WAS THAT A DREAM? NO, IT FELT TOO...REAL.
A NIGHTMARE, THEN. YES, IT WAS A NIGHTMARE.
AND IT HASN'T *FINISHED.*
ANY MINUTE NOW I'LL SEE THE ***HEADLESS MAN OF KIEV*** AND WAKE UP SCREAMING.
SO?
WHY AREN'T I WAKING UP?
COME ON, ANGELINA.
LET ***IMSET*** TAKE THE LIVER, THE LUNGS GO TO ***H'PY,*** THE STOMACH BELONGS TO...
WAKE THE HELL UP!

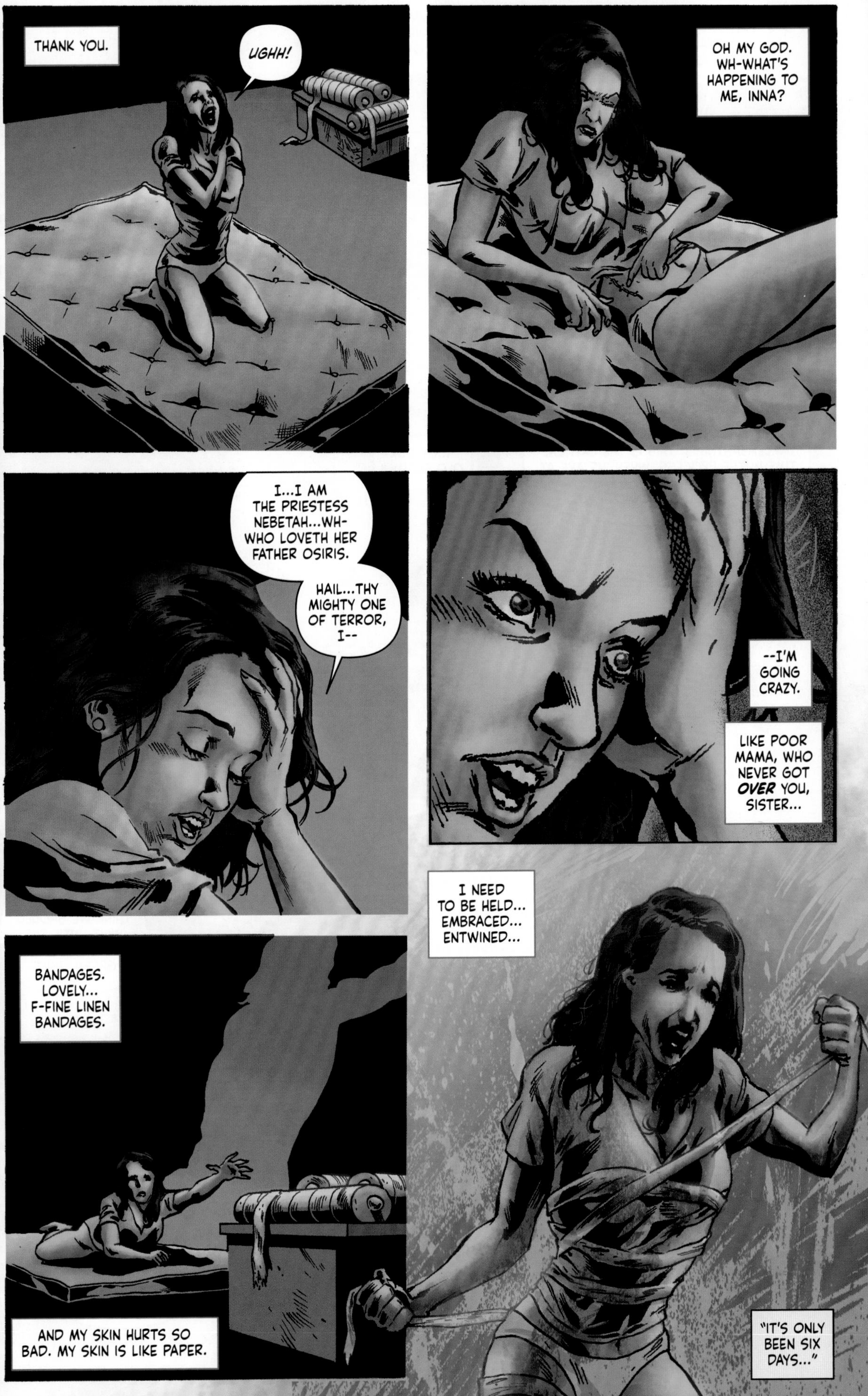
THANK YOU.
UGHH!
OH MY GOD. WH-WHAT'S HAPPENING TO ME, INNA?
I...I AM THE PRIESTESS NEBETAH...WH-WHO LOVETH HER FATHER OSIRIS.
HAIL...THY MIGHTY ONE OF TERROR, I--
--I'M GOING CRAZY.
LIKE POOR MAMA, WHO NEVER GOT ***OVER*** YOU, SISTER...
BANDAGES. LOVELY... F-FINE LINEN BANDAGES.
AND MY SKIN HURTS SO BAD. MY SKIN IS LIKE PAPER.
I NEED TO BE HELD... EMBRACED... ENTWINED...
"IT'S ONLY BEEN SIX DAYS..."

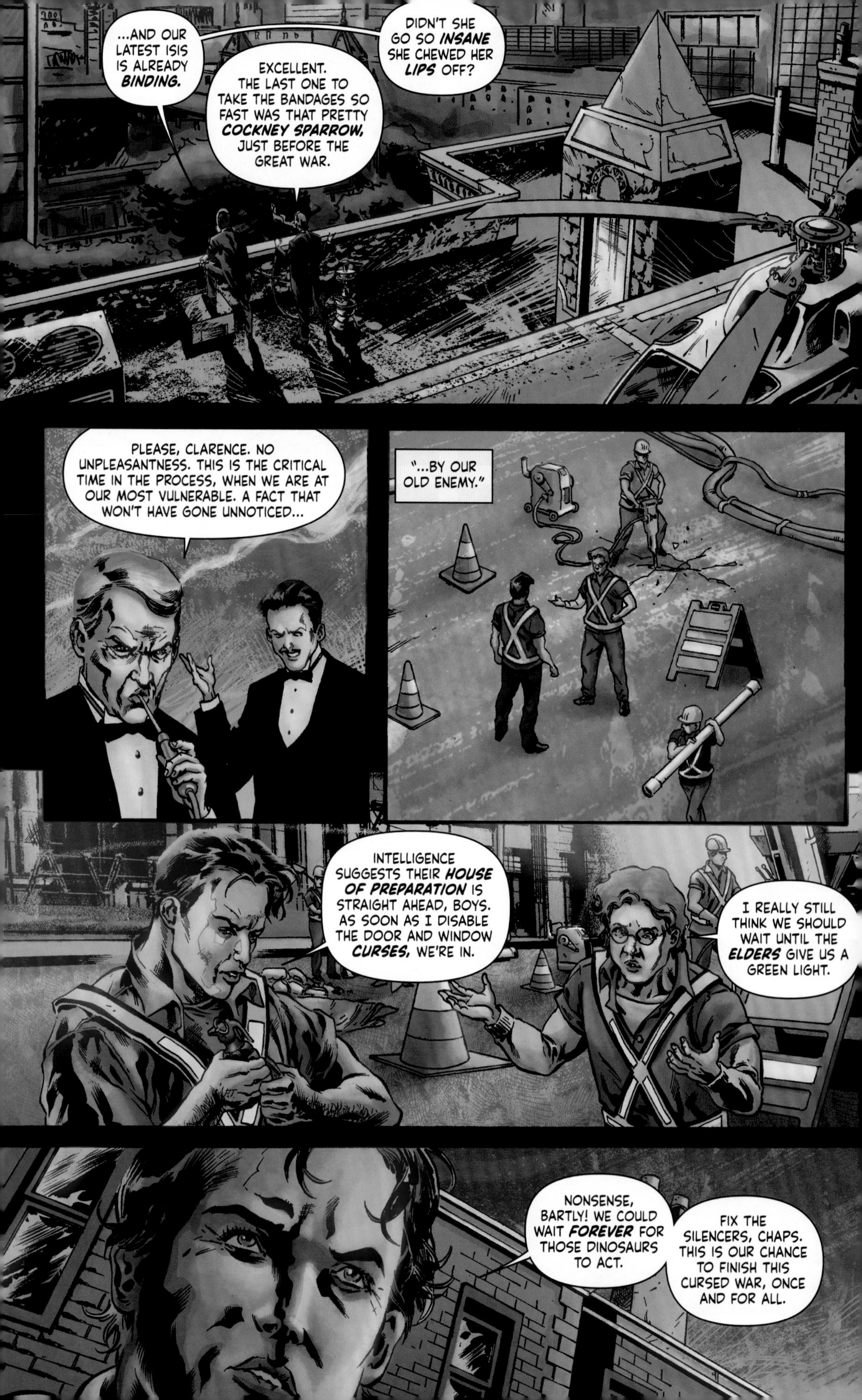
...AND OUR LATEST ISIS IS ALREADY BINDING.
EXCELLENT. THE LAST ONE TO TAKE THE BANDAGES SO FAST WAS THAT PRETTY COCKNEY SPARROW, JUST BEFORE THE GREAT WAR.
DIDN'T SHE GO SO INSANE SHE CHEWED HER LIPS OFF?
PLEASE, CLARENCE. NO UNPLEASANTNESS. THIS IS THE CRITICAL TIME IN THE PROCESS, WHEN WE ARE AT OUR MOST VULNERABLE. A FACT THAT WON'T HAVE GONE UNNOTICED...
"...BY OUR OLD ENEMY."
INTELLIGENCE SUGGESTS THEIR HOUSE OF PREPARATION IS STRAIGHT AHEAD, BOYS. AS SOON AS I DISABLE THE DOOR AND WINDOW CURSES, WE'RE IN.
I REALLY STILL THINK WE SHOULD WAIT UNTIL THE ELDERS GIVE US A GREEN LIGHT.
NONSENSE, BARTLY! WE COULD WAIT FOREVER FOR THOSE DINOSAURS TO ACT.
FIX THE SILENCERS, CHAPS. THIS IS OUR CHANCE TO FINISH THIS CURSED WAR, ONCE AND FOR ALL.

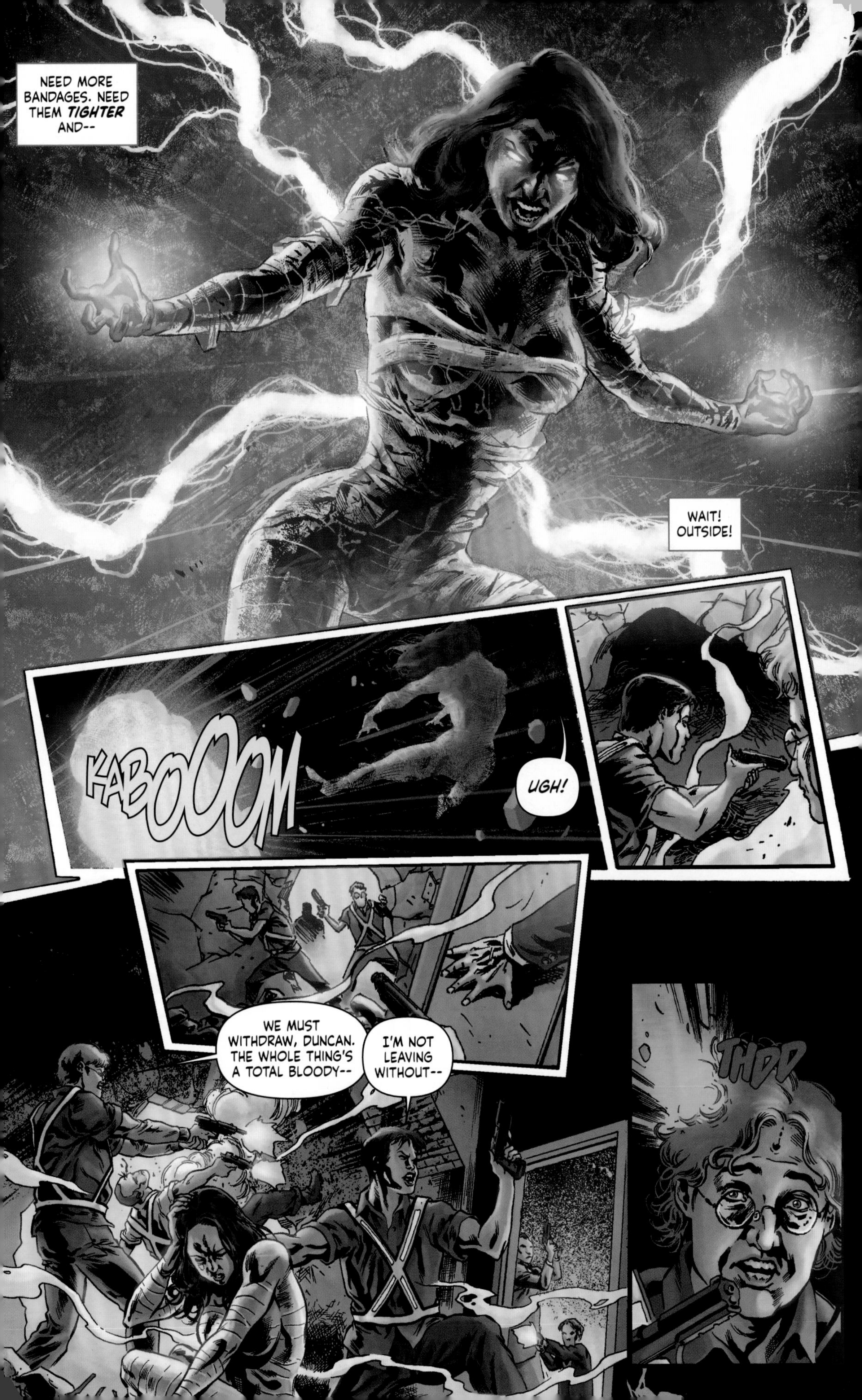

NEED MORE BANDAGES. NEED THEM *TIGHTER* AND--
WAIT! OUTSIDE!
KABOOOM
UGH!
WE MUST WITHDRAW, DUNCAN. THE WHOLE THING'S A TOTAL BLOODY--
I'M NOT LEAVING WITHOUT--
THDD

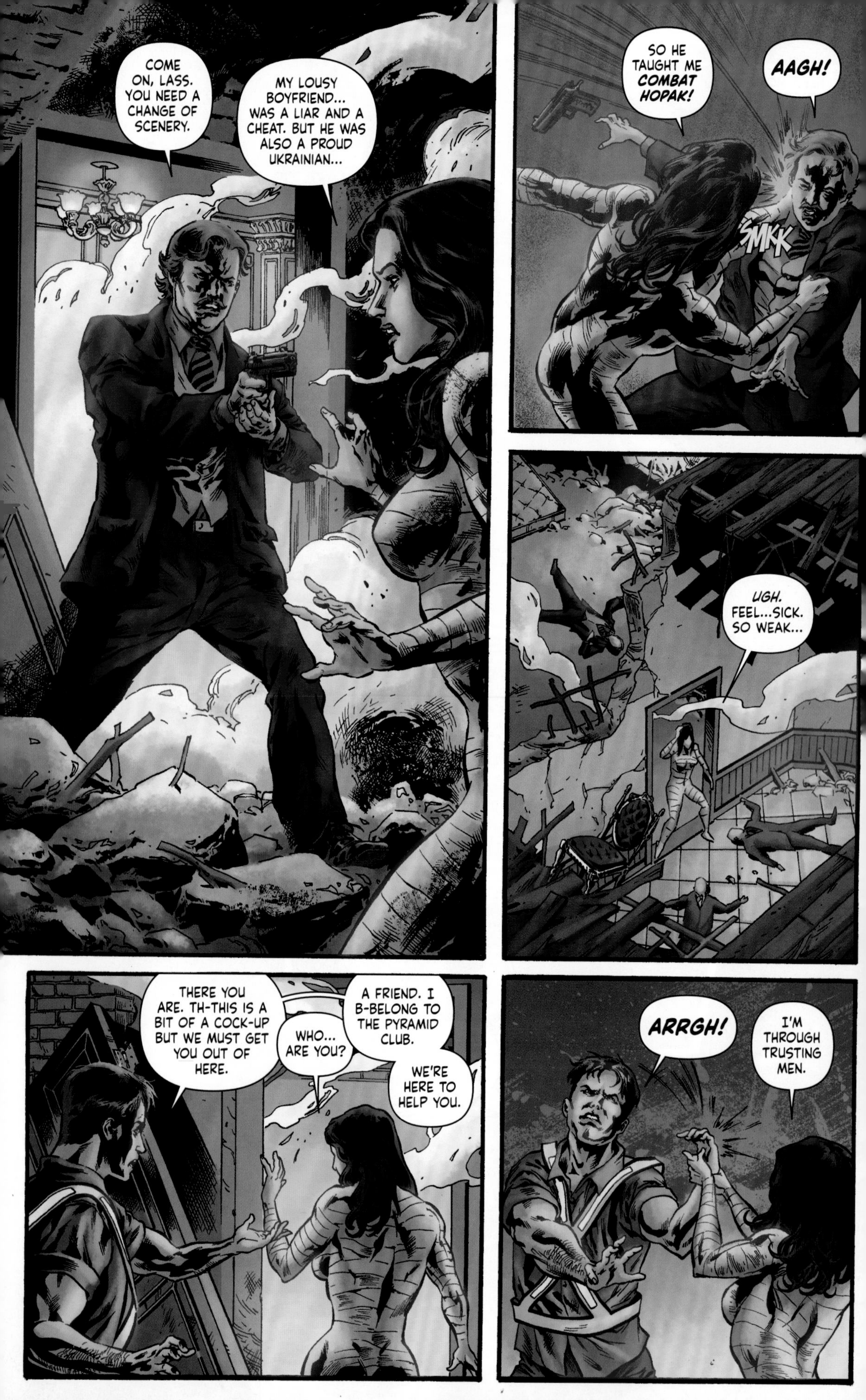
COME ON, LASS. YOU NEED A CHANGE OF SCENERY.
MY LOUSY BOYFRIEND... WAS A LIAR AND A CHEAT. BUT HE WAS ALSO A PROUD UKRAINIAN...
SO HE TAUGHT ME COMBAT HOPAK!
AAGH!
SMKK
UGH. FEEL...SICK. SO WEAK...
THERE YOU ARE. TH-THIS IS A BIT OF A COCK-UP BUT WE MUST GET YOU OUT OF HERE.
WHO... ARE YOU?
A FRIEND. I B-BELONG TO THE PYRAMID CLUB.
WE'RE HERE TO HELP YOU.
ARRGH!
I'M THROUGH TRUSTING MEN.

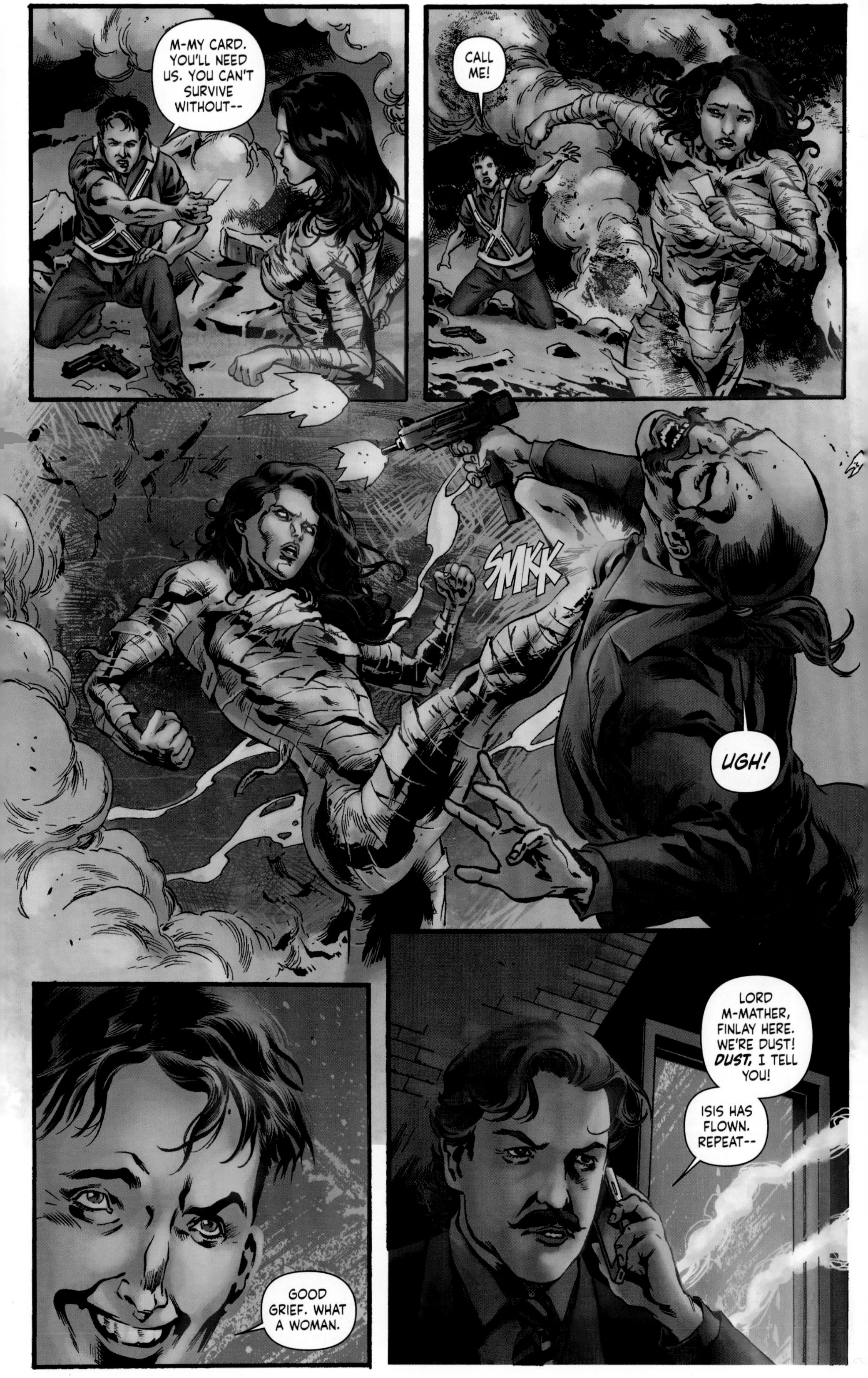
M-MY CARD. YOU'LL NEED US. YOU CAN'T SURVIVE WITHOUT--
CALL ME!
SMKK
UGH!
GOOD GRIEF. WHAT A WOMAN.
LORD M-MATHER, FINLAY HERE. WE'RE DUST! DUST, I TELL YOU!
ISIS HAS FLOWN. REPEAT--

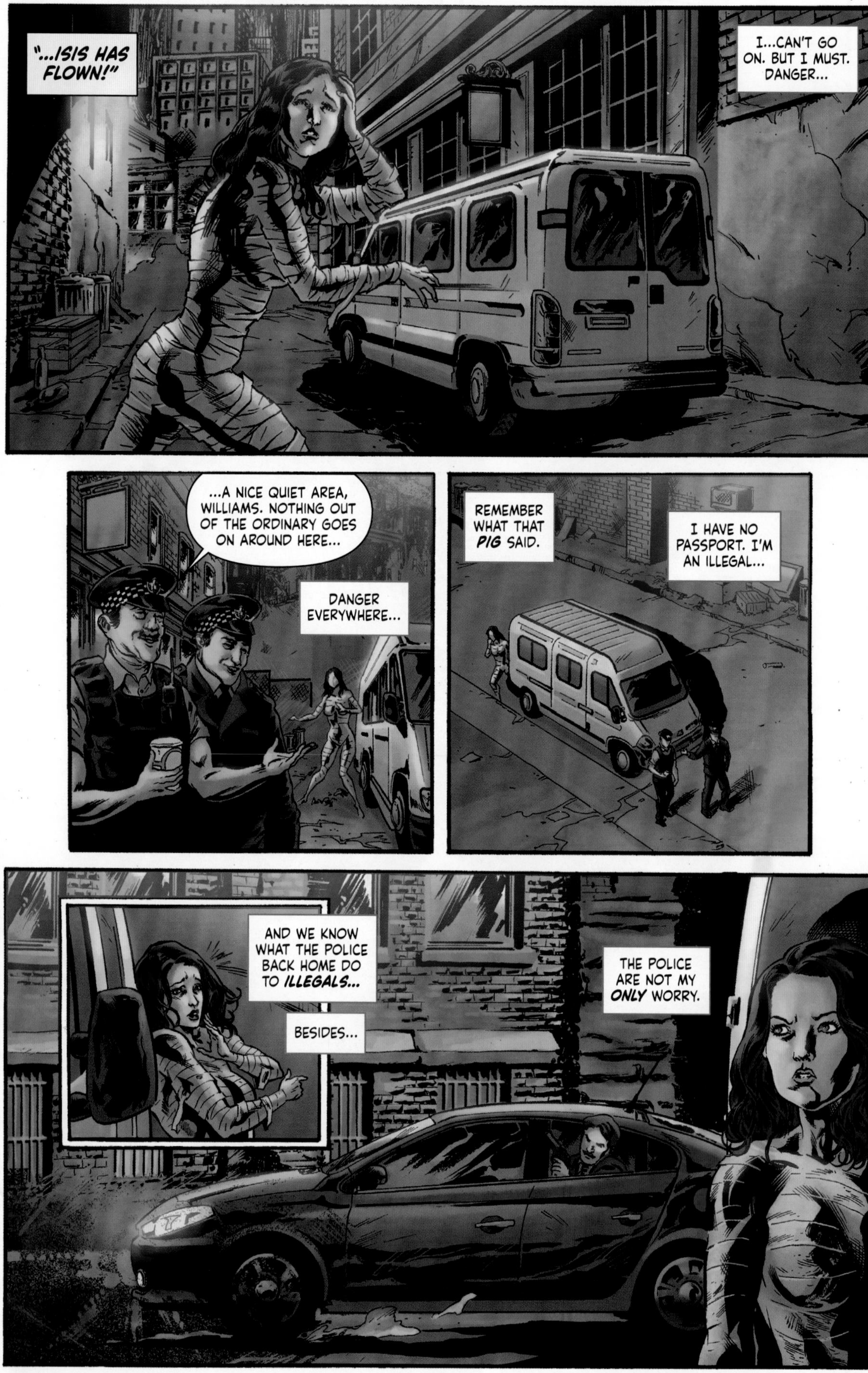
"...ISIS HAS FLOWN!"
I...CAN'T GO ON. BUT I MUST. DANGER...
...A NICE QUIET AREA, WILLIAMS. NOTHING OUT OF THE ORDINARY GOES ON AROUND HERE...
DANGER EVERYWHERE...
REMEMBER WHAT THAT PIG SAID.
I HAVE NO PASSPORT. I'M AN ILLEGAL...
AND WE KNOW WHAT THE POLICE BACK HOME DO TO ILLEGALS...
BESIDES...
THE POLICE ARE NOT MY ONLY WORRY.

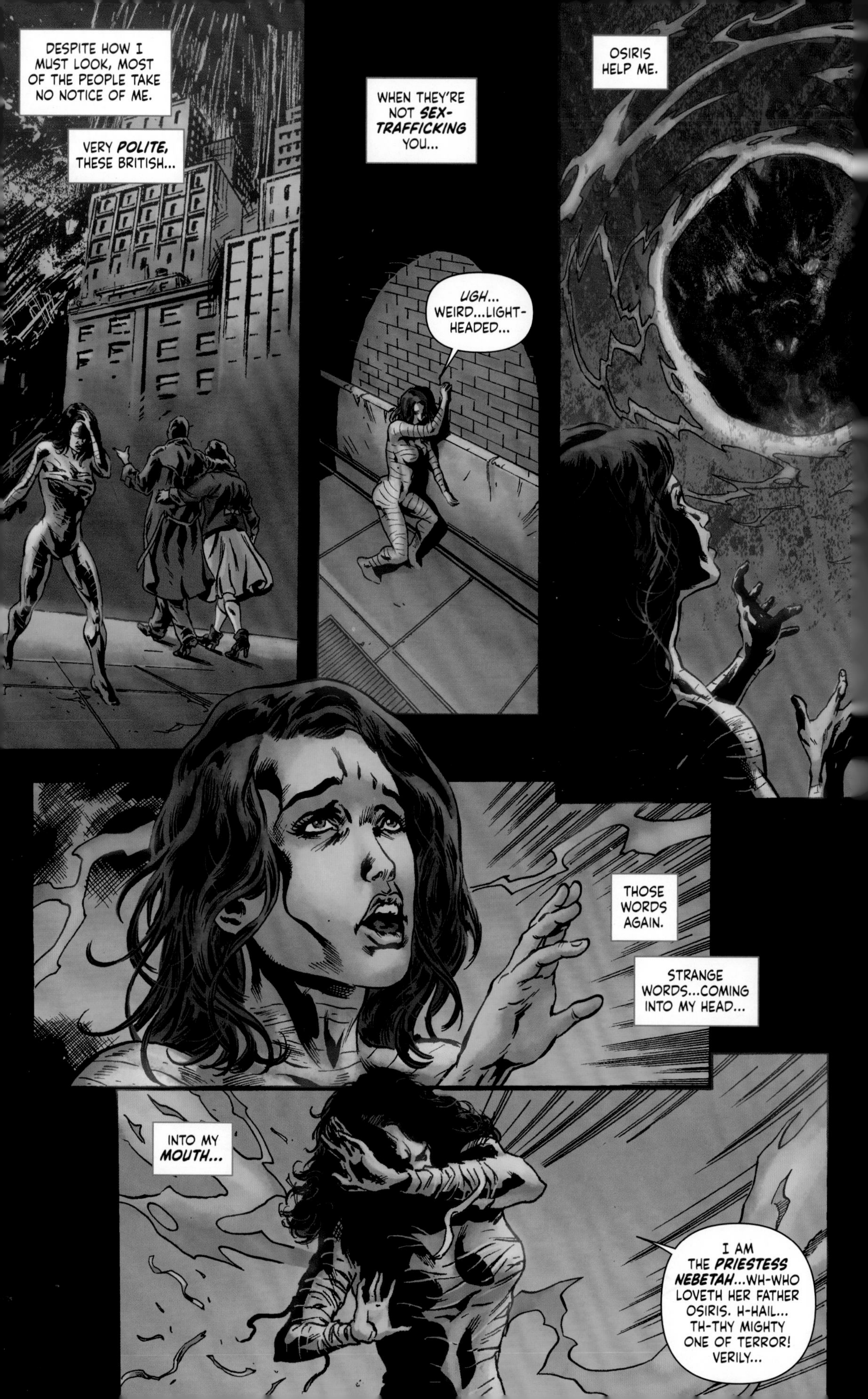
DESPITE HOW I MUST LOOK, MOST OF THE PEOPLE TAKE NO NOTICE OF ME.
VERY **POLITE,** THESE BRITISH...
WHEN THEY'RE NOT ***SEX-TRAFFICKING*** YOU...
UGH... WEIRD...LIGHT-HEADED...
OSIRIS HELP ME.
THOSE WORDS AGAIN.
STRANGE WORDS...COMING INTO MY HEAD...
INTO MY ***MOUTH...***
I AM THE ***PRIESTESS NEBETAH***...WH-WHO LOVETH HER FATHER OSIRIS. H-HAIL... TH-THY MIGHTY ONE OF TERROR! VERILY...

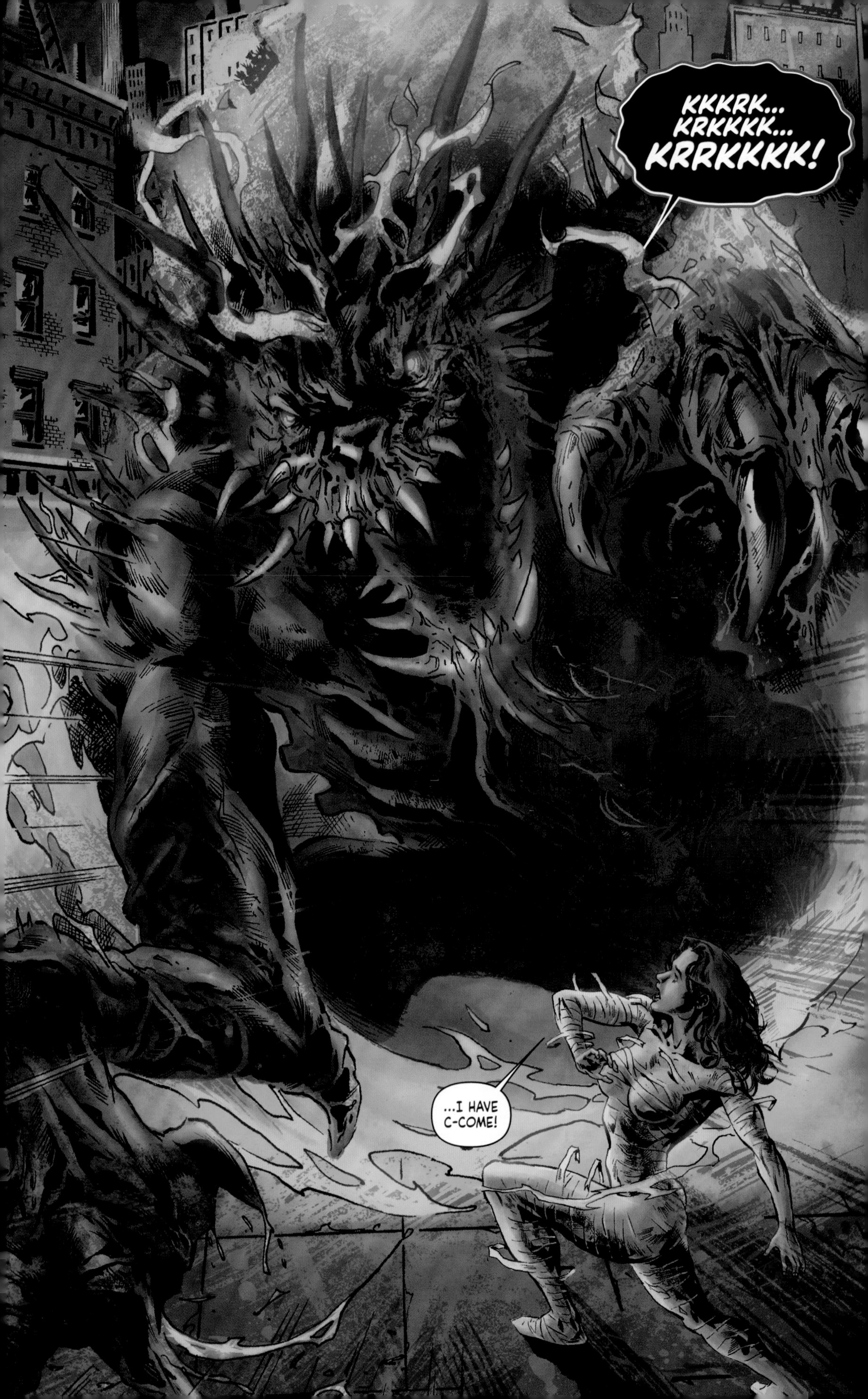
KKKRK...
KRKKKK...
KRRKKKK!
...I HAVE
C-COME!

PART II

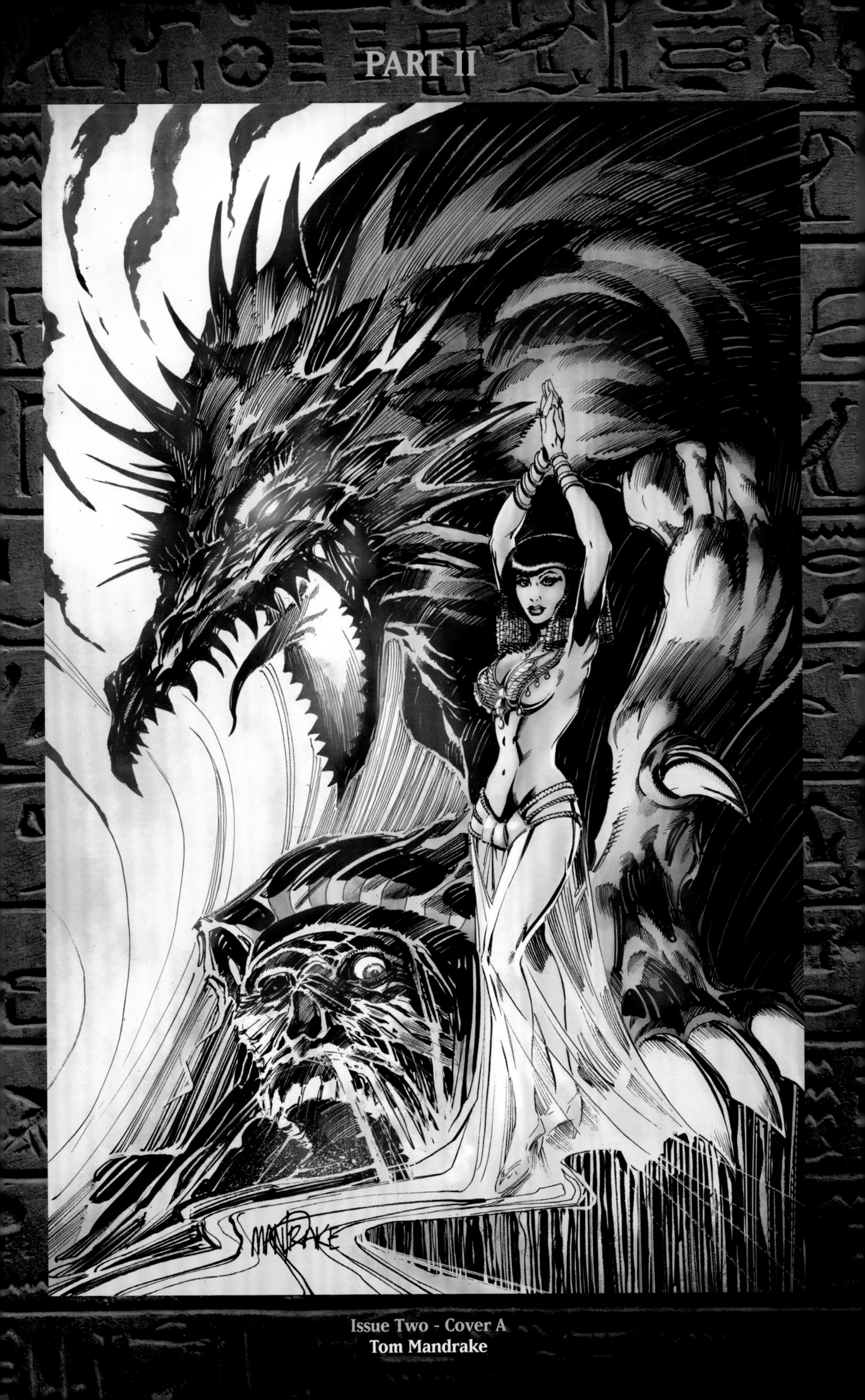
MANDRAKE

Issue Two - Cover A
Tom Mandrake

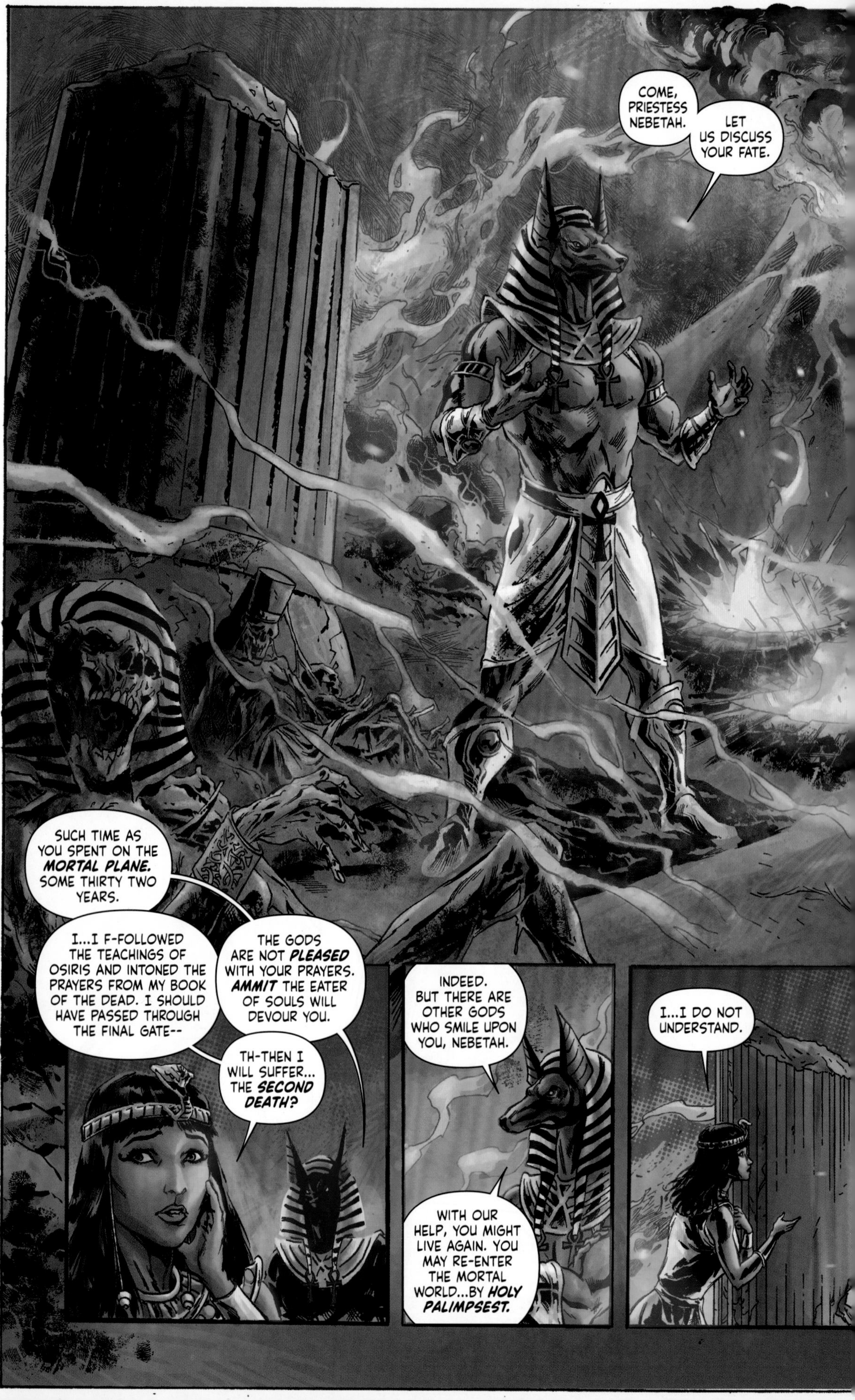

COME, PRIESTESS NEBETAH.
LET US DISCUSS YOUR FATE.
SUCH TIME AS YOU SPENT ON THE **MORTAL PLANE.** SOME THIRTY TWO YEARS.
I...I F-FOLLOWED THE TEACHINGS OF OSIRIS AND INTONED THE PRAYERS FROM MY BOOK OF THE DEAD. I SHOULD HAVE PASSED THROUGH THE FINAL GATE--
THE GODS ARE NOT **PLEASED** WITH YOUR PRAYERS. **AMMIT** THE EATER OF SOULS WILL DEVOUR YOU.
TH-THEN I WILL SUFFER... THE **SECOND DEATH?**
INDEED. BUT THERE ARE OTHER GODS WHO SMILE UPON YOU, NEBETAH.
WITH OUR HELP, YOU MIGHT LIVE AGAIN. YOU MAY RE-ENTER THE MORTAL WORLD...BY **HOLY PALIMPSEST.**
I...I DO NOT UNDERSTAND.

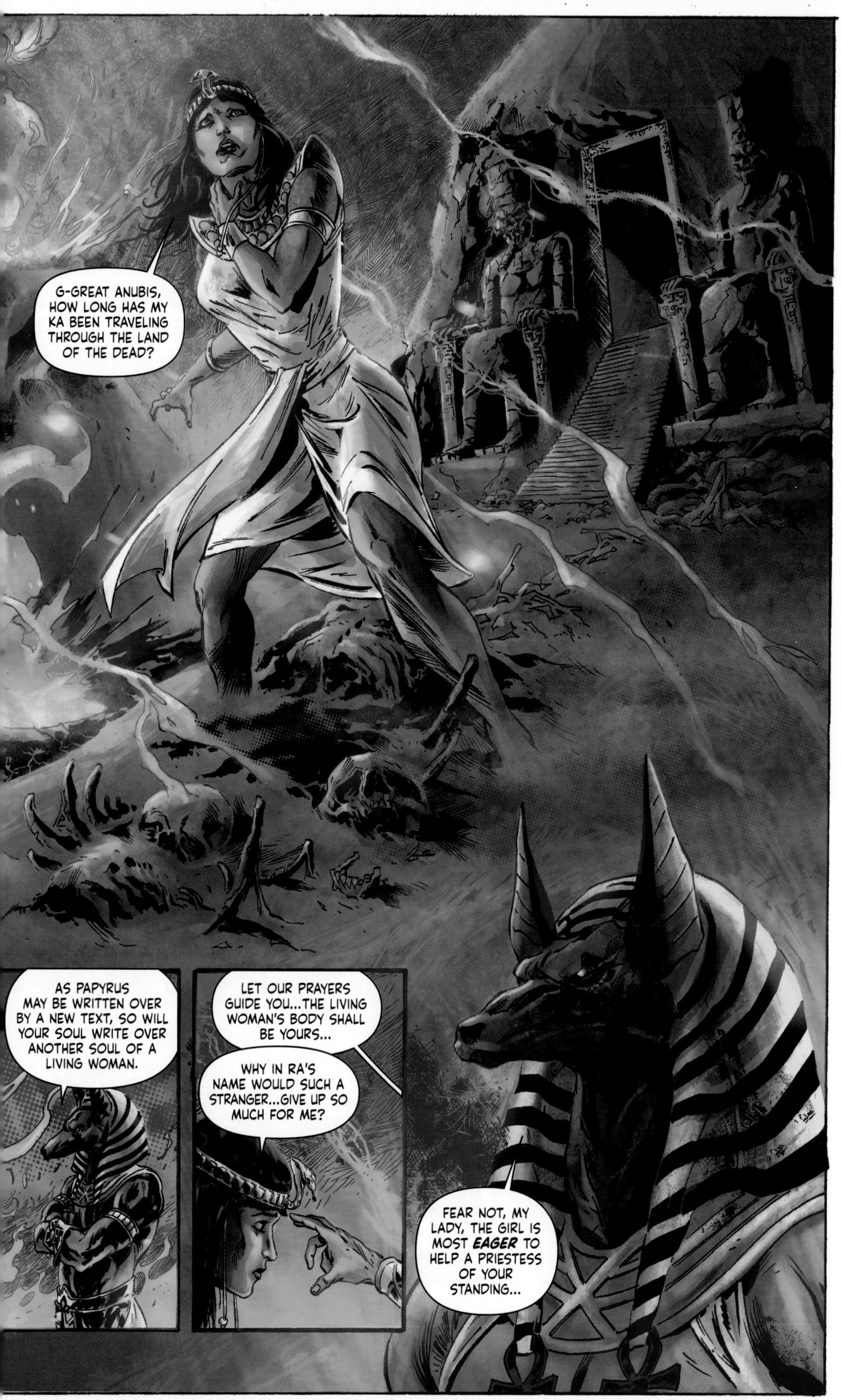
G-GREAT ANUBIS, HOW LONG HAS MY KA BEEN TRAVELING THROUGH THE LAND OF THE DEAD?
AS PAPYRUS MAY BE WRITTEN OVER BY A NEW TEXT, SO WILL YOUR SOUL WRITE OVER ANOTHER SOUL OF A LIVING WOMAN.
LET OUR PRAYERS GUIDE YOU...THE LIVING WOMAN'S BODY SHALL BE YOURS...
WHY IN RA'S NAME WOULD SUCH A STRANGER...GIVE UP SO MUCH FOR ME?
FEAR NOT, MY LADY, THE GIRL IS MOST **EAGER** TO HELP A PRIESTESS OF YOUR STANDING...

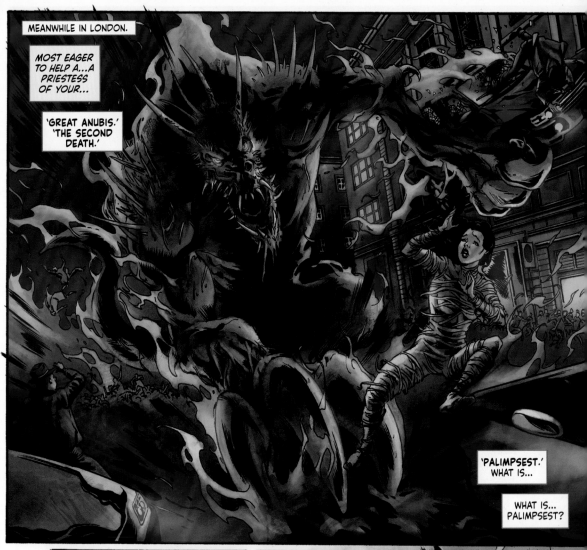

MEANWHILE IN LONDON.

MOST EAGER TO HELP A...A PRIESTESS OF YOUR...

'GREAT ANUBIS.' 'THE SECOND DEATH.'

'PALIMPSEST.' WHAT IS...

WHAT IS... PALIMPSEST?

WHAT STRANGE MEMORIES... ARE THESE?

OH MY GOD. *AMAZING.*

WEAK... MUST... MUST...

"...DO SOMETHING..."

KSSSSH

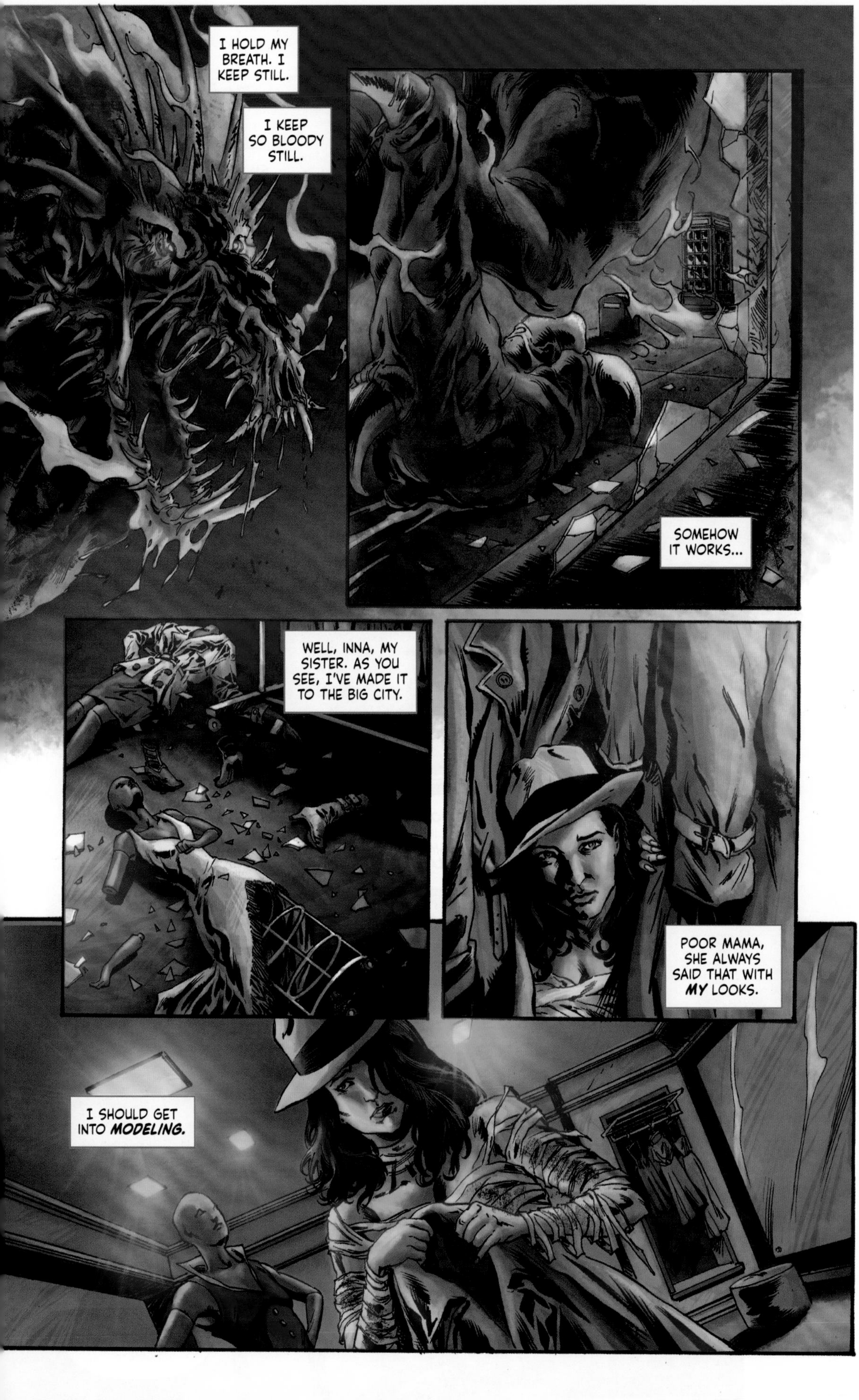
I HOLD MY BREATH. I KEEP STILL.
I KEEP SO BLOODY STILL.
SOMEHOW IT WORKS...
WELL, INNA, MY SISTER. AS YOU SEE, I'VE MADE IT TO THE BIG CITY.
POOR MAMA, SHE ALWAYS SAID THAT WITH *MY* LOOKS.
I SHOULD GET INTO *MODELING.*

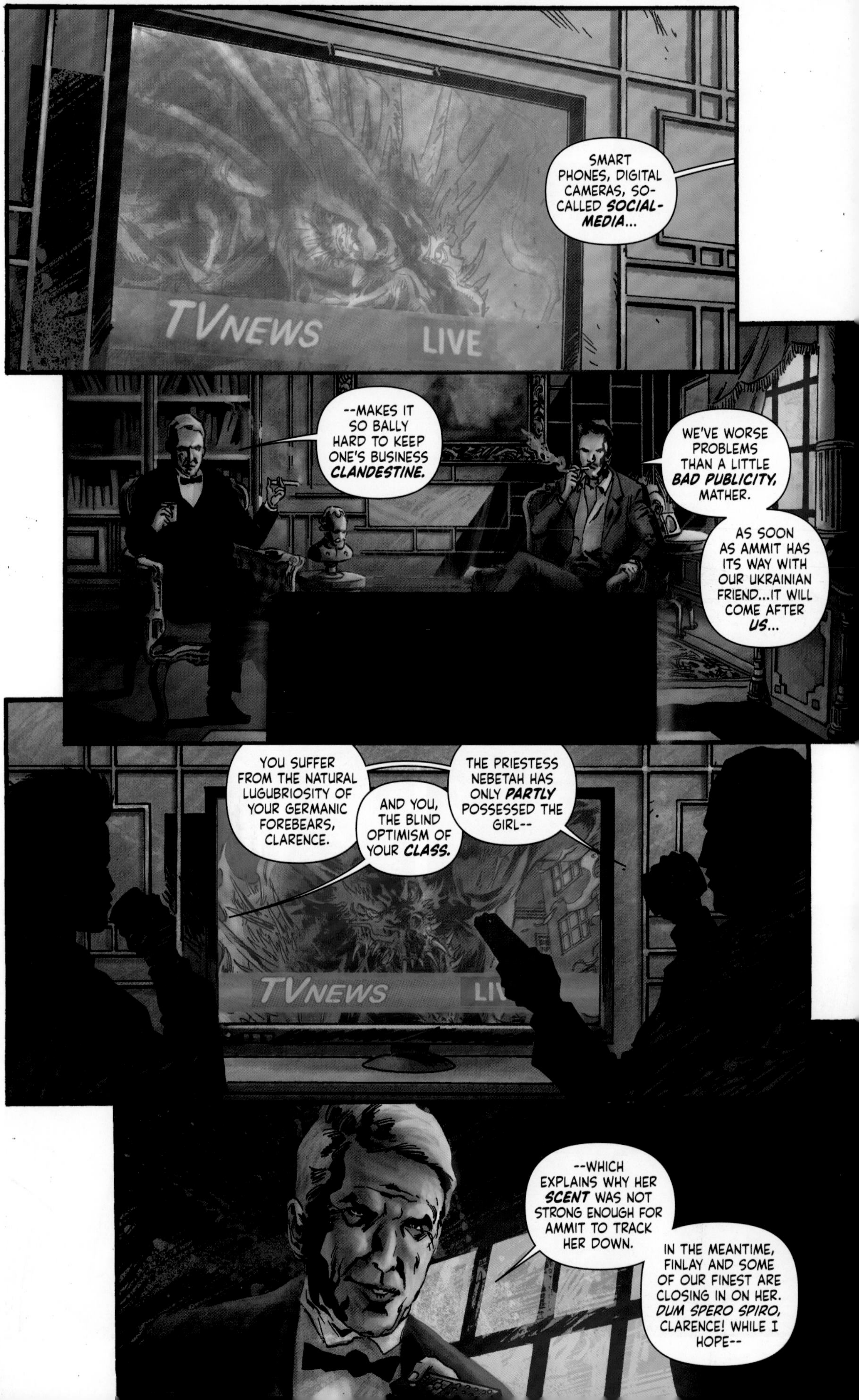
SMART PHONES, DIGITAL CAMERAS, SO-CALLED SOCIAL-MEDIA...
TVNEWS
LIVE
--MAKES IT SO BALLY HARD TO KEEP ONE'S BUSINESS CLANDESTINE.
WE'VE WORSE PROBLEMS THAN A LITTLE BAD PUBLICITY, MATHER.
AS SOON AS AMMIT HAS ITS WAY WITH OUR UKRAINIAN FRIEND...IT WILL COME AFTER US...
YOU SUFFER FROM THE NATURAL LUGUBRIOSITY OF YOUR GERMANIC FOREBEARS, CLARENCE.
AND YOU, THE BLIND OPTIMISM OF YOUR CLASS.
THE PRIESTESS NEBETAH HAS ONLY PARTLY POSSESSED THE GIRL--
TVNEWS
--WHICH EXPLAINS WHY HER SCENT WAS NOT STRONG ENOUGH FOR AMMIT TO TRACK HER DOWN.
IN THE MEANTIME, FINLAY AND SOME OF OUR FINEST ARE CLOSING IN ON HER. DUM SPERO SPIRO, CLARENCE! WHILE I HOPE--

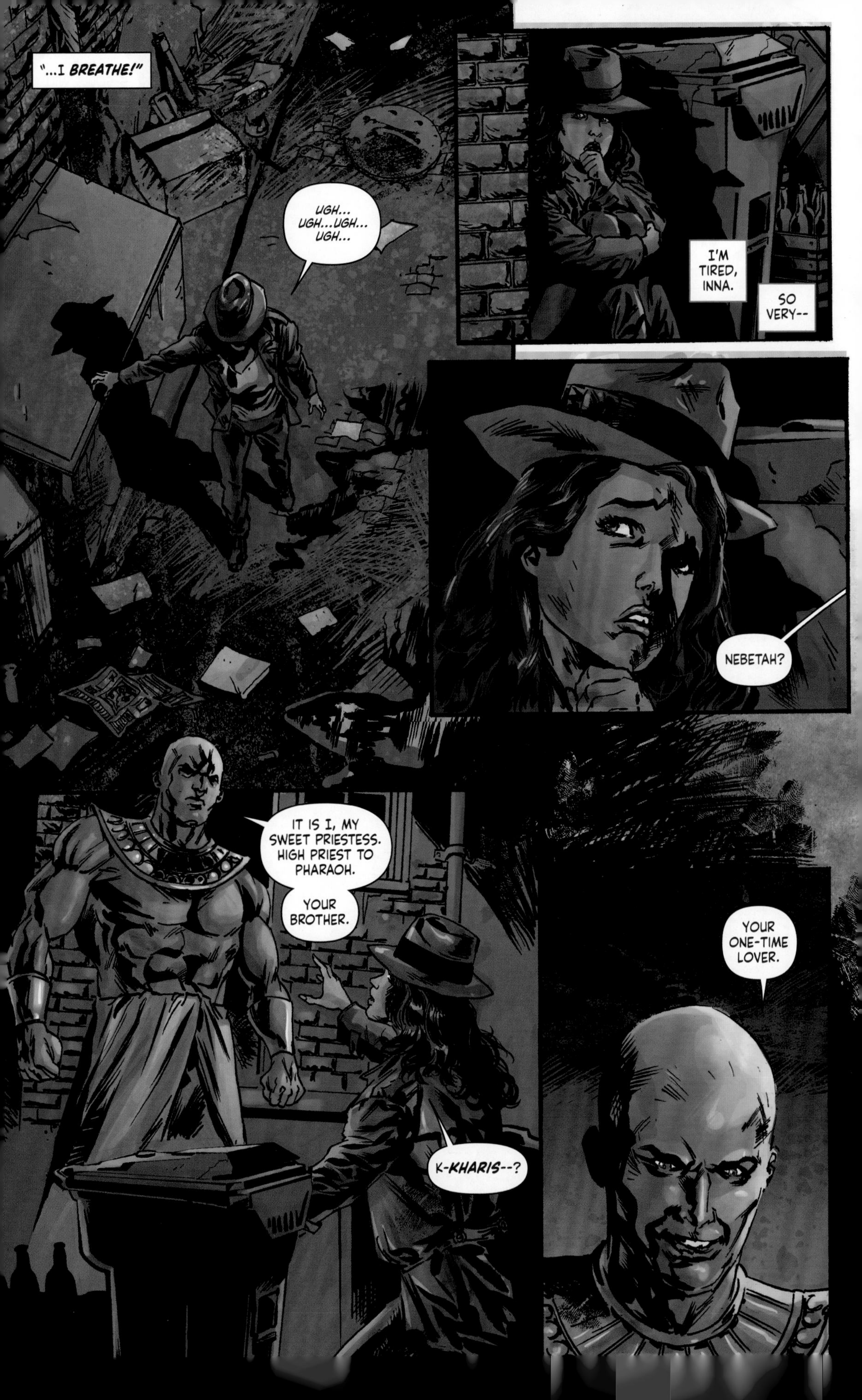
"...I BREATHE!"
UGH... UGH...UGH... UGH...
I'M TIRED, INNA.
SO VERY--
NEBETAH?
IT IS I, MY SWEET PRIESTESS. HIGH PRIEST TO PHARAOH.
YOUR BROTHER.
K-KHARIS--?
YOUR ONE-TIME LOVER.

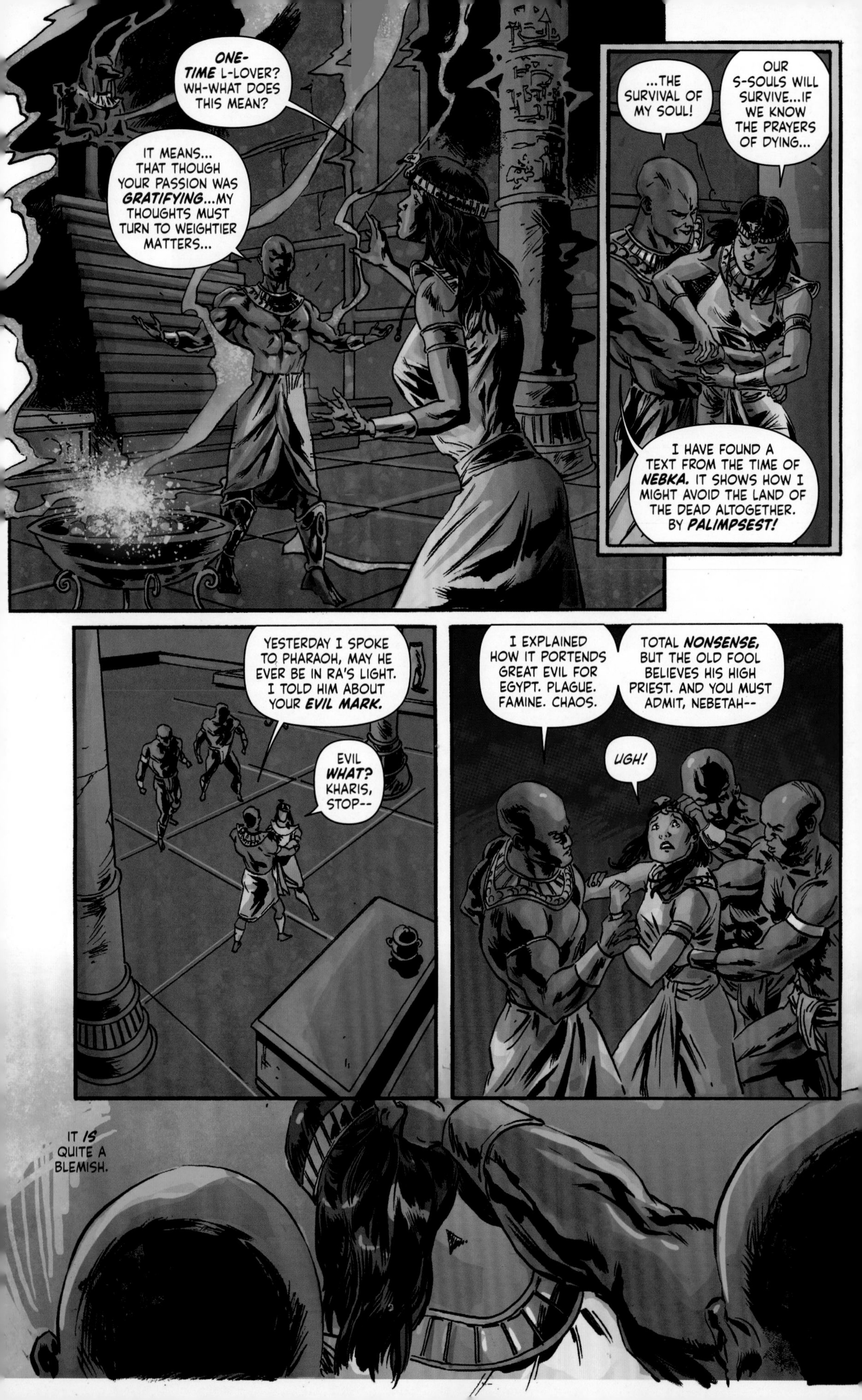
ONE-TIME L-LOVER? WH-WHAT DOES THIS MEAN?
IT MEANS... THAT THOUGH YOUR PASSION WAS GRATIFYING...MY THOUGHTS MUST TURN TO WEIGHTIER MATTERS...
...THE SURVIVAL OF MY SOUL!
OUR S-SOULS WILL SURVIVE...IF WE KNOW THE PRAYERS OF DYING...
I HAVE FOUND A TEXT FROM THE TIME OF NEBKA. IT SHOWS HOW I MIGHT AVOID THE LAND OF THE DEAD ALTOGETHER. BY PALIMPSEST!
YESTERDAY I SPOKE TO PHARAOH, MAY HE EVER BE IN RA'S LIGHT. I TOLD HIM ABOUT YOUR EVIL MARK.
EVIL WHAT? KHARIS, STOP--
I EXPLAINED HOW IT PORTENDS GREAT EVIL FOR EGYPT. PLAGUE. FAMINE. CHAOS.
TOTAL NONSENSE, BUT THE OLD FOOL BELIEVES HIS HIGH PRIEST. AND YOU MUST ADMIT, NEBETAH--
UGH!
IT IS QUITE A BLEMISH.

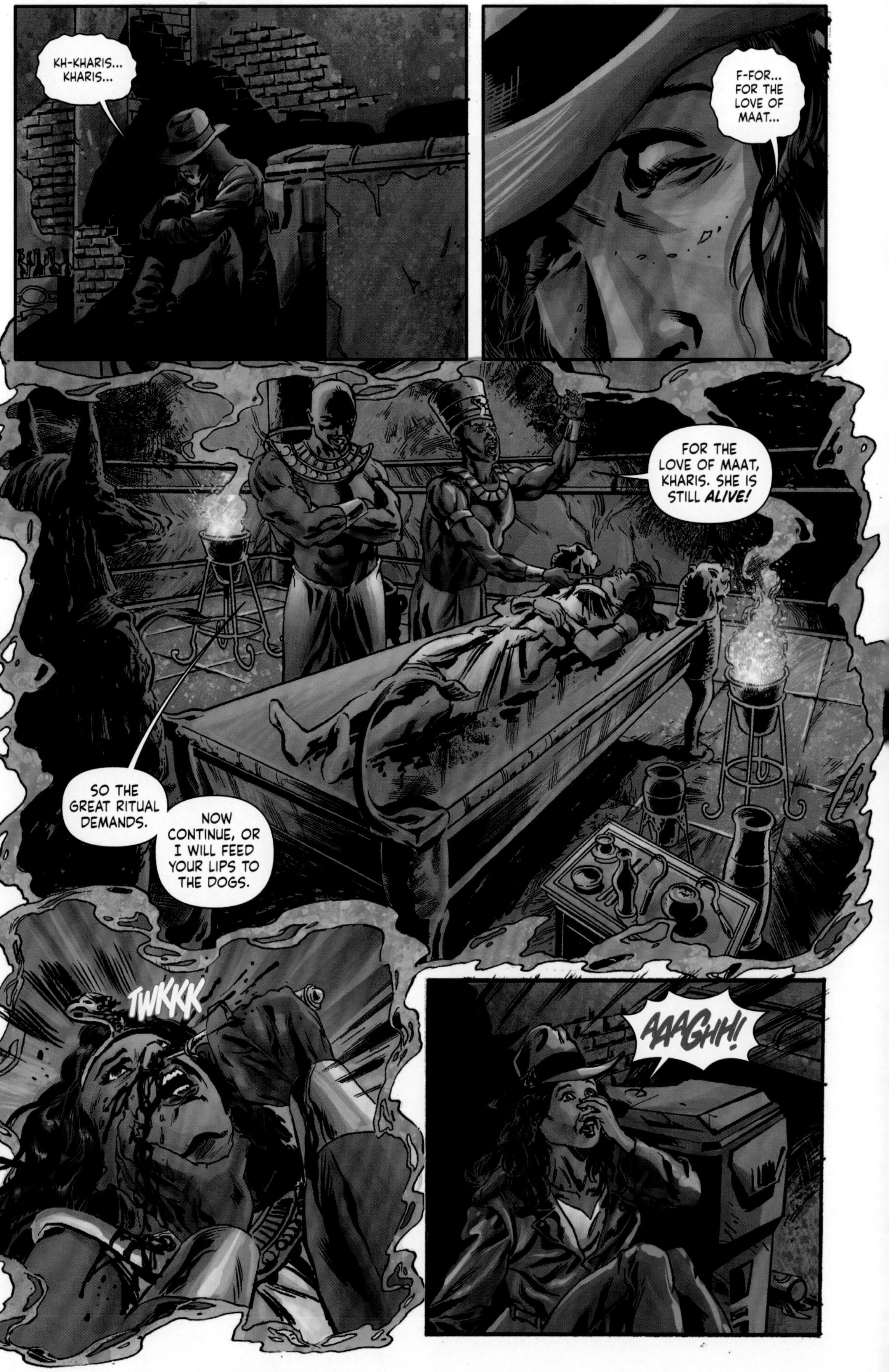
KH-KHARIS... KHARIS...
F-FOR... FOR THE LOVE OF MAAT...
FOR THE LOVE OF MAAT, KHARIS. SHE IS STILL *ALIVE!*
SO THE GREAT RITUAL DEMANDS.
NOW CONTINUE, OR I WILL FEED YOUR LIPS TO THE DOGS.
TWKKK
AAAGHH!

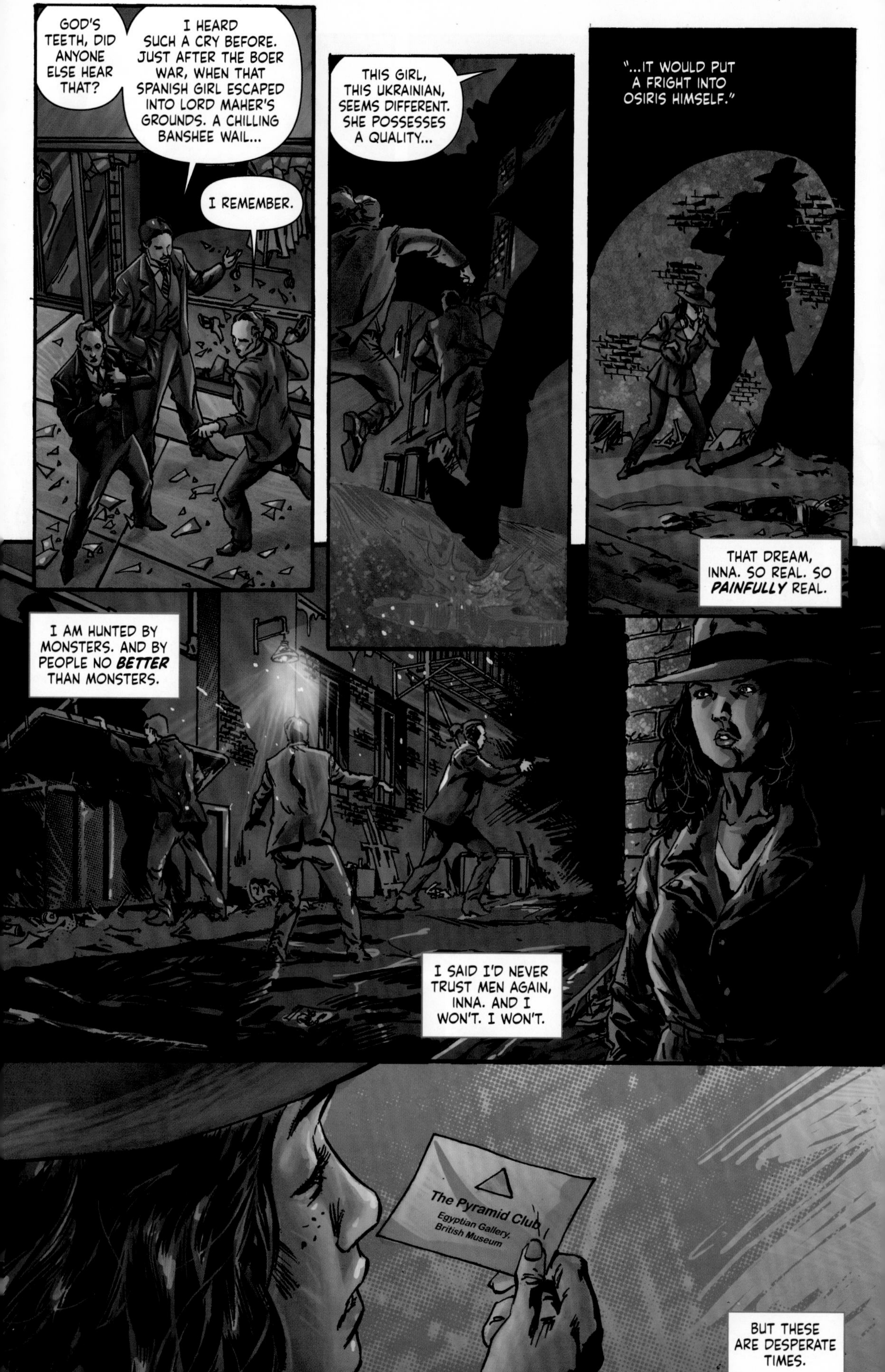
GOD'S TEETH, DID ANYONE ELSE HEAR THAT?
I HEARD SUCH A CRY BEFORE. JUST AFTER THE BOER WAR, WHEN THAT SPANISH GIRL ESCAPED INTO LORD MAHER'S GROUNDS. A CHILLING BANSHEE WAIL...
I REMEMBER.
THIS GIRL, THIS UKRAINIAN, SEEMS DIFFERENT. SHE POSSESSES A QUALITY...
"...IT WOULD PUT A FRIGHT INTO OSIRIS HIMSELF."
THAT DREAM, INNA. SO REAL. SO *PAINFULLY* REAL.
I AM HUNTED BY MONSTERS. AND BY PEOPLE NO *BETTER* THAN MONSTERS.
I SAID I'D NEVER TRUST MEN AGAIN, INNA. AND I WON'T. I WON'T.
The Pyramid Club
Egyptian Gallery, British Museum
BUT THESE ARE DESPERATE TIMES.

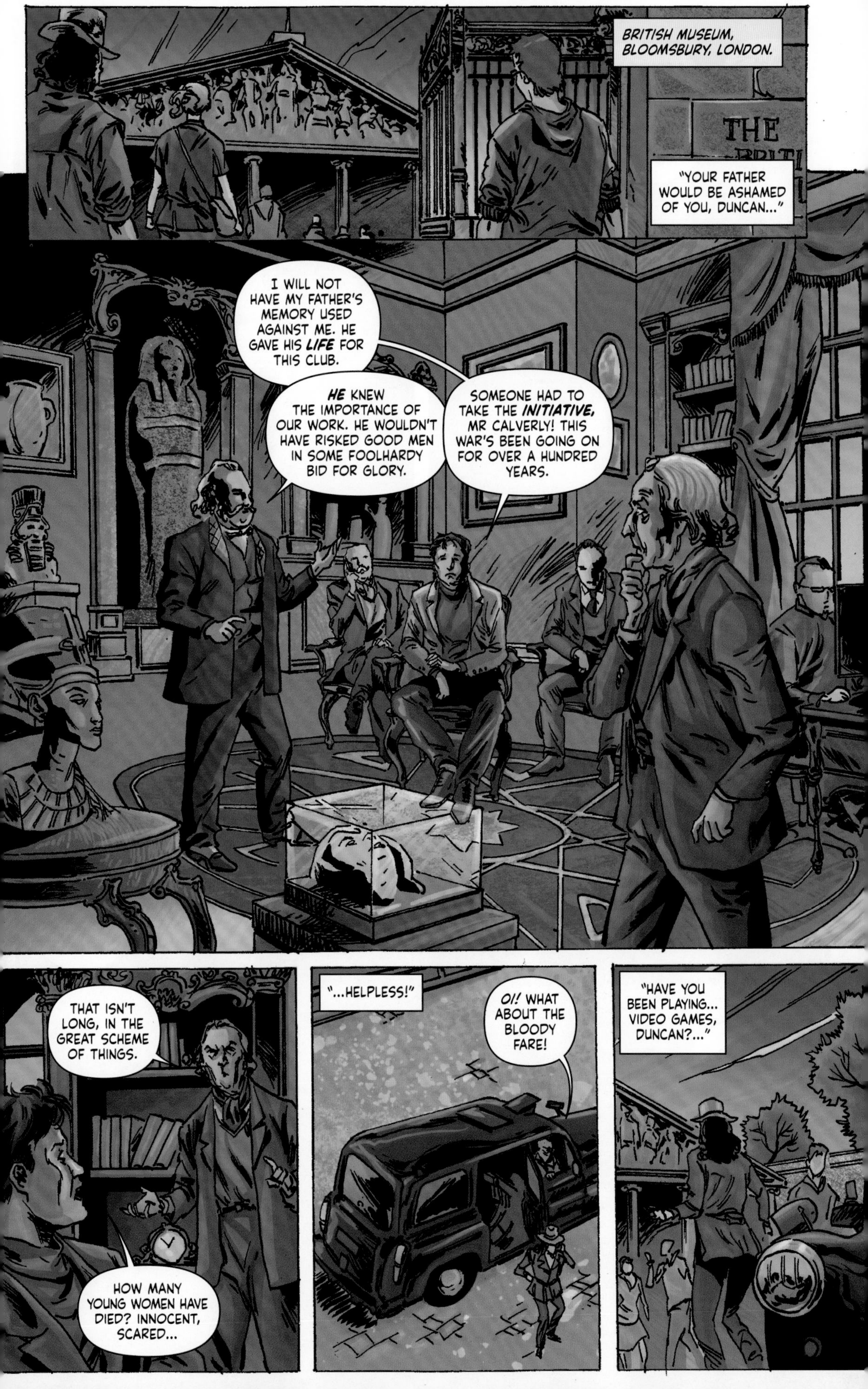
BRITISH MUSEUM, BLOOMSBURY, LONDON.
"YOUR FATHER WOULD BE ASHAMED OF YOU, DUNCAN..."
I WILL NOT HAVE MY FATHER'S MEMORY USED AGAINST ME. HE GAVE HIS *LIFE* FOR THIS CLUB.
HE KNEW THE IMPORTANCE OF OUR WORK. HE WOULDN'T HAVE RISKED GOOD MEN IN SOME FOOLHARDY BID FOR GLORY.
SOMEONE HAD TO TAKE THE *INITIATIVE,* MR CALVERLY! THIS WAR'S BEEN GOING ON FOR OVER A HUNDRED YEARS.
THAT ISN'T LONG, IN THE GREAT SCHEME OF THINGS.
HOW MANY YOUNG WOMEN HAVE DIED? INNOCENT, SCARED...
"...HELPLESS!"
OI! WHAT ABOUT THE BLOODY FARE!
"HAVE YOU BEEN PLAYING... VIDEO GAMES, DUNCAN?..."

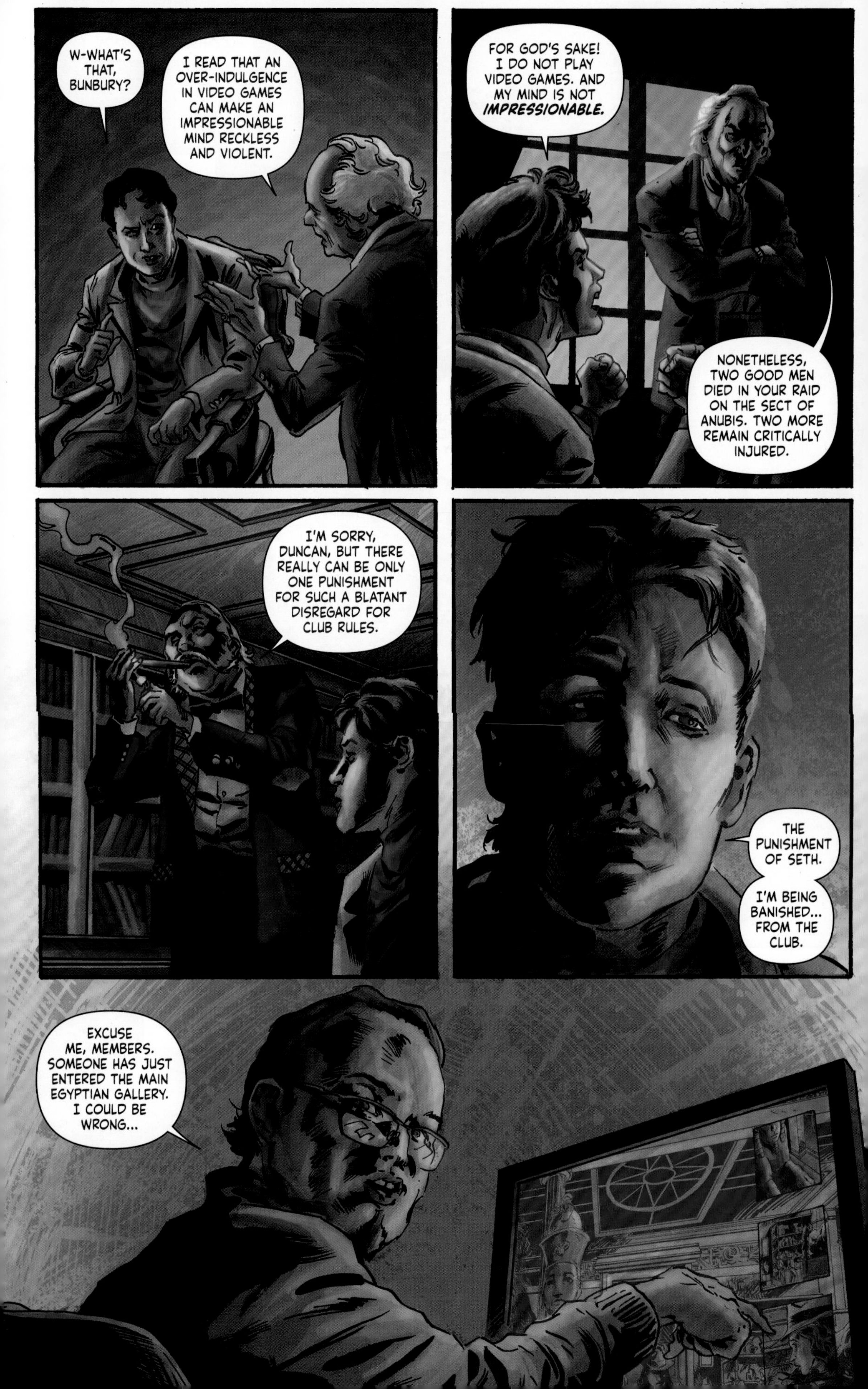
W-WHAT'S THAT, BUNBURY?
I READ THAT AN OVER-INDULGENCE IN VIDEO GAMES CAN MAKE AN IMPRESSIONABLE MIND RECKLESS AND VIOLENT.
FOR GOD'S SAKE! I DO NOT PLAY VIDEO GAMES. AND MY MIND IS NOT *IMPRESSIONABLE.*
NONETHELESS, TWO GOOD MEN DIED IN YOUR RAID ON THE SECT OF ANUBIS. TWO MORE REMAIN CRITICALLY INJURED.
I'M SORRY, DUNCAN, BUT THERE REALLY CAN BE ONLY ONE PUNISHMENT FOR SUCH A BLATANT DISREGARD FOR CLUB RULES.
THE PUNISHMENT OF SETH.
I'M BEING BANISHED... FROM THE CLUB.
EXCUSE ME, MEMBERS. SOMEONE HAS JUST ENTERED THE MAIN EGYPTIAN GALLERY. I COULD BE WRONG...

"...BUT I DO BELIEVE SHE'S BEEN TOUCHED BY OUR *ENEMY*..."

IT'S HER! THE GIRL! I *TOLD* YOU SHE WAS BEAUTIFUL!

DUNCAN, THEY INFORM ME YOU ARE ATTRACTIVE TO THE FEMALE SEX. USE YOUR...*CHARM* TO LURE HER IN HERE.

I SHALL DEAL WITH HER MYSELF.

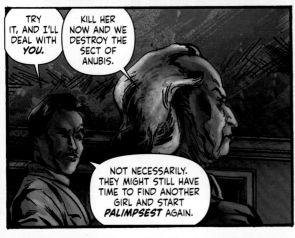

TRY IT, AND I'LL DEAL WITH *YOU*.

KILL HER NOW AND WE DESTROY THE SECT OF ANUBIS.

NOT NECESSARILY. THEY MIGHT STILL HAVE TIME TO FIND ANOTHER GIRL AND START *PALIMPSEST* AGAIN.

GENTLEMEN, GENTLEMEN. THERE IS *ANOTHER* WAY...

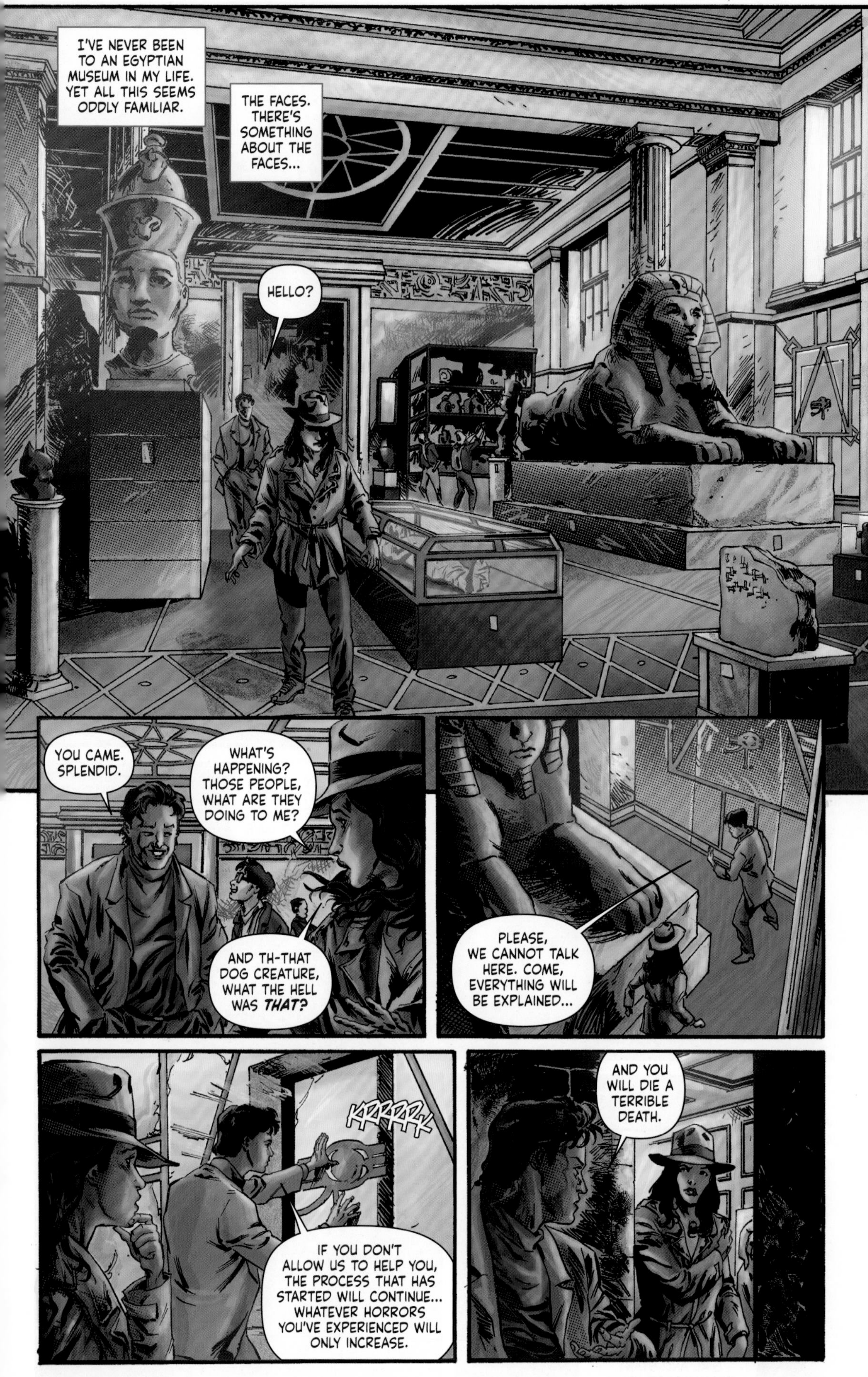
I'VE NEVER BEEN TO AN EGYPTIAN MUSEUM IN MY LIFE. YET ALL THIS SEEMS ODDLY FAMILIAR.
THE FACES. THERE'S SOMETHING ABOUT THE FACES...
HELLO?
YOU CAME. SPLENDID.
WHAT'S HAPPENING? THOSE PEOPLE, WHAT ARE THEY DOING TO ME?
AND TH-THAT DOG CREATURE, WHAT THE HELL WAS *THAT?*
PLEASE, WE CANNOT TALK HERE. COME, EVERYTHING WILL BE EXPLAINED...
KRRRRK
IF YOU DON'T ALLOW US TO HELP YOU, THE PROCESS THAT HAS STARTED WILL CONTINUE... WHATEVER HORRORS YOU'VE EXPERIENCED WILL ONLY INCREASE.
AND YOU WILL DIE A TERRIBLE DEATH.

YOU SEE, INNA?

I'M DUNCAN. AND YOU ARE?

NONE OF YOUR GODDAMN BUSINESS. I'M NOT SAYING ANYTHING UNTIL I GET SOME QUESTIONS ANSWERED.

DESPERATE TIMES.

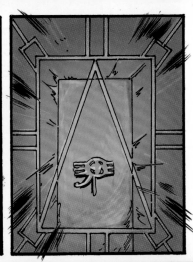

WHAT *IS* THIS PLACE?

THE HEADQUARTERS OF THE PYRAMID CLUB. FOUNDED IN 1883 TO FIGHT THE *SECT OF ANUBIS.* THEY'RE THE FIENDS WHO'VE BEEN HURTING YOU.

HERE WE ARE. I SHOULD WARN YOU, MY COLLEAGUES ARE A LITTLE... CRUSTY.

THE IDEA OF *WOMEN'S LIBERATION* HAS SOMEWHAT PASSED THEM BY.

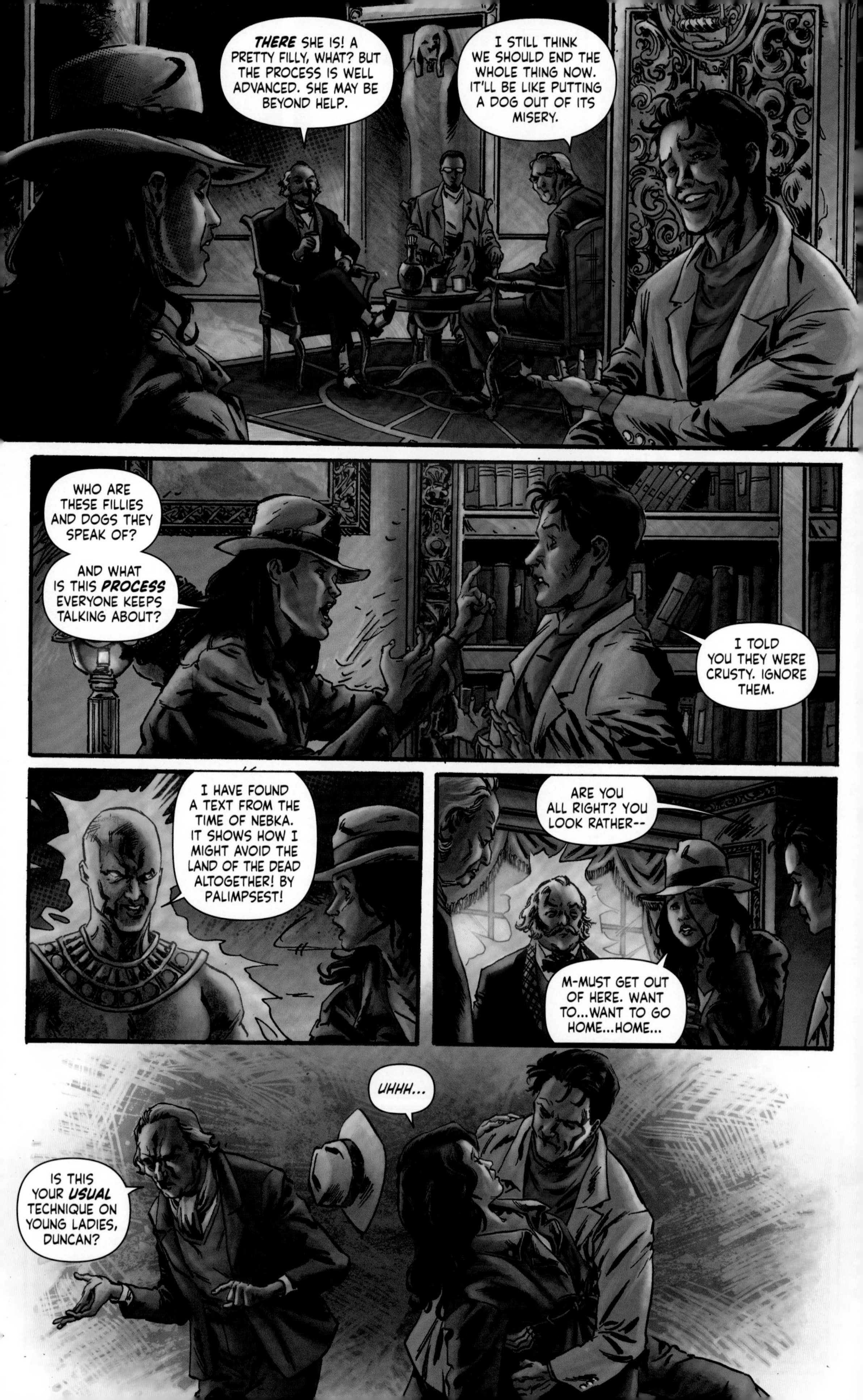
THERE SHE IS! A PRETTY FILLY, WHAT? BUT THE PROCESS IS WELL ADVANCED. SHE MAY BE BEYOND HELP.
I STILL THINK WE SHOULD END THE WHOLE THING NOW. IT'LL BE LIKE PUTTING A DOG OUT OF ITS MISERY.
WHO ARE THESE FILLIES AND DOGS THEY SPEAK OF?
AND WHAT IS THIS PROCESS EVERYONE KEEPS TALKING ABOUT?
I TOLD YOU THEY WERE CRUSTY. IGNORE THEM.
I HAVE FOUND A TEXT FROM THE TIME OF NEBKA. IT SHOWS HOW I MIGHT AVOID THE LAND OF THE DEAD ALTOGETHER! BY PALIMPSEST!
ARE YOU ALL RIGHT? YOU LOOK RATHER--
M-MUST GET OUT OF HERE. WANT TO...WANT TO GO HOME...HOME...
UHHH...
IS THIS YOUR USUAL TECHNIQUE ON YOUNG LADIES, DUNCAN?

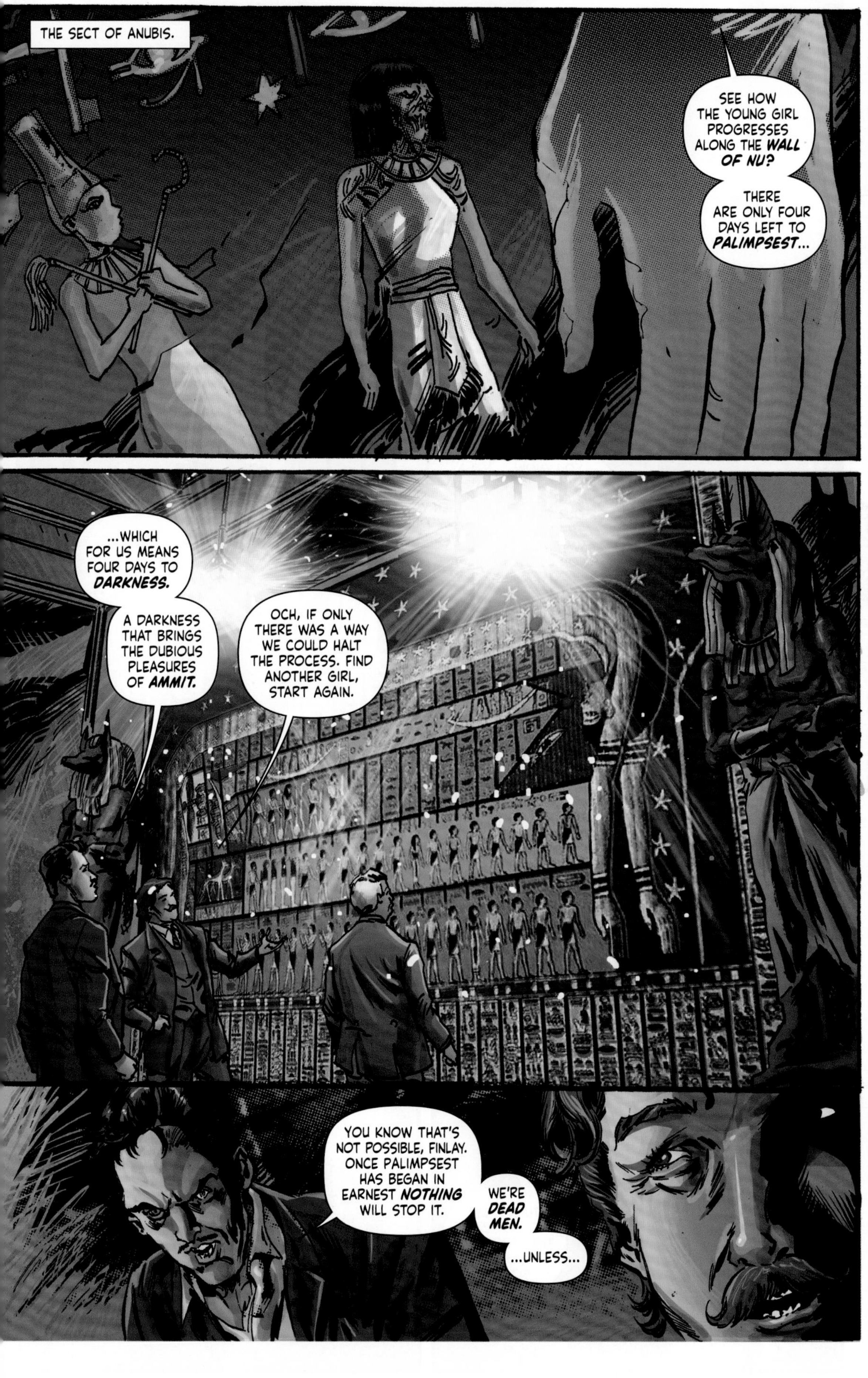
THE SECT OF ANUBIS.
SEE HOW THE YOUNG GIRL PROGRESSES ALONG THE WALL OF NU?
THERE ARE ONLY FOUR DAYS LEFT TO PALIMPSEST...
...WHICH FOR US MEANS FOUR DAYS TO DARKNESS.
A DARKNESS THAT BRINGS THE DUBIOUS PLEASURES OF AMMIT.
OCH, IF ONLY THERE WAS A WAY WE COULD HALT THE PROCESS. FIND ANOTHER GIRL, START AGAIN.
YOU KNOW THAT'S NOT POSSIBLE, FINLAY. ONCE PALIMPSEST HAS BEGAN IN EARNEST NOTHING WILL STOP IT.
WE'RE DEAD MEN.
...UNLESS...

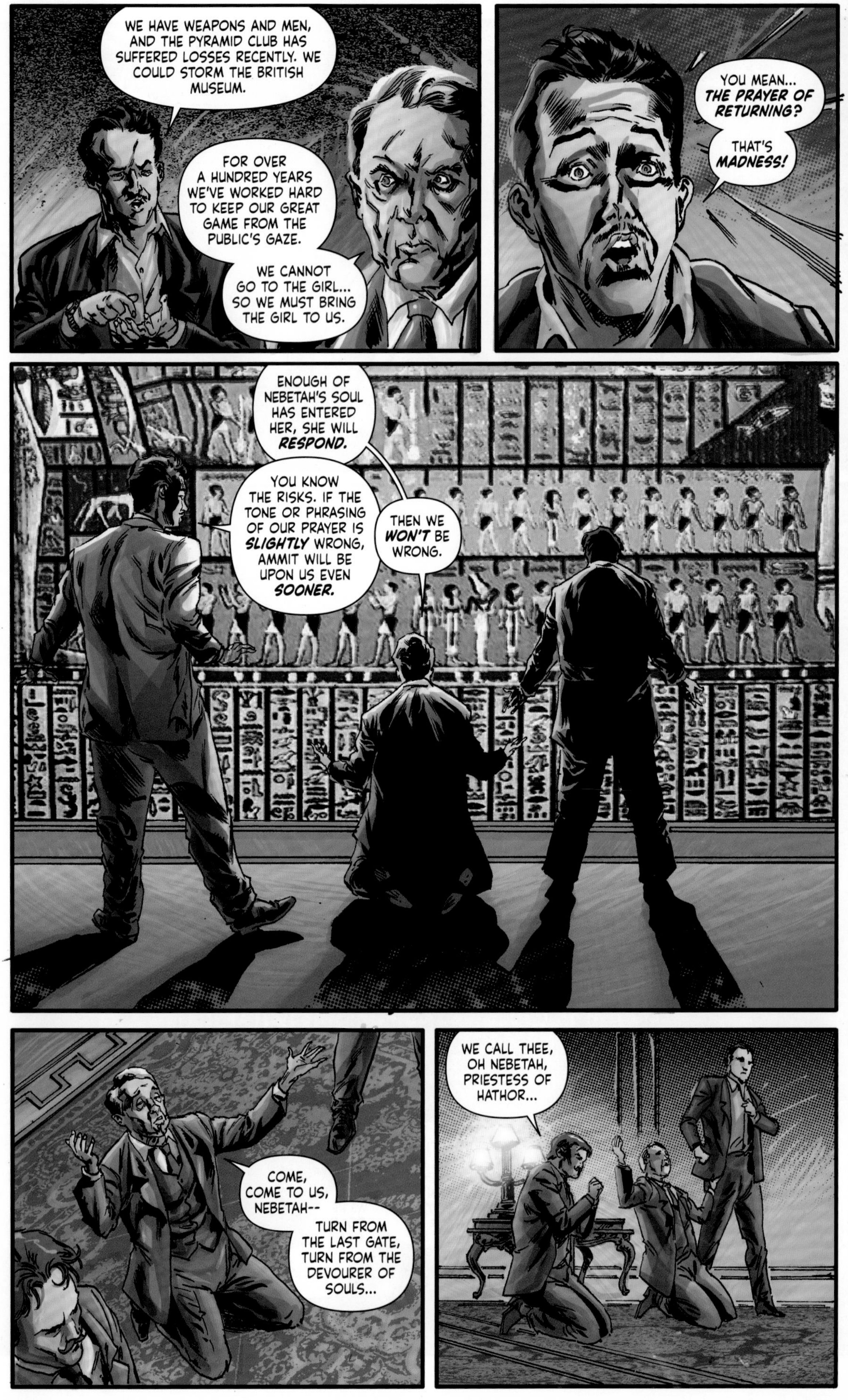
WE HAVE WEAPONS AND MEN, AND THE PYRAMID CLUB HAS SUFFERED LOSSES RECENTLY. WE COULD STORM THE BRITISH MUSEUM.
FOR OVER A HUNDRED YEARS WE'VE WORKED HARD TO KEEP OUR GREAT GAME FROM THE PUBLIC'S GAZE.
WE CANNOT GO TO THE GIRL... SO WE MUST BRING THE GIRL TO US.
YOU MEAN... THE PRAYER OF RETURNING?
THAT'S MADNESS!
ENOUGH OF NEBETAH'S SOUL HAS ENTERED HER, SHE WILL RESPOND.
YOU KNOW THE RISKS. IF THE TONE OR PHRASING OF OUR PRAYER IS SLIGHTLY WRONG, AMMIT WILL BE UPON US EVEN SOONER.
THEN WE WON'T BE WRONG.
COME, COME TO US, NEBETAH--
TURN FROM THE LAST GATE, TURN FROM THE DEVOURER OF SOULS...
WE CALL THEE, OH NEBETAH, PRIESTESS OF HATHOR...

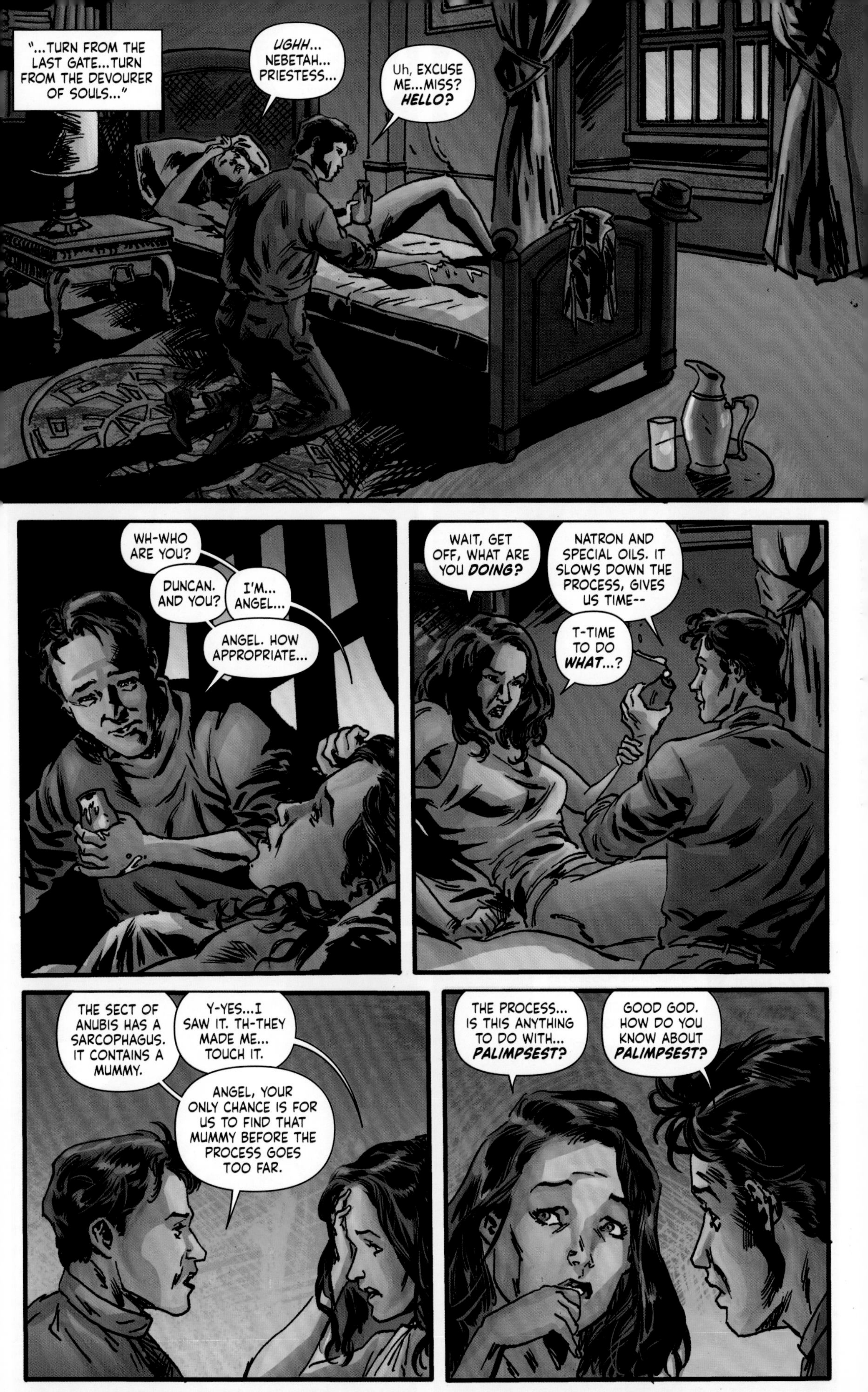
"...TURN FROM THE LAST GATE...TURN FROM THE DEVOURER OF SOULS..."
UGHH... NEBETAH... PRIESTESS...
Uh, EXCUSE ME...MISS? HELLO?
WH-WHO ARE YOU?
DUNCAN. AND YOU?
I'M... ANGEL...
ANGEL. HOW APPROPRIATE...
WAIT, GET OFF, WHAT ARE YOU DOING?
NATRON AND SPECIAL OILS. IT SLOWS DOWN THE PROCESS, GIVES US TIME--
T-TIME TO DO WHAT...?
THE SECT OF ANUBIS HAS A SARCOPHAGUS. IT CONTAINS A MUMMY.
Y-YES...I SAW IT. TH-THEY MADE ME... TOUCH IT.
ANGEL, YOUR ONLY CHANCE IS FOR US TO FIND THAT MUMMY BEFORE THE PROCESS GOES TOO FAR.
THE PROCESS... IS THIS ANYTHING TO DO WITH... PALIMPSEST?
GOOD GOD. HOW DO YOU KNOW ABOUT PALIMPSEST?

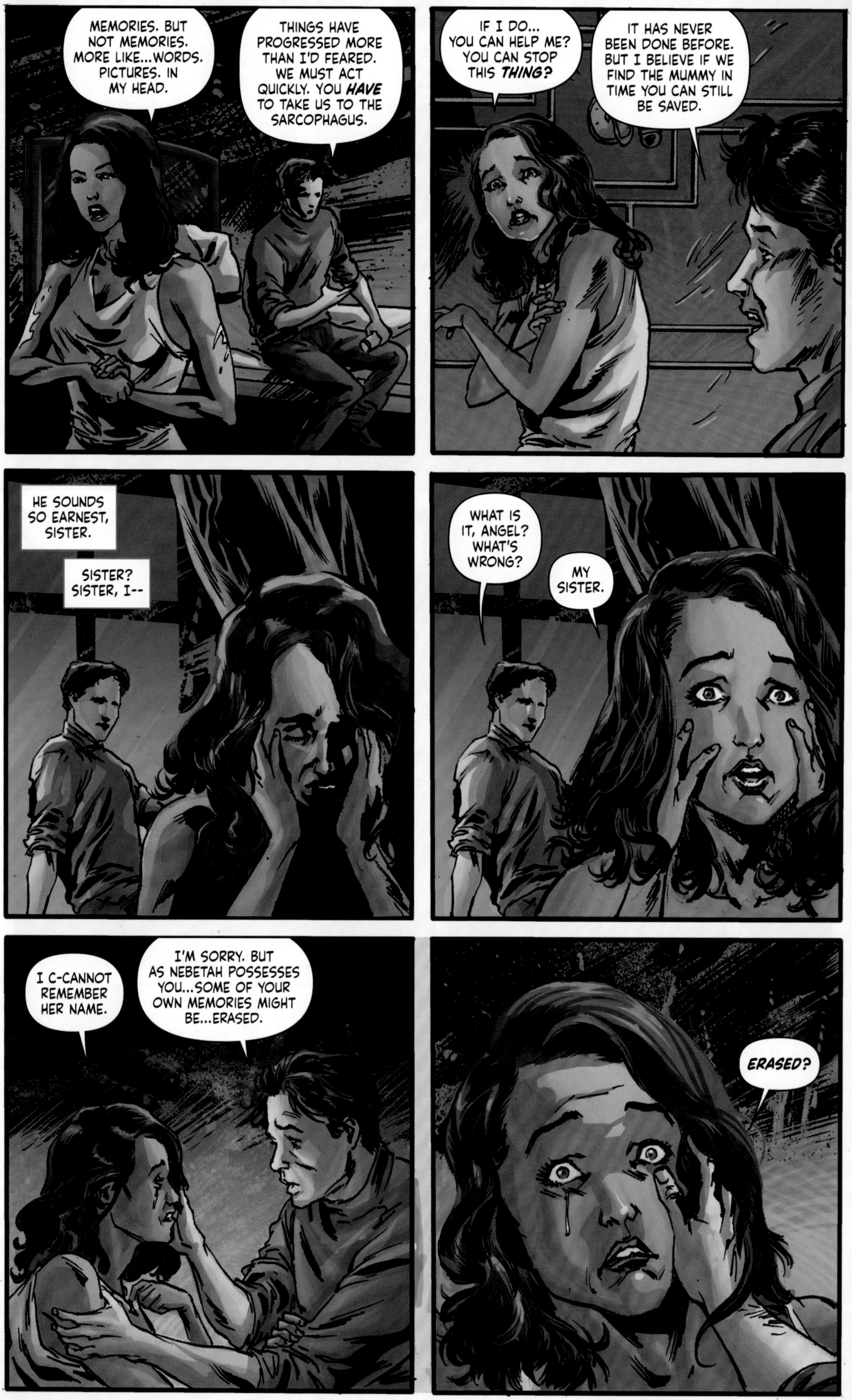
MEMORIES. BUT NOT MEMORIES. MORE LIKE...WORDS. PICTURES. IN MY HEAD.
THINGS HAVE PROGRESSED MORE THAN I'D FEARED. WE MUST ACT QUICKLY. YOU *HAVE* TO TAKE US TO THE SARCOPHAGUS.
IF I DO... YOU CAN HELP ME? YOU CAN STOP THIS *THING?*
IT HAS NEVER BEEN DONE BEFORE. BUT I BELIEVE IF WE FIND THE MUMMY IN TIME YOU CAN STILL BE SAVED.
HE SOUNDS SO EARNEST, SISTER.
SISTER? SISTER, I--
WHAT IS IT, ANGEL? WHAT'S WRONG?
MY SISTER.
I C-CANNOT REMEMBER HER NAME.
I'M SORRY. BUT AS NEBETAH POSSESSES YOU...SOME OF YOUR OWN MEMORIES MIGHT BE...ERASED.
ERASED?

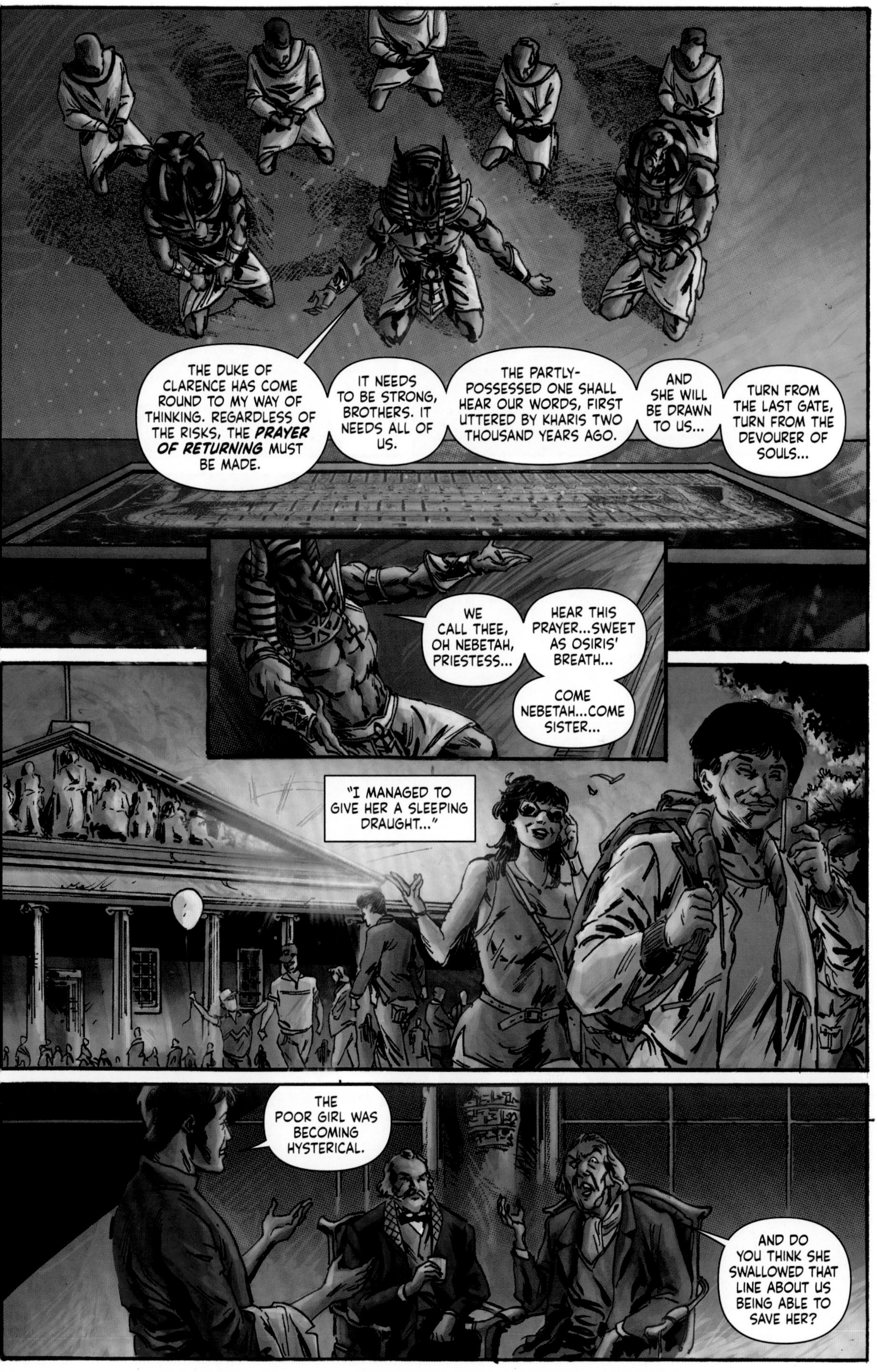
THE DUKE OF CLARENCE HAS COME ROUND TO MY WAY OF THINKING. REGARDLESS OF THE RISKS, THE **PRAYER OF RETURNING** MUST BE MADE.
IT NEEDS TO BE STRONG, BROTHERS. IT NEEDS ALL OF US.
THE PARTLY-POSSESSED ONE SHALL HEAR OUR WORDS, FIRST UTTERED BY KHARIS TWO THOUSAND YEARS AGO.
AND SHE WILL BE DRAWN TO US...
TURN FROM THE LAST GATE, TURN FROM THE DEVOURER OF SOULS...
WE CALL THEE, OH NEBETAH, PRIESTESS...
HEAR THIS PRAYER...SWEET AS OSIRIS' BREATH...
COME NEBETAH...COME SISTER...
"I MANAGED TO GIVE HER A SLEEPING DRAUGHT..."
THE POOR GIRL WAS BECOMING HYSTERICAL.
AND DO YOU THINK SHE SWALLOWED THAT LINE ABOUT US BEING ABLE TO SAVE HER?

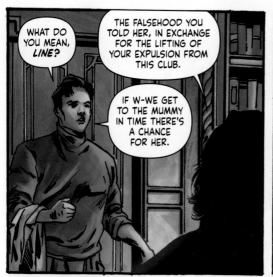

WHAT DO YOU MEAN, *LINE?*

THE FALSEHOOD YOU TOLD HER, IN EXCHANGE FOR THE LIFTING OF YOUR EXPULSION FROM THIS CLUB.

IF W-WE GET TO THE MUMMY IN TIME THERE'S A CHANCE FOR HER.

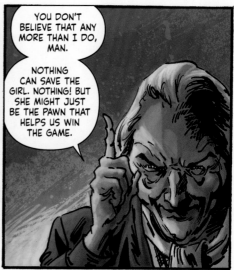

YOU DON'T BELIEVE THAT ANY MORE THAN I DO, MAN.

NOTHING CAN SAVE THE GIRL. NOTHING! BUT SHE MIGHT JUST BE THE PAWN THAT HELPS US WIN THE GAME.

GAME! THAT'S ALL THIS BLOODY WELL IS TO YOU FOSSILS. A GAME!

DAMN HIM, DAMN HIM TO HELL.

BUT--

BUT WHAT IF HE'S RIGHT?

WHAT IF I'M LYING TO MYSELF...*AND* TO ANGEL?

ANGEL?

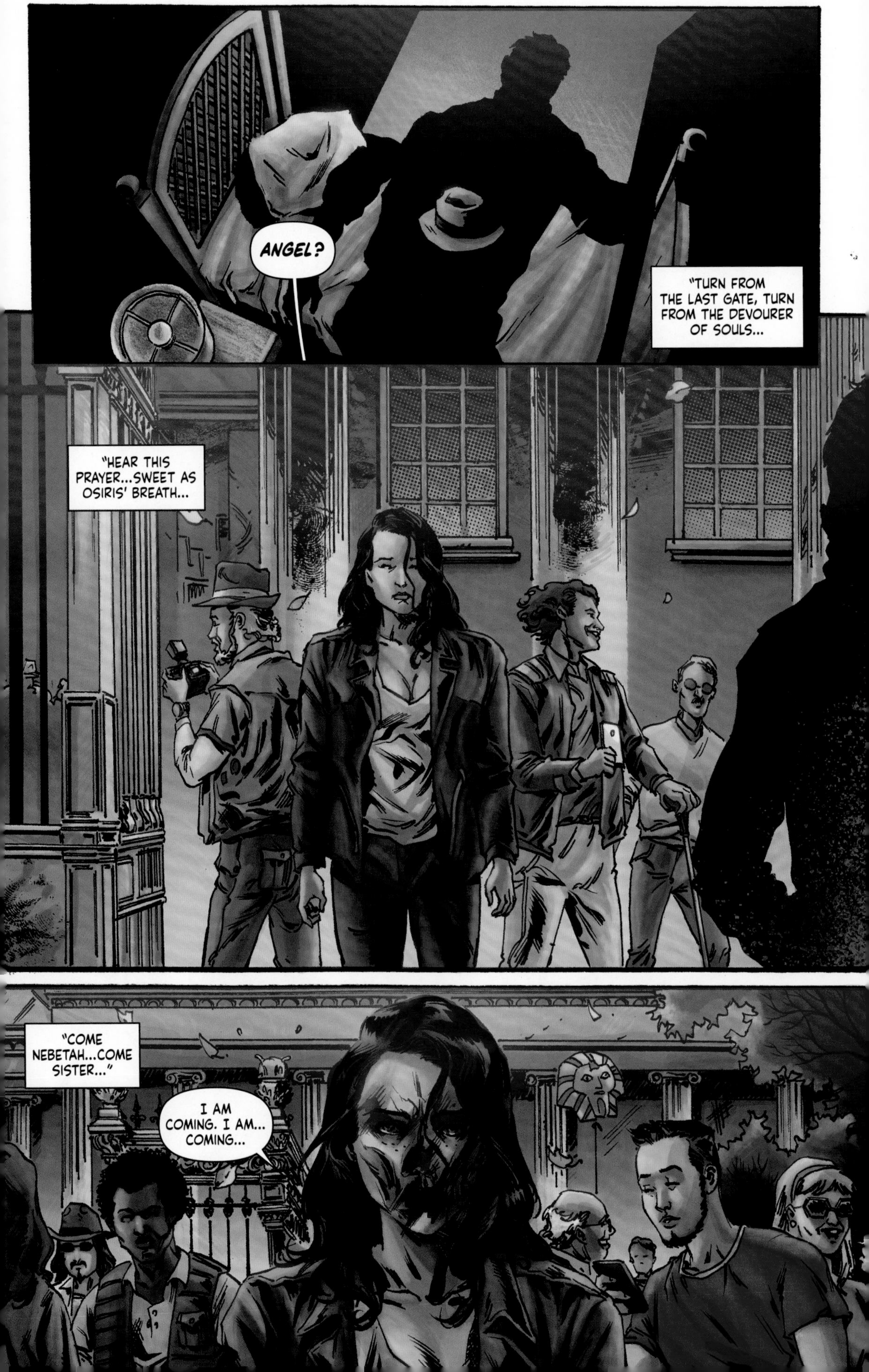
ANGEL?
"TURN FROM THE LAST GATE, TURN FROM THE DEVOURER OF SOULS...
"HEAR THIS PRAYER...SWEET AS OSIRIS' BREATH...
"COME NEBETAH...COME SISTER..."
I AM COMING. I AM... COMING...

PART III

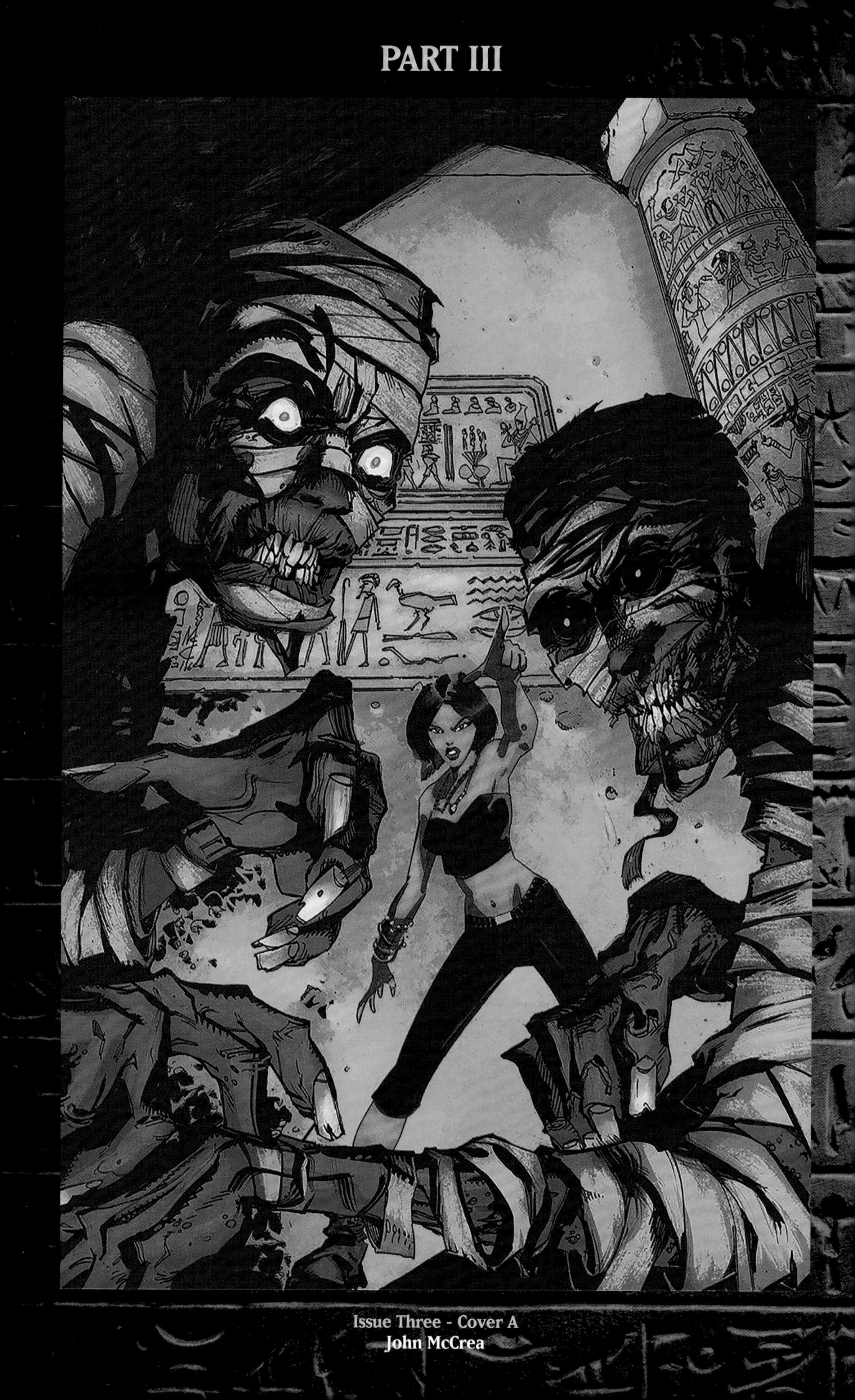

Issue Three - Cover A
John McCrea

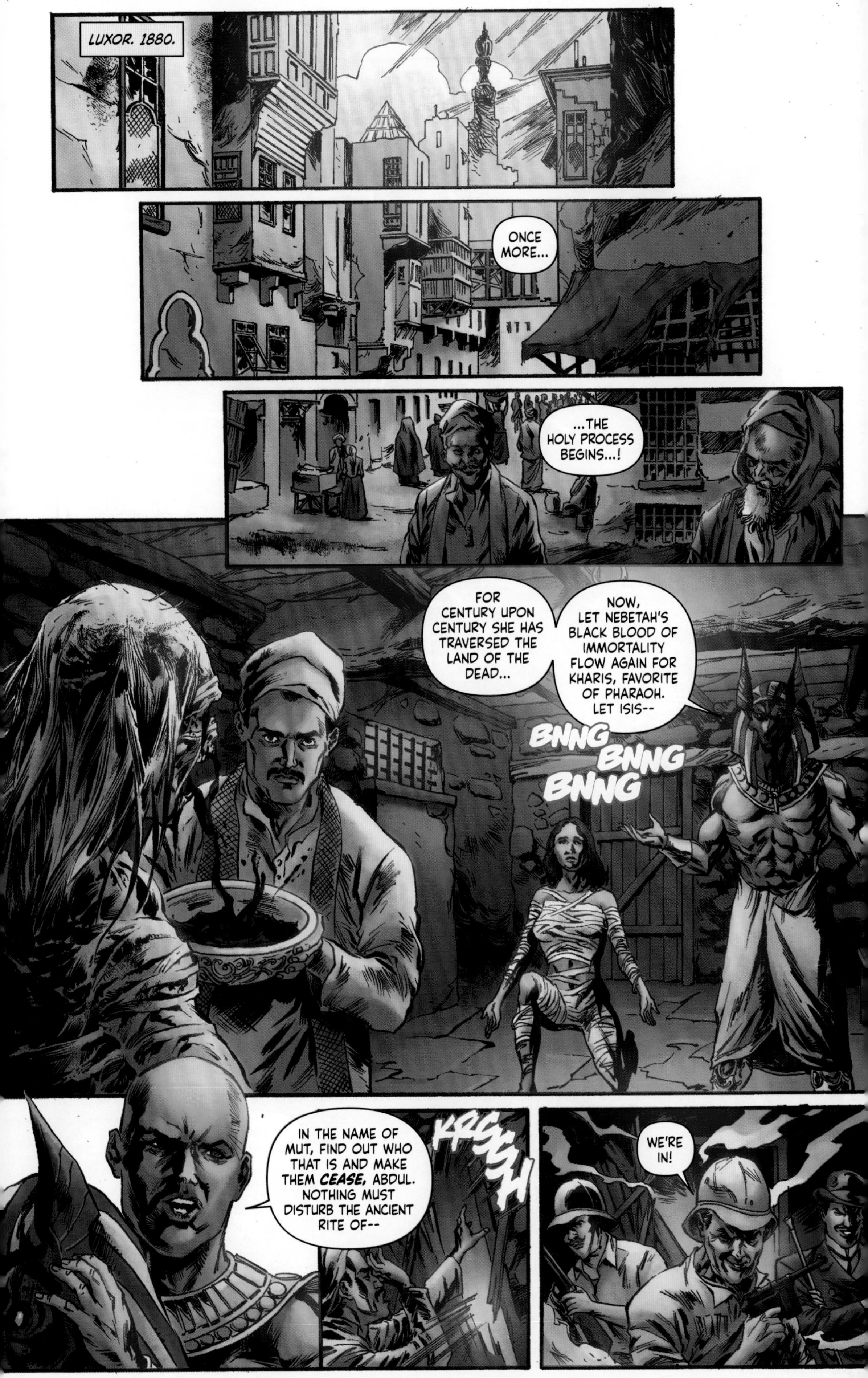
LUXOR. 1880.
ONCE MORE...
...THE HOLY PROCESS BEGINS...!
FOR CENTURY UPON CENTURY SHE HAS TRAVERSED THE LAND OF THE DEAD...
NOW, LET NEBETAH'S BLACK BLOOD OF IMMORTALITY FLOW AGAIN FOR KHARIS, FAVORITE OF PHARAOH. LET ISIS--
BNNG BNNG BNNG
IN THE NAME OF MUT, FIND OUT WHO THAT IS AND MAKE THEM *CEASE,* ABDUL. NOTHING MUST DISTURB THE ANCIENT RITE OF--
KRSSSH
WE'RE IN!

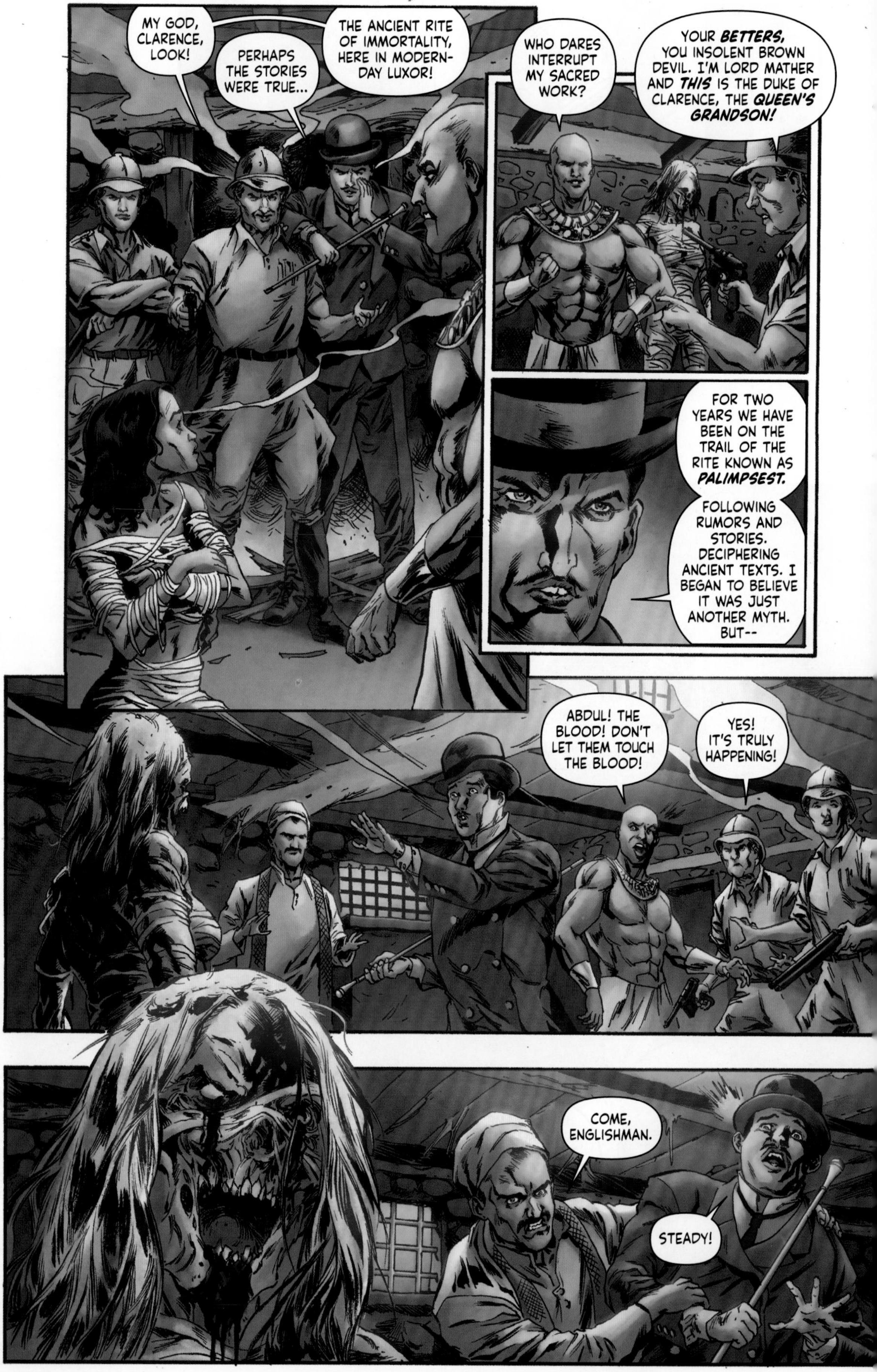
MY GOD, CLARENCE, LOOK!
PERHAPS THE STORIES WERE TRUE...
THE ANCIENT RITE OF IMMORTALITY, HERE IN MODERN-DAY LUXOR!
WHO DARES INTERRUPT MY SACRED WORK?
YOUR BETTERS, YOU INSOLENT BROWN DEVIL. I'M LORD MATHER AND THIS IS THE DUKE OF CLARENCE, THE QUEEN'S GRANDSON!
FOR TWO YEARS WE HAVE BEEN ON THE TRAIL OF THE RITE KNOWN AS PALIMPSEST.
FOLLOWING RUMORS AND STORIES. DECIPHERING ANCIENT TEXTS. I BEGAN TO BELIEVE IT WAS JUST ANOTHER MYTH. BUT--
ABDUL! THE BLOOD! DON'T LET THEM TOUCH THE BLOOD!
YES! IT'S TRULY HAPPENING!
COME, ENGLISHMAN.
STEADY!

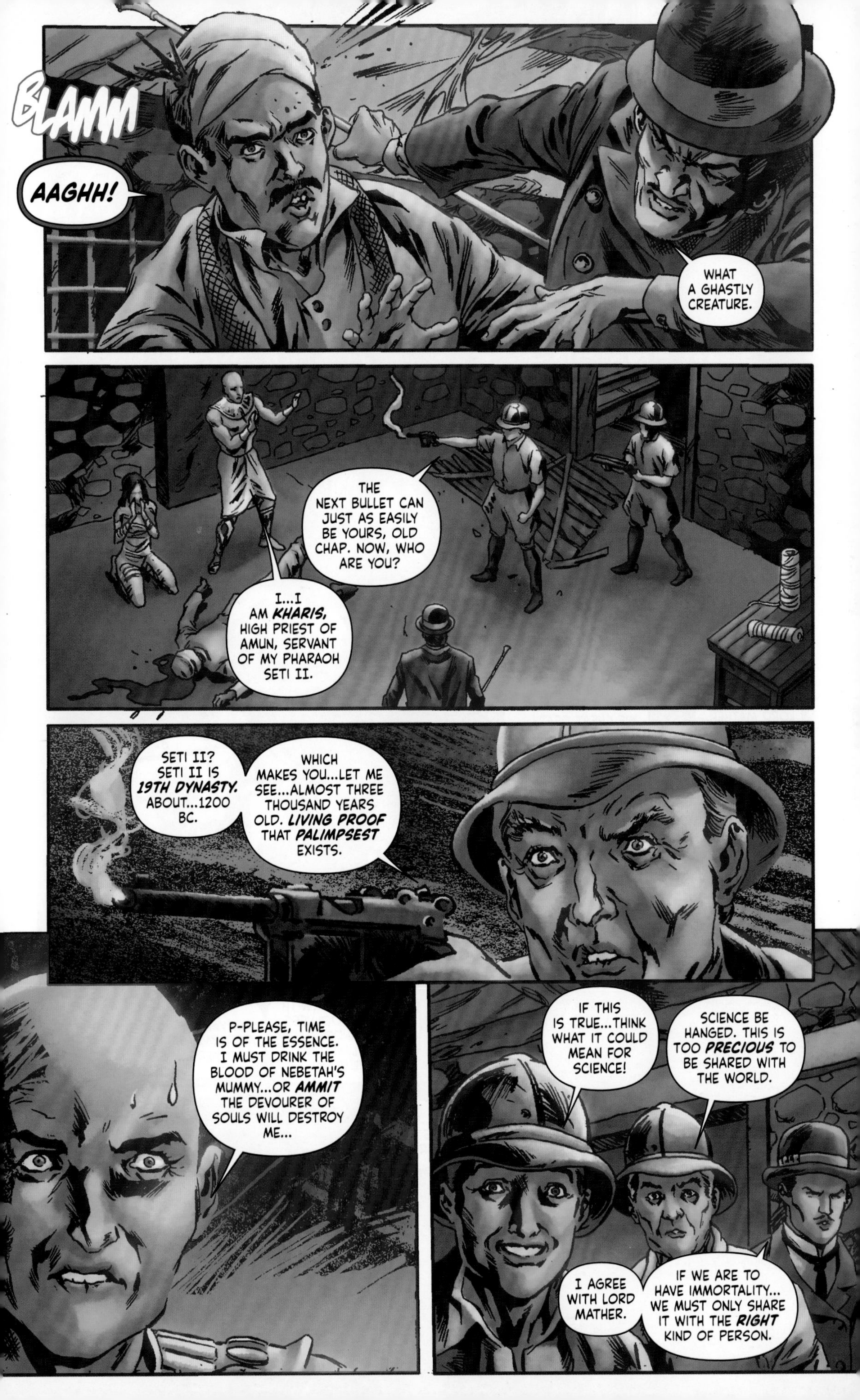
BLAMM
AAGHH!
WHAT A GHASTLY CREATURE.
THE NEXT BULLET CAN JUST AS EASILY BE YOURS, OLD CHAP. NOW, WHO ARE YOU?
I...I AM KHARIS, HIGH PRIEST OF AMUN, SERVANT OF MY PHARAOH SETI II.
SETI II? SETI II IS 19TH DYNASTY. ABOUT...1200 BC.
WHICH MAKES YOU...LET ME SEE...ALMOST THREE THOUSAND YEARS OLD. LIVING PROOF THAT PALIMPSEST EXISTS.
P-PLEASE, TIME IS OF THE ESSENCE. I MUST DRINK THE BLOOD OF NEBETAH'S MUMMY...OR AMMIT THE DEVOURER OF SOULS WILL DESTROY ME...
IF THIS IS TRUE...THINK WHAT IT COULD MEAN FOR SCIENCE!
SCIENCE BE HANGED. THIS IS TOO PRECIOUS TO BE SHARED WITH THE WORLD.
I AGREE WITH LORD MATHER.
IF WE ARE TO HAVE IMMORTALITY... WE MUST ONLY SHARE IT WITH THE RIGHT KIND OF PERSON.

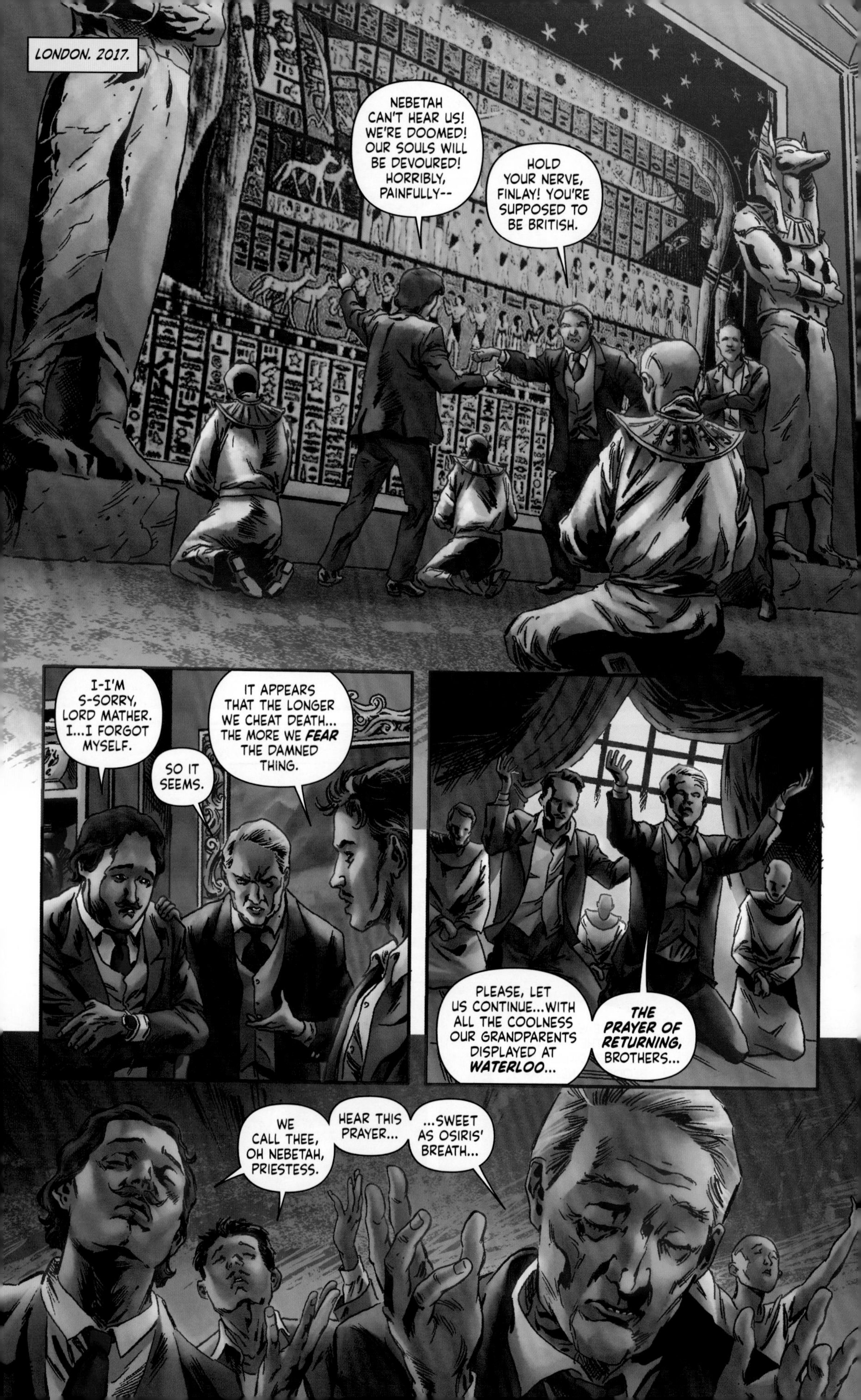

LONDON. 2017.
NEBETAH CAN'T HEAR US! WE'RE DOOMED! OUR SOULS WILL BE DEVOURED! HORRIBLY, PAINFULLY--
HOLD YOUR NERVE, FINLAY! YOU'RE SUPPOSED TO BE BRITISH.
I-I'M S-SORRY, LORD MATHER. I...I FORGOT MYSELF.
SO IT SEEMS.
IT APPEARS THAT THE LONGER WE CHEAT DEATH... THE MORE WE FEAR THE DAMNED THING.
PLEASE, LET US CONTINUE...WITH ALL THE COOLNESS OUR GRANDPARENTS DISPLAYED AT WATERLOO...
THE PRAYER OF RETURNING, BROTHERS...
WE CALL THEE, OH NEBETAH, PRIESTESS.
HEAR THIS PRAYER...
...SWEET AS OSIRIS' BREATH...

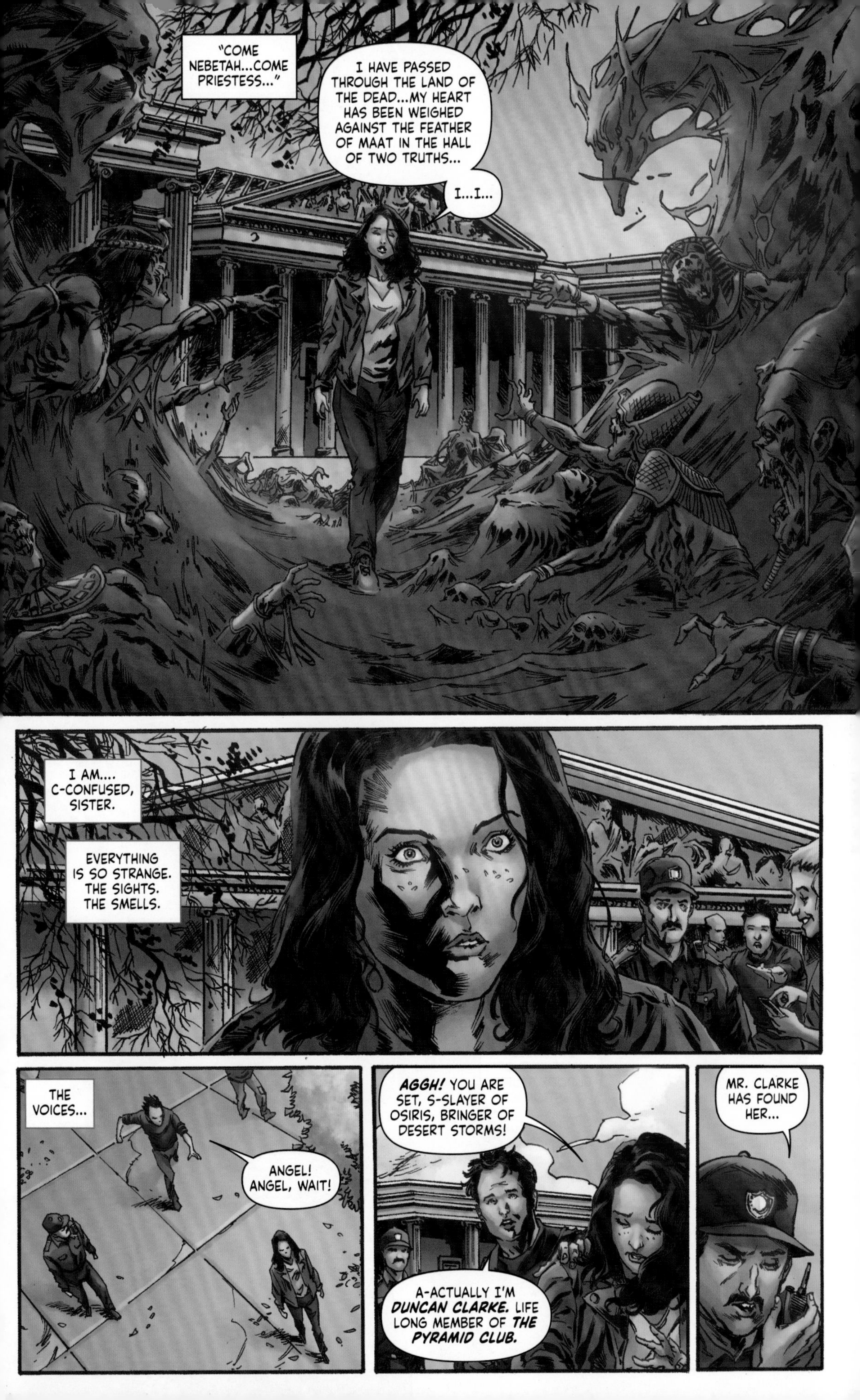
"COME NEBETAH...COME PRIESTESS..."
I HAVE PASSED THROUGH THE LAND OF THE DEAD...MY HEART HAS BEEN WEIGHED AGAINST THE FEATHER OF MAAT IN THE HALL OF TWO TRUTHS...
I...I...
I AM.... C-CONFUSED, SISTER.
EVERYTHING IS SO STRANGE. THE SIGHTS. THE SMELLS.
THE VOICES...
ANGEL! ANGEL, WAIT!
AGGH! YOU ARE SET, S-SLAYER OF OSIRIS, BRINGER OF DESERT STORMS!
A-ACTUALLY I'M DUNCAN CLARKE. LIFE LONG MEMBER OF THE PYRAMID CLUB.
MR. CLARKE HAS FOUND HER...

...BUT SHE SEEMS TO BE IN A PRETTY BAD WAY.

WE'RE IN LUCK, CALVERLY!

IF IT LOOKS LIKE HE'S LOSING HER, INFORM US IMMEDIATELY, MICHAEL. OTHERWISE...

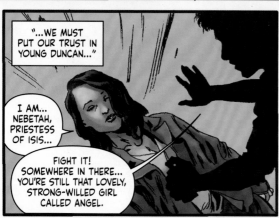

"...WE MUST PUT OUR TRUST IN YOUNG DUNCAN..."

I AM... NEBETAH, PRIESTESS OF ISIS...

FIGHT IT! SOMEWHERE IN THERE... YOU'RE STILL THAT LOVELY, STRONG-WILLED GIRL CALLED ANGEL.

AGGHH!

I HAVE SOMETHING HERE THAT MIGHT HELP...

NATRON AND SPICES, CORE INGREDIENTS OF THE MUMMIFICATION PROCESS, MIXED WITH CRUSHED HIEROGLYPHS.

IS IT YOU ANGEL?

OF COURSE I'M ANGEL. WHAT KIND OF BLOODY STUPID QUESTION IS--

I...UGH... I FEEL SO...

"OH GREAT HORUS, OH TERRIBLE ANUBIS..."

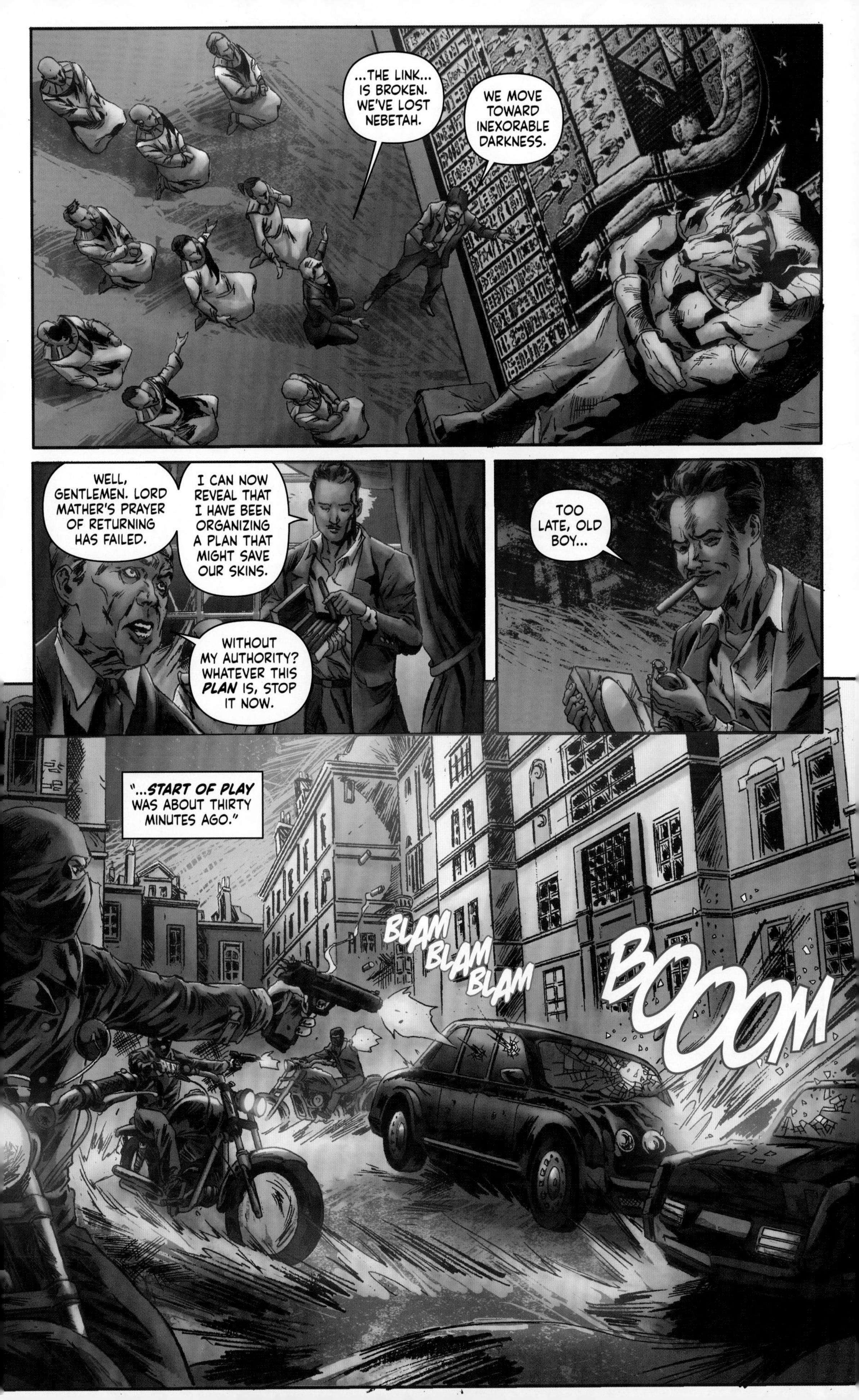
...THE LINK... IS BROKEN. WE'VE LOST NEBETAH.
WE MOVE TOWARD INEXORABLE DARKNESS.
WELL, GENTLEMEN. LORD MATHER'S PRAYER OF RETURNING HAS FAILED.
I CAN NOW REVEAL THAT I HAVE BEEN ORGANIZING A PLAN THAT MIGHT SAVE OUR SKINS.
WITHOUT MY AUTHORITY? WHATEVER THIS PLAN IS, STOP IT NOW.
TOO LATE, OLD BOY...
"...START OF PLAY WAS ABOUT THIRTY MINUTES AGO."
BLAM BLAM BLAM
BOOOOM

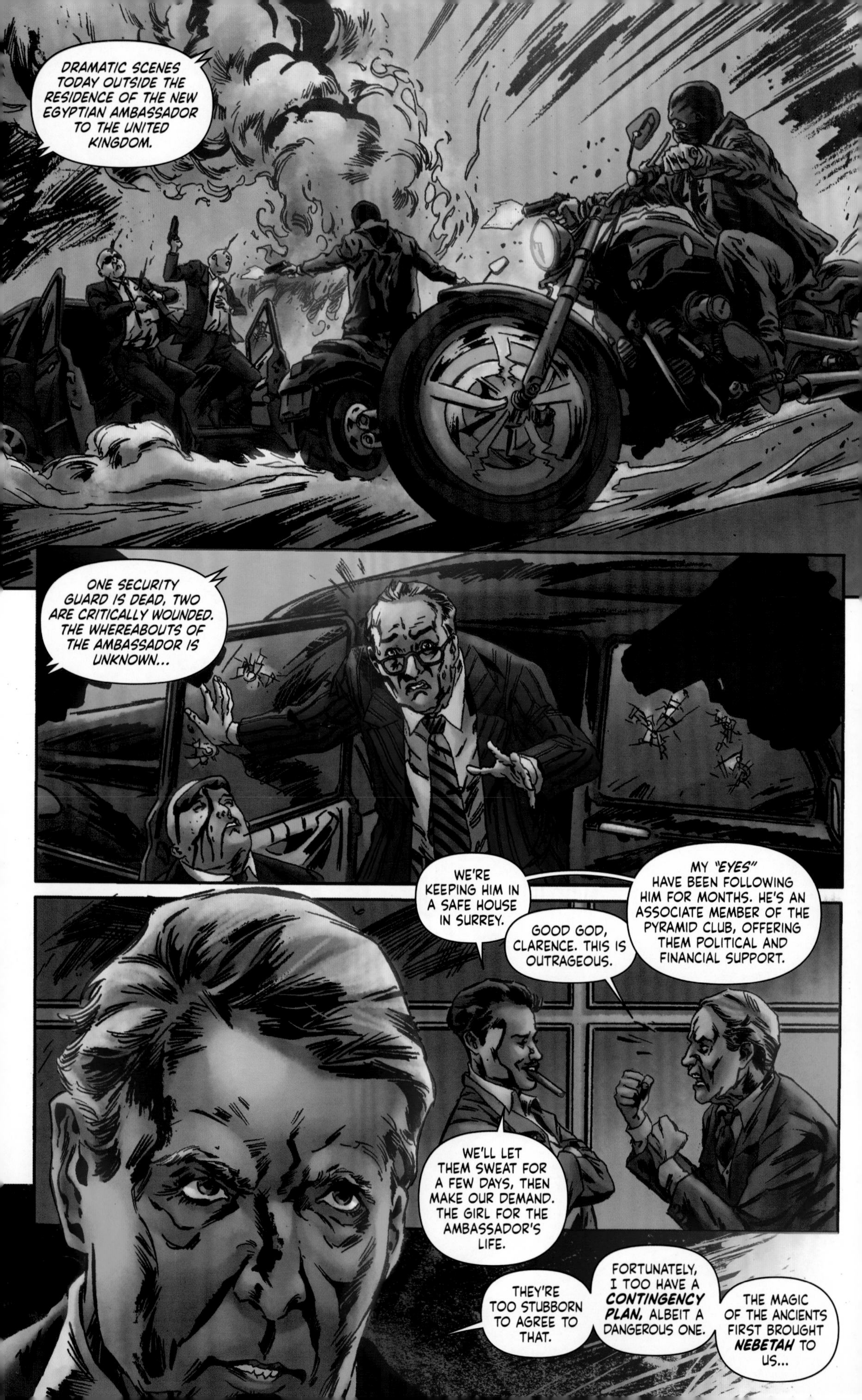
DRAMATIC SCENES TODAY OUTSIDE THE RESIDENCE OF THE NEW EGYPTIAN AMBASSADOR TO THE UNITED KINGDOM.
ONE SECURITY GUARD IS DEAD, TWO ARE CRITICALLY WOUNDED. THE WHEREABOUTS OF THE AMBASSADOR IS UNKNOWN...
MY "EYES" HAVE BEEN FOLLOWING HIM FOR MONTHS. HE'S AN ASSOCIATE MEMBER OF THE PYRAMID CLUB, OFFERING THEM POLITICAL AND FINANCIAL SUPPORT.
WE'RE KEEPING HIM IN A SAFE HOUSE IN SURREY.
GOOD GOD, CLARENCE. THIS IS OUTRAGEOUS.
WE'LL LET THEM SWEAT FOR A FEW DAYS, THEN MAKE OUR DEMAND. THE GIRL FOR THE AMBASSADOR'S LIFE.
THEY'RE TOO STUBBORN TO AGREE TO THAT.
FORTUNATELY, I TOO HAVE A CONTINGENCY PLAN, ALBEIT A DANGEROUS ONE.
THE MAGIC OF THE ANCIENTS FIRST BROUGHT NEBETAH TO US...

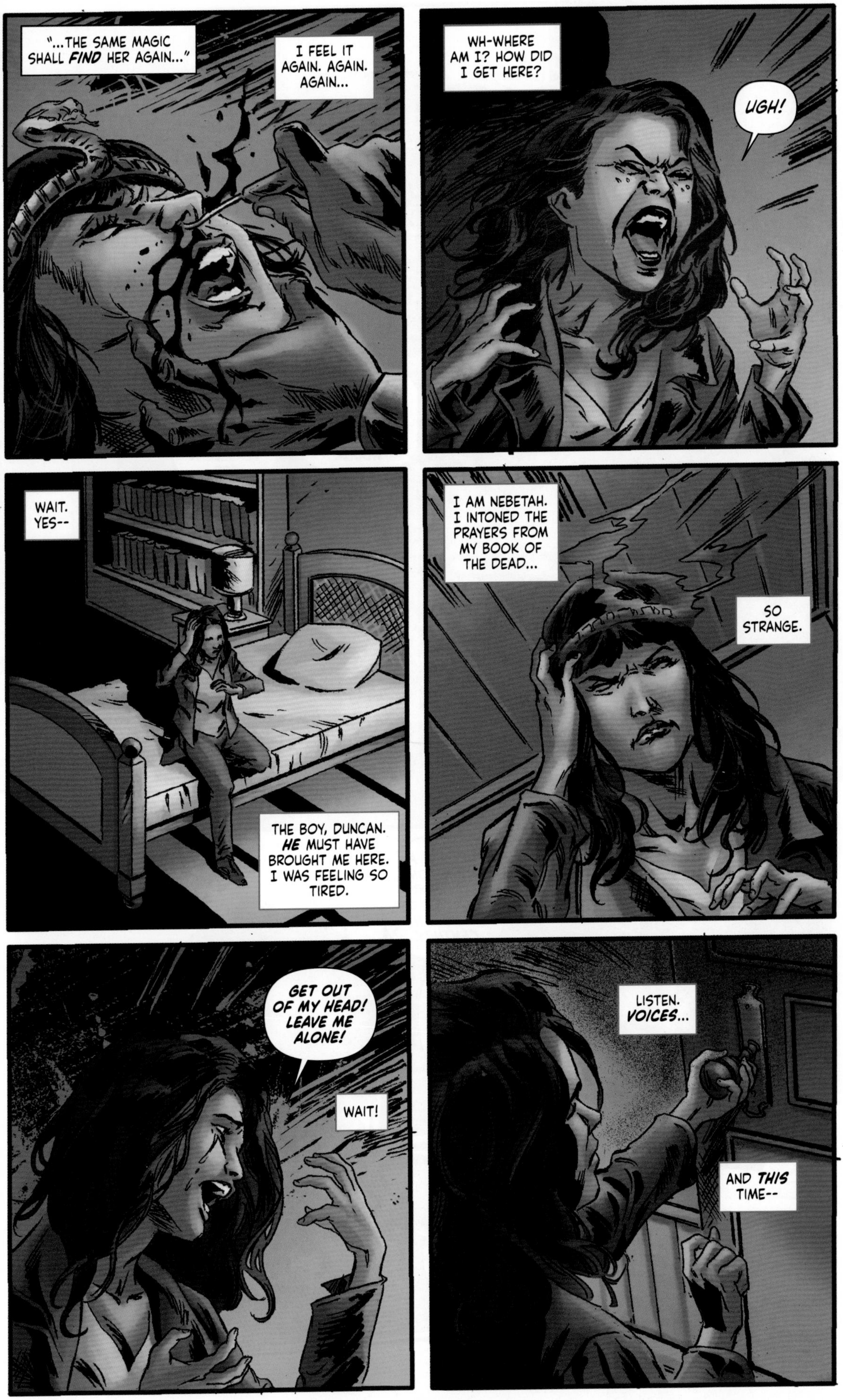
"...THE SAME MAGIC SHALL FIND HER AGAIN..."
I FEEL IT AGAIN. AGAIN. AGAIN...
WH-WHERE AM I? HOW DID I GET HERE?
UGH!
WAIT. YES--
THE BOY, DUNCAN. HE MUST HAVE BROUGHT ME HERE. I WAS FEELING SO TIRED.
I AM NEBETAH. I INTONED THE PRAYERS FROM MY BOOK OF THE DEAD...
SO STRANGE.
GET OUT OF MY HEAD! LEAVE ME ALONE!
WAIT!
LISTEN. VOICES...
AND THIS TIME--

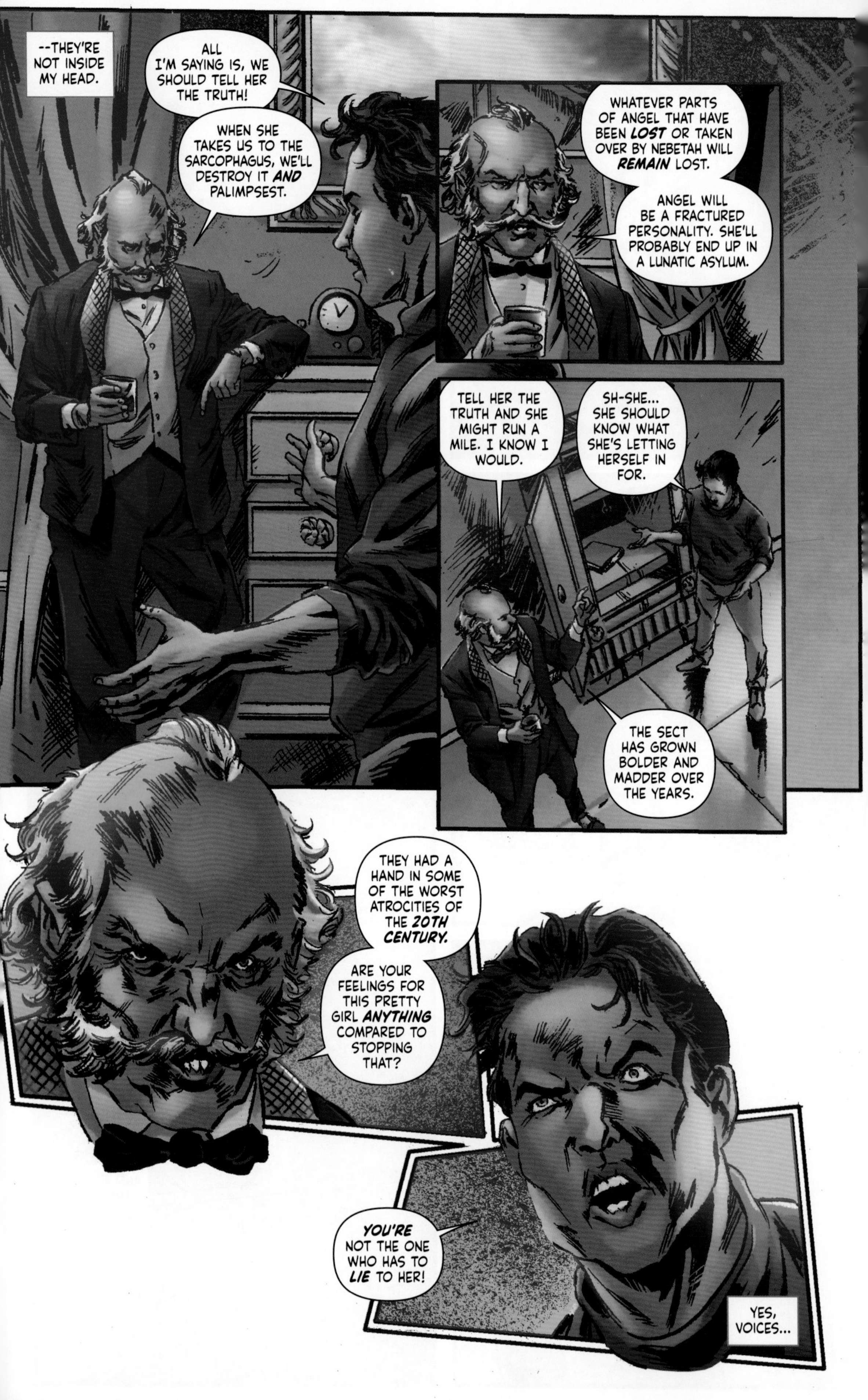
--THEY'RE NOT INSIDE MY HEAD.
ALL I'M SAYING IS, WE SHOULD TELL HER THE TRUTH!
WHEN SHE TAKES US TO THE SARCOPHAGUS, WE'LL DESTROY IT AND PALIMPSEST.
WHATEVER PARTS OF ANGEL THAT HAVE BEEN LOST OR TAKEN OVER BY NEBETAH WILL REMAIN LOST.
ANGEL WILL BE A FRACTURED PERSONALITY. SHE'LL PROBABLY END UP IN A LUNATIC ASYLUM.
TELL HER THE TRUTH AND SHE MIGHT RUN A MILE. I KNOW I WOULD.
SH-SHE... SHE SHOULD KNOW WHAT SHE'S LETTING HERSELF IN FOR.
THE SECT HAS GROWN BOLDER AND MADDER OVER THE YEARS.
THEY HAD A HAND IN SOME OF THE WORST ATROCITIES OF THE 20TH CENTURY.
ARE YOUR FEELINGS FOR THIS PRETTY GIRL ANYTHING COMPARED TO STOPPING THAT?
YOU'RE NOT THE ONE WHO HAS TO LIE TO HER!
YES, VOICES...

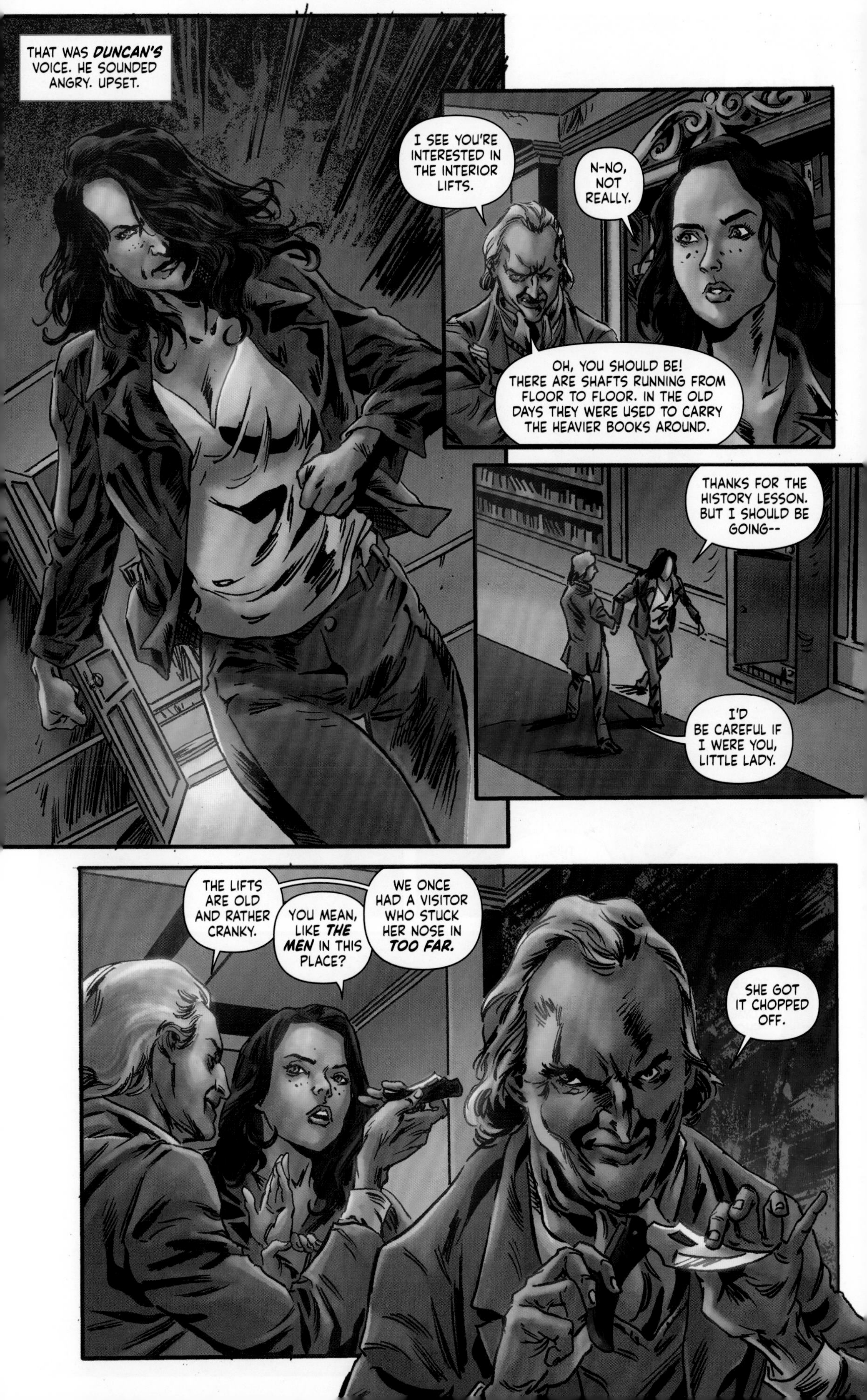
THAT WAS **DUNCAN'S** VOICE. HE SOUNDED ANGRY. UPSET.
I SEE YOU'RE INTERESTED IN THE INTERIOR LIFTS.
N-NO, NOT REALLY.
OH, YOU SHOULD BE! THERE ARE SHAFTS RUNNING FROM FLOOR TO FLOOR. IN THE OLD DAYS THEY WERE USED TO CARRY THE HEAVIER BOOKS AROUND.
THANKS FOR THE HISTORY LESSON. BUT I SHOULD BE GOING--
I'D BE CAREFUL IF I WERE YOU, LITTLE LADY.
THE LIFTS ARE OLD AND RATHER CRANKY.
YOU MEAN, LIKE **THE MEN** IN THIS PLACE?
WE ONCE HAD A VISITOR WHO STUCK HER NOSE IN **TOO FAR.**
SHE GOT IT CHOPPED OFF.

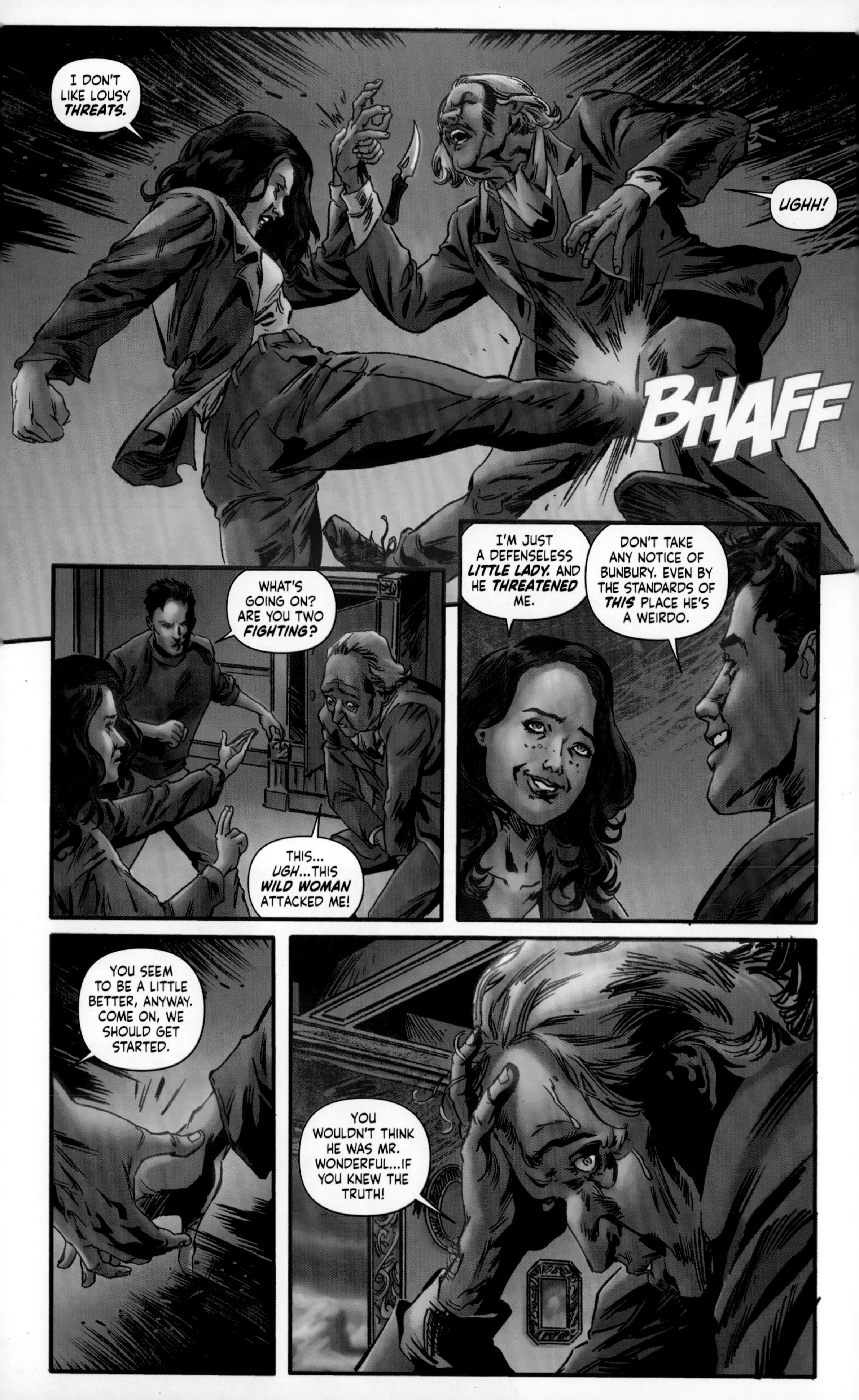
I DON'T LIKE LOUSY THREATS.
UGHH!
BHAFF
WHAT'S GOING ON? ARE YOU TWO FIGHTING?
THIS... UGH...THIS WILD WOMAN ATTACKED ME!
I'M JUST A DEFENSELESS LITTLE LADY. AND HE THREATENED ME.
DON'T TAKE ANY NOTICE OF BUNBURY. EVEN BY THE STANDARDS OF THIS PLACE HE'S A WEIRDO.
YOU SEEM TO BE A LITTLE BETTER, ANYWAY. COME ON, WE SHOULD GET STARTED.
YOU WOULDN'T THINK HE WAS MR. WONDERFUL...IF YOU KNEW THE TRUTH!

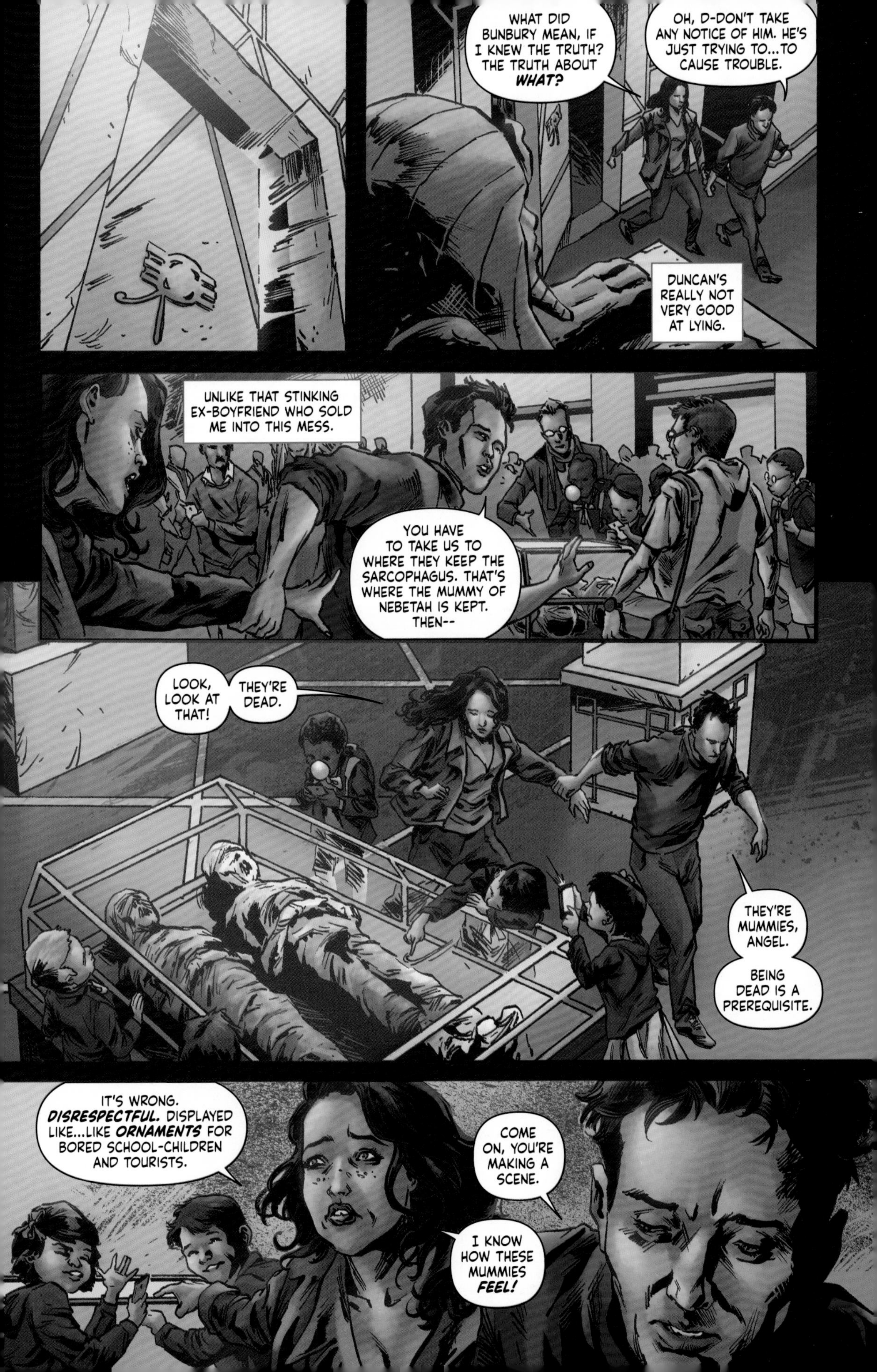
WHAT DID BUNBURY MEAN, IF I KNEW THE TRUTH? THE TRUTH ABOUT WHAT?
OH, D-DON'T TAKE ANY NOTICE OF HIM. HE'S JUST TRYING TO...TO CAUSE TROUBLE.
DUNCAN'S REALLY NOT VERY GOOD AT LYING.
UNLIKE THAT STINKING EX-BOYFRIEND WHO SOLD ME INTO THIS MESS.
YOU HAVE TO TAKE US TO WHERE THEY KEEP THE SARCOPHAGUS. THAT'S WHERE THE MUMMY OF NEBETAH IS KEPT. THEN--
LOOK, LOOK AT THAT!
THEY'RE DEAD.
THEY'RE MUMMIES, ANGEL.
BEING DEAD IS A PREREQUISITE.
IT'S WRONG. DISRESPECTFUL. DISPLAYED LIKE...LIKE ORNAMENTS FOR BORED SCHOOL-CHILDREN AND TOURISTS.
COME ON, YOU'RE MAKING A SCENE.
I KNOW HOW THESE MUMMIES FEEL!

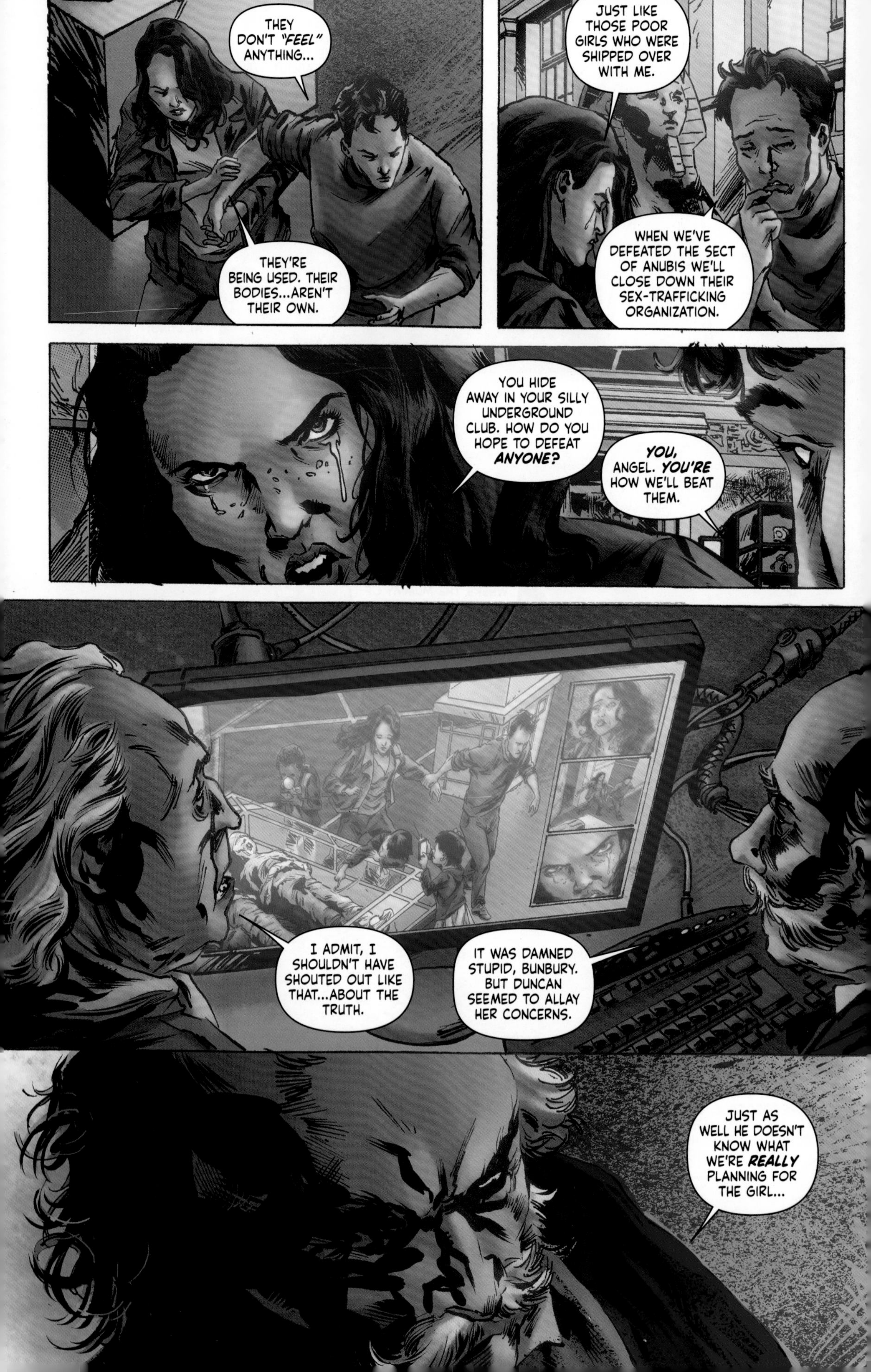
THEY DON'T "FEEL" ANYTHING...
THEY'RE BEING USED. THEIR BODIES...AREN'T THEIR OWN.
JUST LIKE THOSE POOR GIRLS WHO WERE SHIPPED OVER WITH ME.
WHEN WE'VE DEFEATED THE SECT OF ANUBIS WE'LL CLOSE DOWN THEIR SEX-TRAFFICKING ORGANIZATION.
YOU HIDE AWAY IN YOUR SILLY UNDERGROUND CLUB. HOW DO YOU HOPE TO DEFEAT ANYONE?
YOU, ANGEL. YOU'RE HOW WE'LL BEAT THEM.
I ADMIT, I SHOULDN'T HAVE SHOUTED OUT LIKE THAT...ABOUT THE TRUTH.
IT WAS DAMNED STUPID, BUNBURY. BUT DUNCAN SEEMED TO ALLAY HER CONCERNS.
JUST AS WELL HE DOESN'T KNOW WHAT WE'RE REALLY PLANNING FOR THE GIRL...

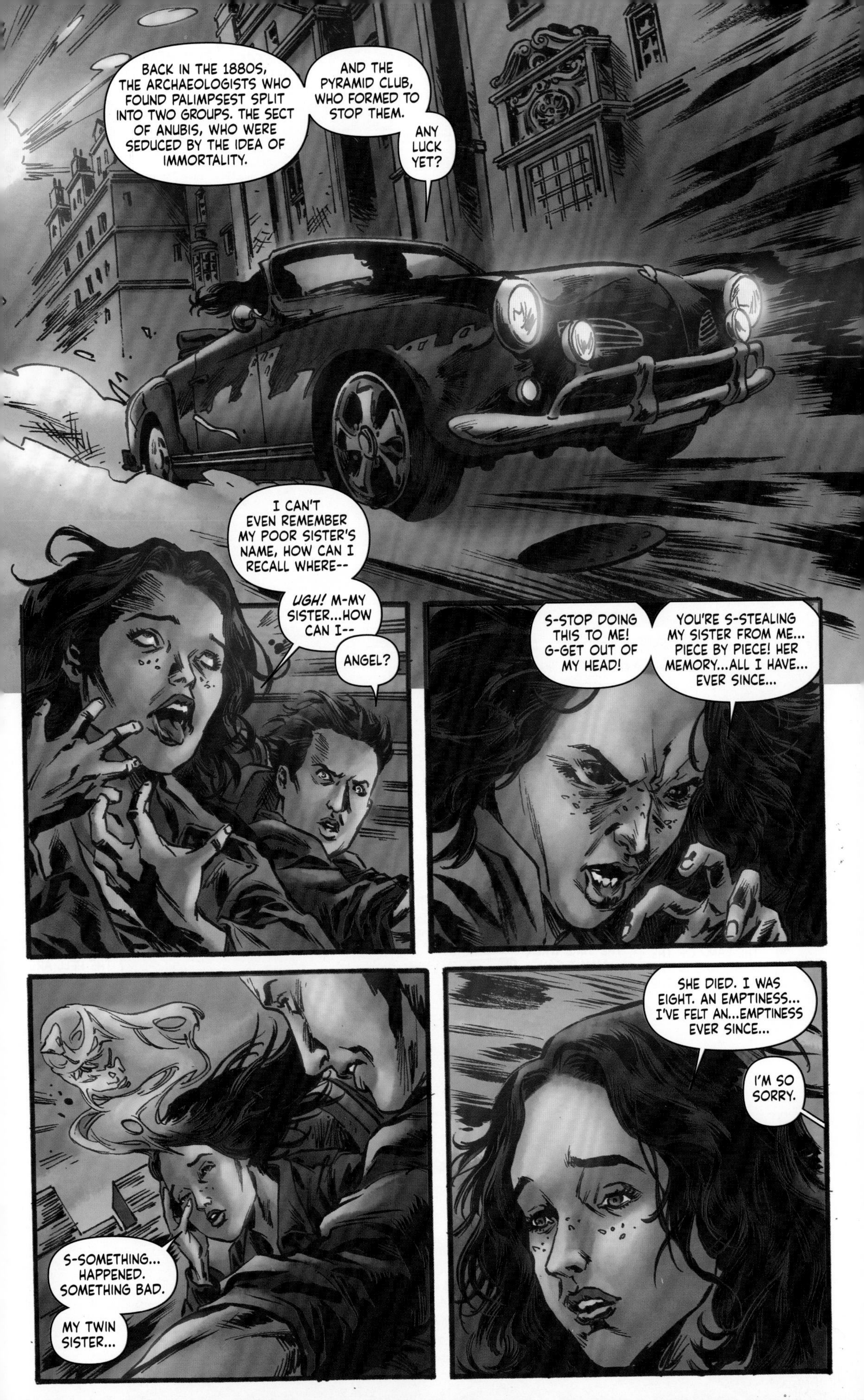
BACK IN THE 1880S, THE ARCHAEOLOGISTS WHO FOUND PALIMPSEST SPLIT INTO TWO GROUPS. THE SECT OF ANUBIS, WHO WERE SEDUCED BY THE IDEA OF IMMORTALITY.
AND THE PYRAMID CLUB, WHO FORMED TO STOP THEM.
ANY LUCK YET?
I CAN'T EVEN REMEMBER MY POOR SISTER'S NAME, HOW CAN I RECALL WHERE--
UGH! M-MY SISTER...HOW CAN I--
ANGEL?
S-STOP DOING THIS TO ME! G-GET OUT OF MY HEAD!
YOU'RE S-STEALING MY SISTER FROM ME... PIECE BY PIECE! HER MEMORY...ALL I HAVE... EVER SINCE...
S-SOMETHING... HAPPENED. SOMETHING BAD.
MY TWIN SISTER...
SHE DIED. I WAS EIGHT. AN EMPTINESS... I'VE FELT AN...EMPTINESS EVER SINCE...
I'M SO SORRY.

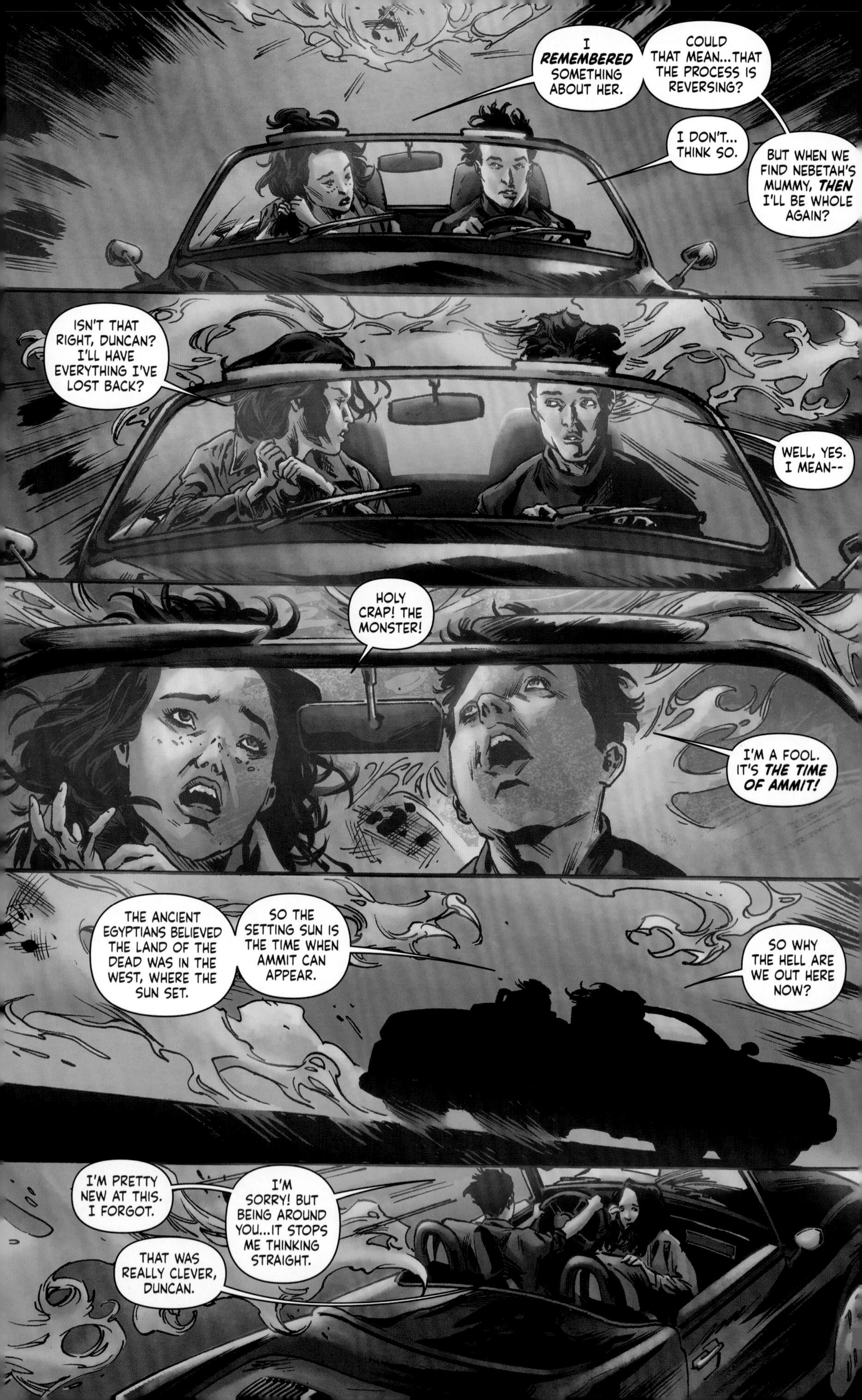
I *REMEMBERED* SOMETHING ABOUT HER.
COULD THAT MEAN...THAT THE PROCESS IS REVERSING?
I DON'T... THINK SO.
BUT WHEN WE FIND NEBETAH'S MUMMY, *THEN* I'LL BE WHOLE AGAIN?
ISN'T THAT RIGHT, DUNCAN? I'LL HAVE EVERYTHING I'VE LOST BACK?
WELL, YES. I MEAN--
HOLY CRAP! THE MONSTER!
I'M A FOOL. IT'S *THE TIME OF AMMIT!*
THE ANCIENT EGYPTIANS BELIEVED THE LAND OF THE DEAD WAS IN THE WEST, WHERE THE SUN SET.
SO THE SETTING SUN IS THE TIME WHEN AMMIT CAN APPEAR.
SO WHY THE HELL ARE WE OUT HERE NOW?
I'M PRETTY NEW AT THIS. I FORGOT.
I'M SORRY! BUT BEING AROUND YOU...IT STOPS ME THINKING STRAIGHT.
THAT WAS REALLY CLEVER, DUNCAN.

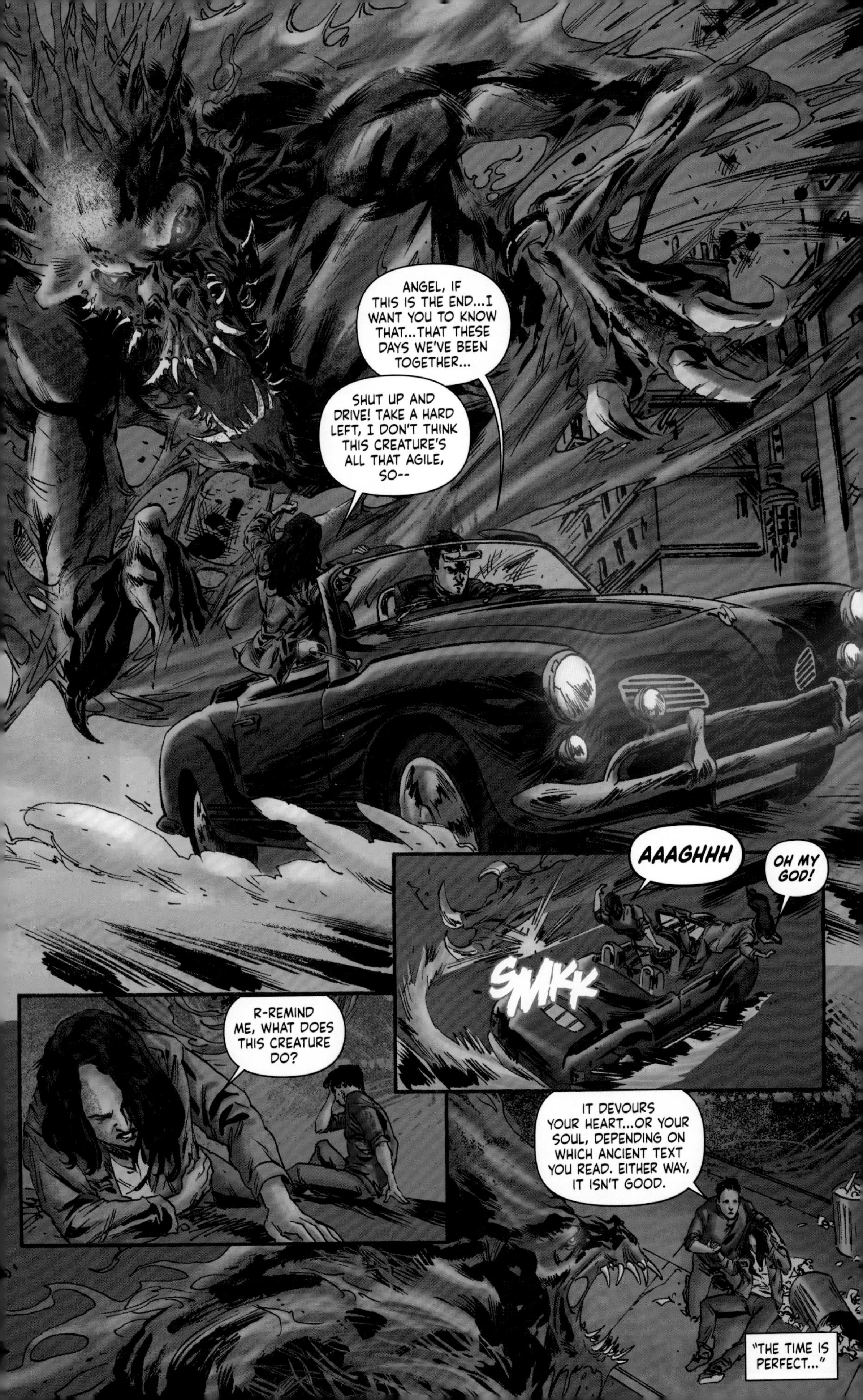
ANGEL, IF THIS IS THE END...I WANT YOU TO KNOW THAT...THAT THESE DAYS WE'VE BEEN TOGETHER...
SHUT UP AND DRIVE! TAKE A HARD LEFT, I DON'T THINK THIS CREATURE'S ALL THAT AGILE, SO--
AAAGHHH
OH MY GOD!
SMKK
R-REMIND ME, WHAT DOES THIS CREATURE DO?
IT DEVOURS YOUR HEART...OR YOUR SOUL, DEPENDING ON WHICH ANCIENT TEXT YOU READ. EITHER WAY, IT ISN'T GOOD.
"THE TIME IS PERFECT..."

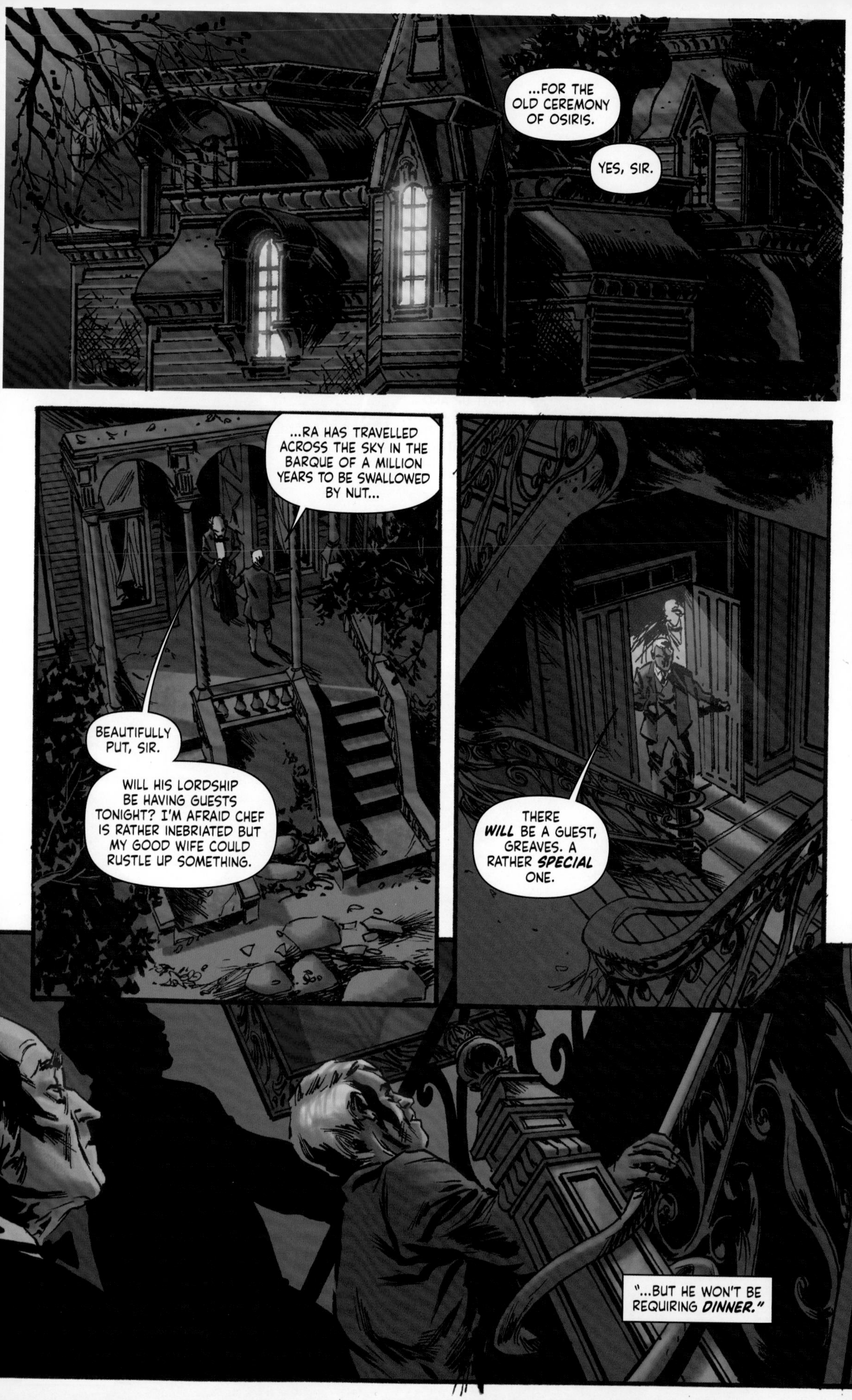
...FOR THE OLD CEREMONY OF OSIRIS.
YES, SIR.
...RA HAS TRAVELLED ACROSS THE SKY IN THE BARQUE OF A MILLION YEARS TO BE SWALLOWED BY NUT...
BEAUTIFULLY PUT, SIR.
WILL HIS LORDSHIP BE HAVING GUESTS TONIGHT? I'M AFRAID CHEF IS RATHER INEBRIATED BUT MY GOOD WIFE COULD RUSTLE UP SOMETHING.
THERE *WILL* BE A GUEST, GREAVES. A RATHER *SPECIAL* ONE.
"...BUT HE WON'T BE REQUIRING *DINNER.*"

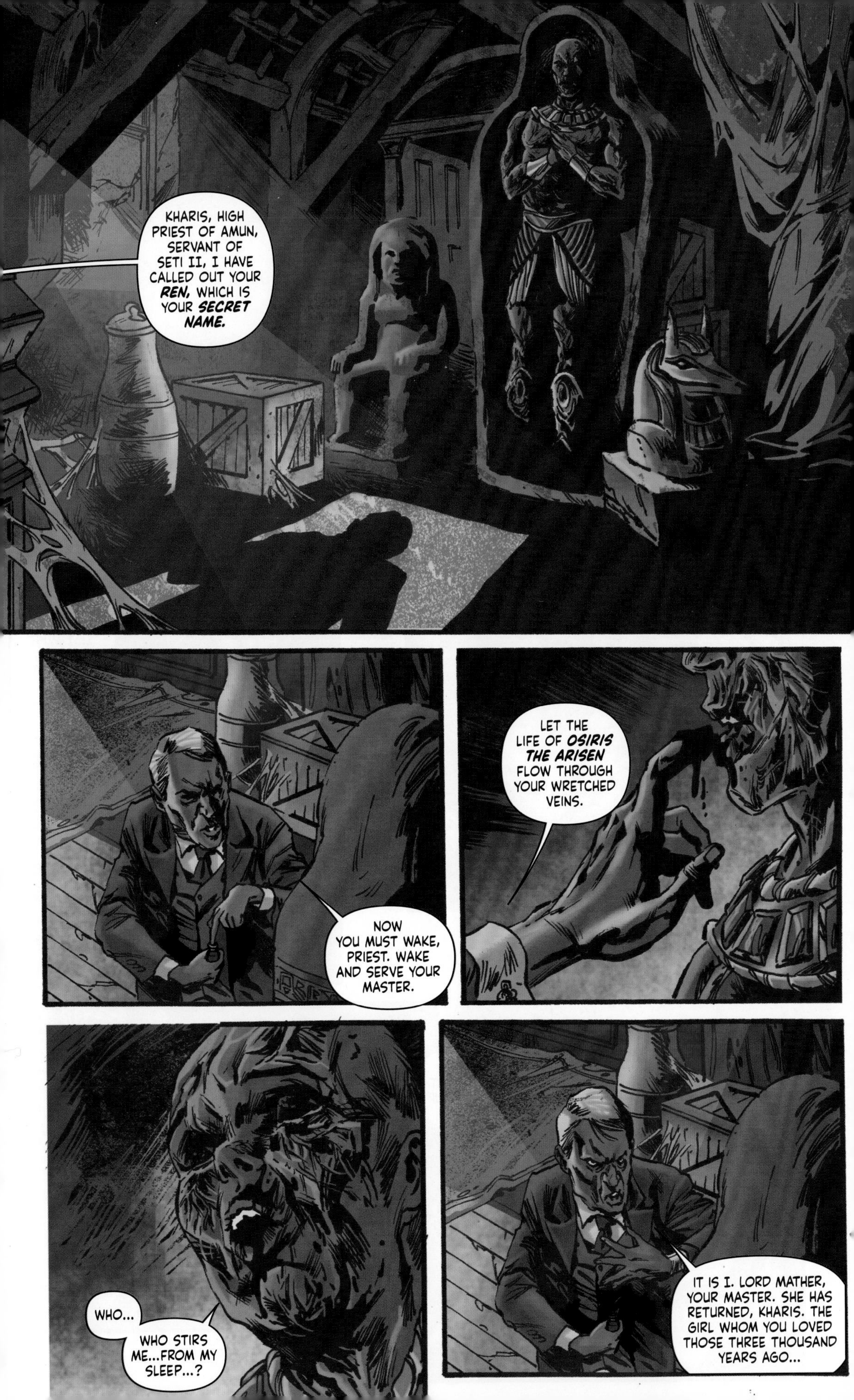
KHARIS, HIGH PRIEST OF AMUN, SERVANT OF SETI II, I HAVE CALLED OUT YOUR ***REN,*** WHICH IS YOUR ***SECRET NAME.***
NOW YOU MUST WAKE, PRIEST. WAKE AND SERVE YOUR MASTER.
LET THE LIFE OF ***OSIRIS THE ARISEN*** FLOW THROUGH YOUR WRETCHED VEINS.
WHO...
WHO STIRS ME...FROM MY SLEEP...?
IT IS I. LORD MATHER, YOUR MASTER. SHE HAS RETURNED, KHARIS. THE GIRL WHOM YOU LOVED THOSE THREE THOUSAND YEARS AGO...

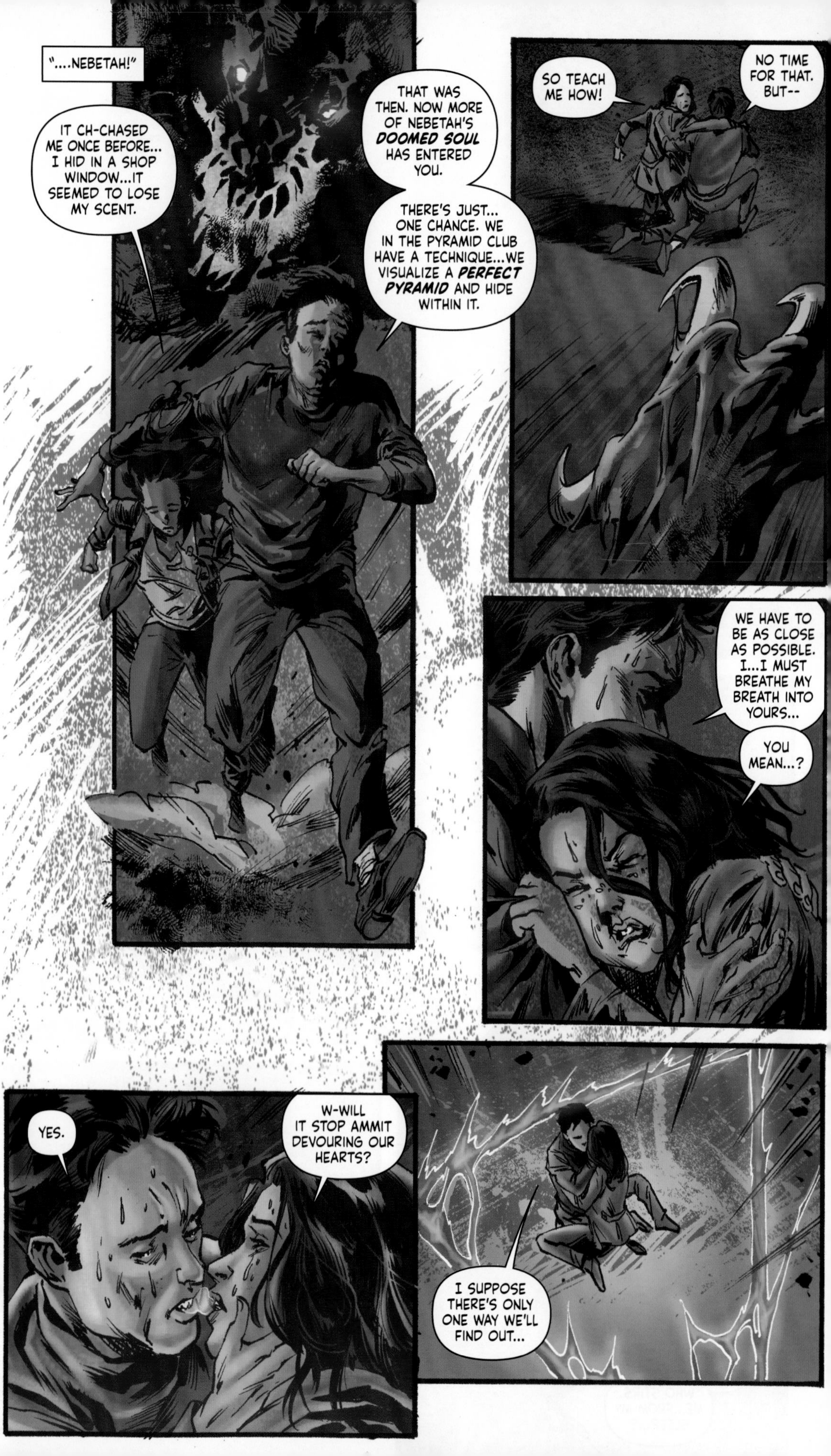
"....NEBETAH!"
IT CH-CHASED ME ONCE BEFORE... I HID IN A SHOP WINDOW...IT SEEMED TO LOSE MY SCENT.
THAT WAS THEN. NOW MORE OF NEBETAH'S DOOMED SOUL HAS ENTERED YOU.
THERE'S JUST... ONE CHANCE. WE IN THE PYRAMID CLUB HAVE A TECHNIQUE...WE VISUALIZE A PERFECT PYRAMID AND HIDE WITHIN IT.
SO TEACH ME HOW!
NO TIME FOR THAT. BUT--
WE HAVE TO BE AS CLOSE AS POSSIBLE. I...I MUST BREATHE MY BREATH INTO YOURS...
YOU MEAN...?
YES.
W-WILL IT STOP AMMIT DEVOURING OUR HEARTS?
I SUPPOSE THERE'S ONLY ONE WAY WE'LL FIND OUT...

TELL ME...HOW IS THIS SO? HOW DO I LIVE?

W-WELL, YEARS AGO YOU KINDLY LET US INTO THE SECRET OF *PALIMPSEST.*

YOU MEAN...YOU TOOK IT FROM ME!

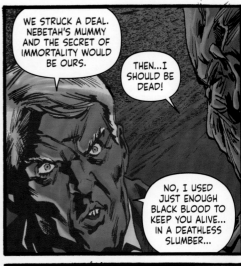

WE STRUCK A DEAL. NEBETAH'S MUMMY AND THE SECRET OF IMMORTALITY WOULD BE OURS.

THEN...I SHOULD BE DEAD!

NO, I USED JUST ENOUGH BLACK BLOOD TO KEEP YOU ALIVE... IN A DEATHLESS SLUMBER...

NO ORDINARY MAN, NO MAN WHO WASN'T A PRIEST OF PHARAOH'S EGYPT, COULD SURVIVE THUS.

I KNEW THAT ONE DAY I MIGHT HAVE A USE FOR YOU. THAT DAY HAS *COME,* KHARIS.

THE PRIESTESS NEBETAH HAS RETURNED. YOU MUST FIND HER.

YOU STOLE PALIMPSEST FROM ME.

IN MY TIME... PHARAOH HAD A *PUNISHMENT* FOR THIEVES...

AAIGH! P-PLEASE, L-LET'S DISCUSS THIS... LIKE C-CIVILIZED PEOPLE...

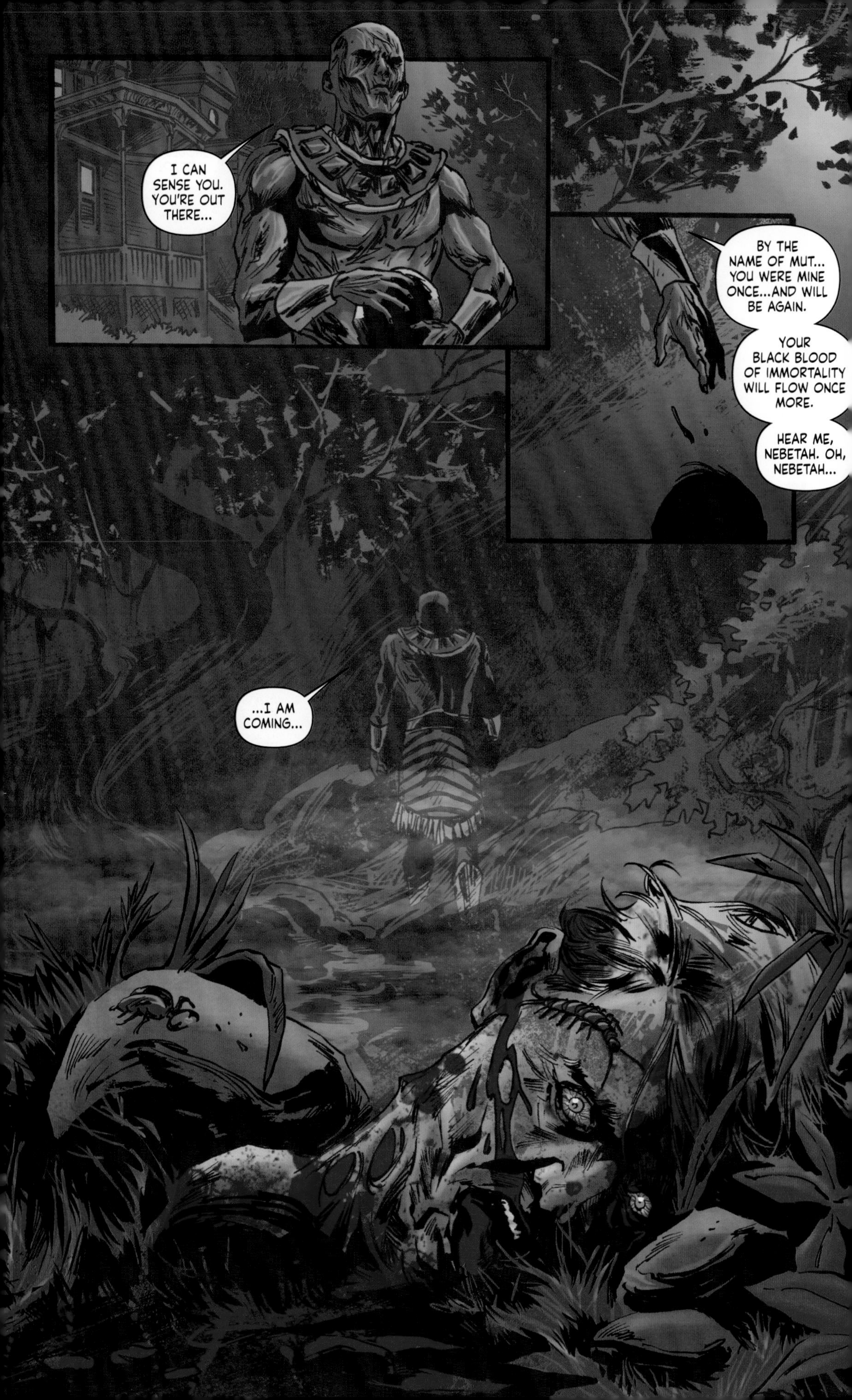
I CAN SENSE YOU. YOU'RE OUT THERE...
BY THE NAME OF MUT... YOU WERE MINE ONCE...AND WILL BE AGAIN.
YOUR BLACK BLOOD OF IMMORTALITY WILL FLOW ONCE MORE.
HEAR ME, NEBETAH. OH, NEBETAH...
...I AM COMING...

PART IV

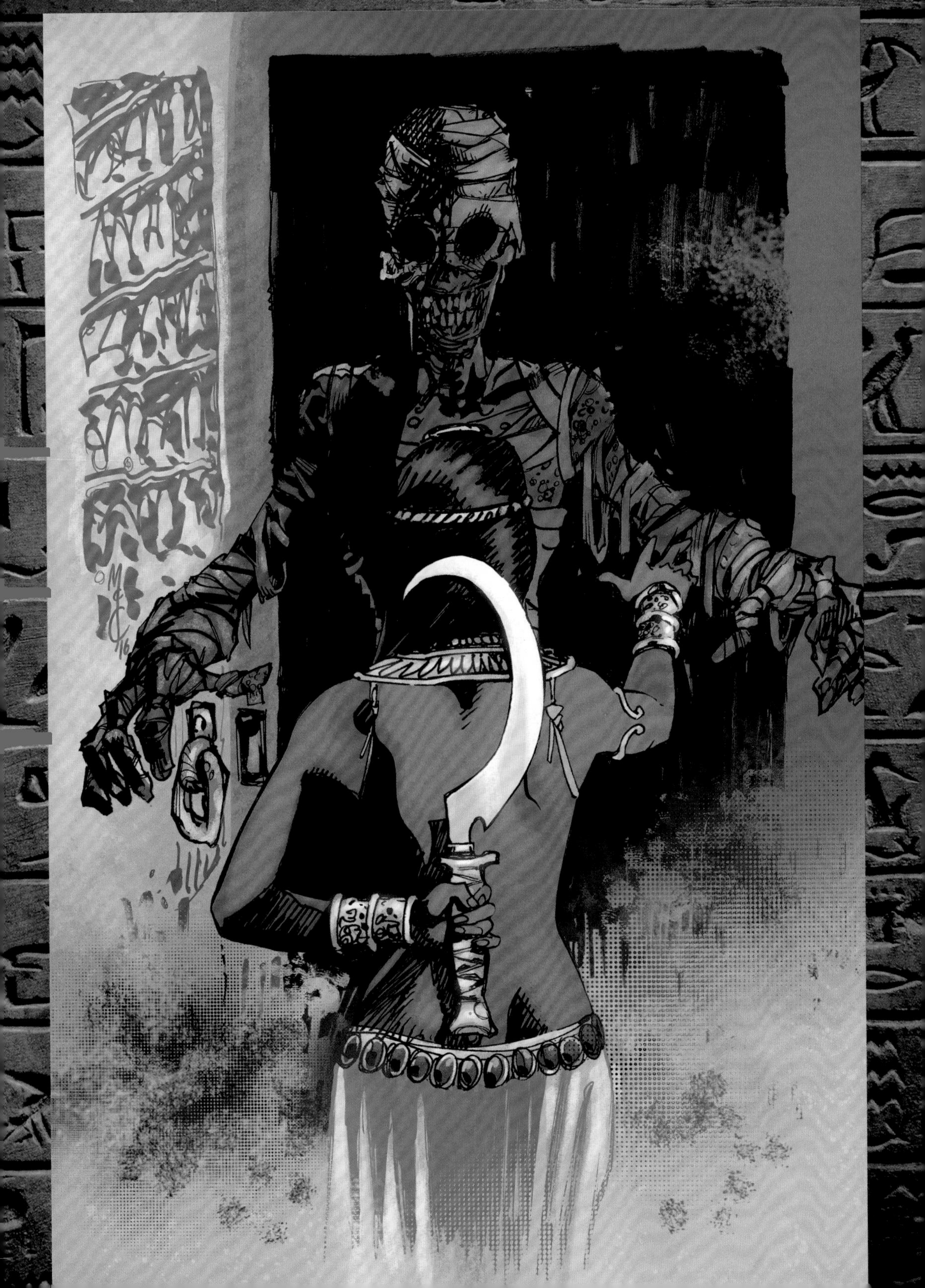

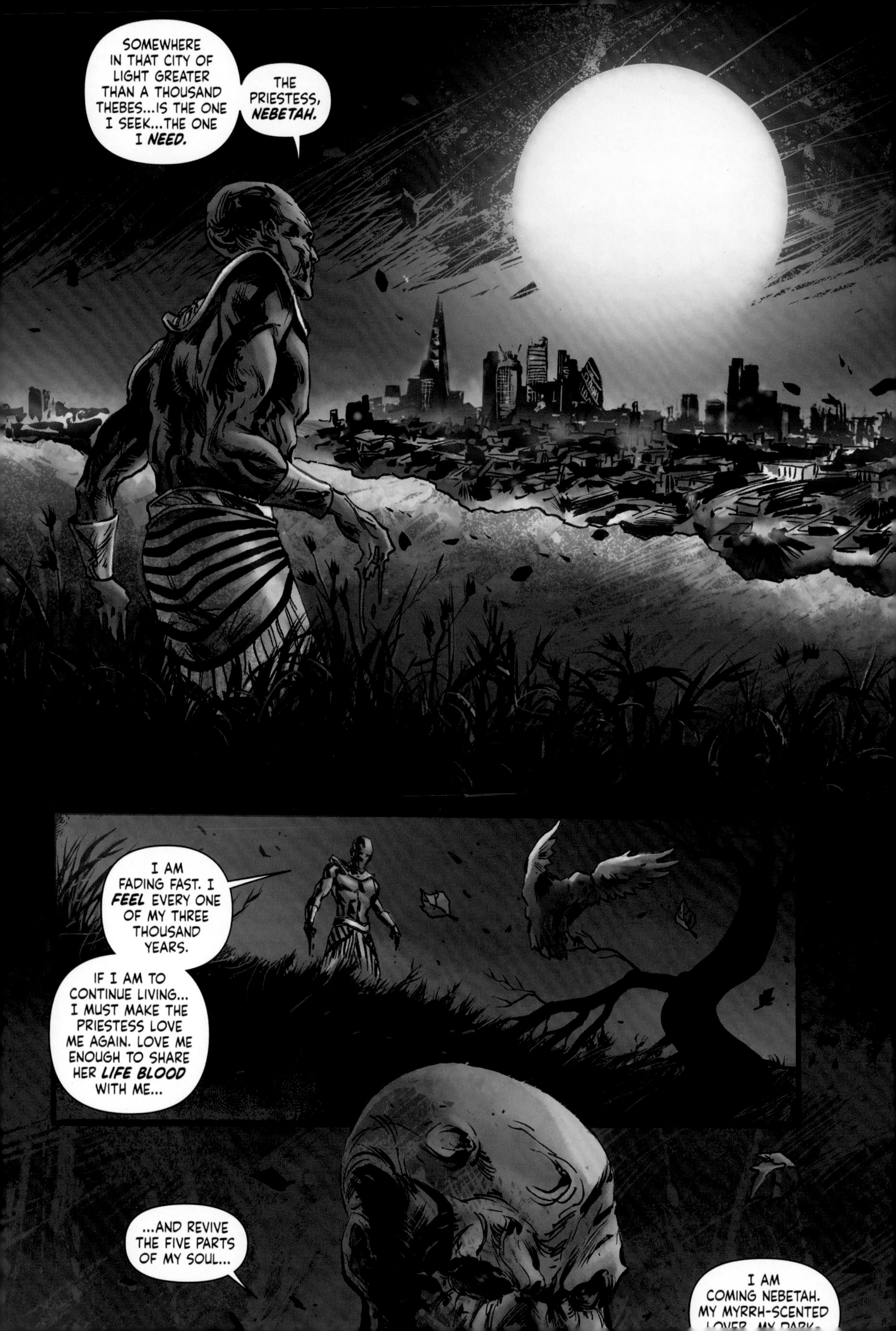

SOMEWHERE IN THAT CITY OF LIGHT GREATER THAN A THOUSAND THEBES...IS THE ONE I SEEK...THE ONE I NEED.
THE PRIESTESS, NEBETAH.
I AM FADING FAST. I FEEL EVERY ONE OF MY THREE THOUSAND YEARS.
IF I AM TO CONTINUE LIVING... I MUST MAKE THE PRIESTESS LOVE ME AGAIN. LOVE ME ENOUGH TO SHARE HER LIFE BLOOD WITH ME...
...AND REVIVE THE FIVE PARTS OF MY SOUL...
I AM COMING NEBETAH. MY MYRRH-SCENTED

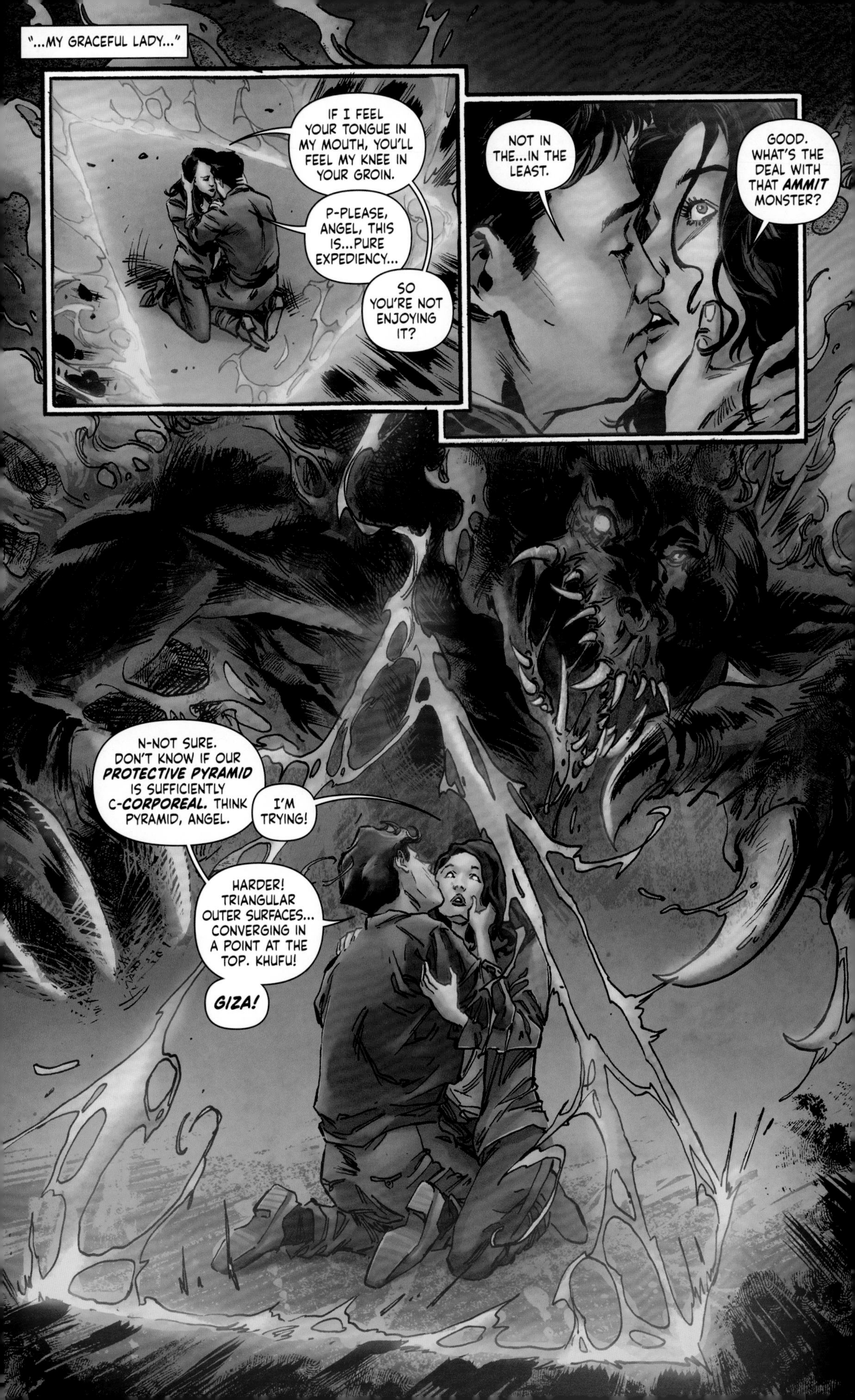
"...MY GRACEFUL LADY..."
IF I FEEL YOUR TONGUE IN MY MOUTH, YOU'LL FEEL MY KNEE IN YOUR GROIN.
P-PLEASE, ANGEL, THIS IS...PURE EXPEDIENCY...
SO YOU'RE NOT ENJOYING IT?
NOT IN THE...IN THE LEAST.
GOOD. WHAT'S THE DEAL WITH THAT AMMIT MONSTER?
N-NOT SURE. DON'T KNOW IF OUR PROTECTIVE PYRAMID IS SUFFICIENTLY C-CORPOREAL. THINK PYRAMID, ANGEL.
I'M TRYING!
HARDER! TRIANGULAR OUTER SURFACES... CONVERGING IN A POINT AT THE TOP. KHUFU!
GIZA!

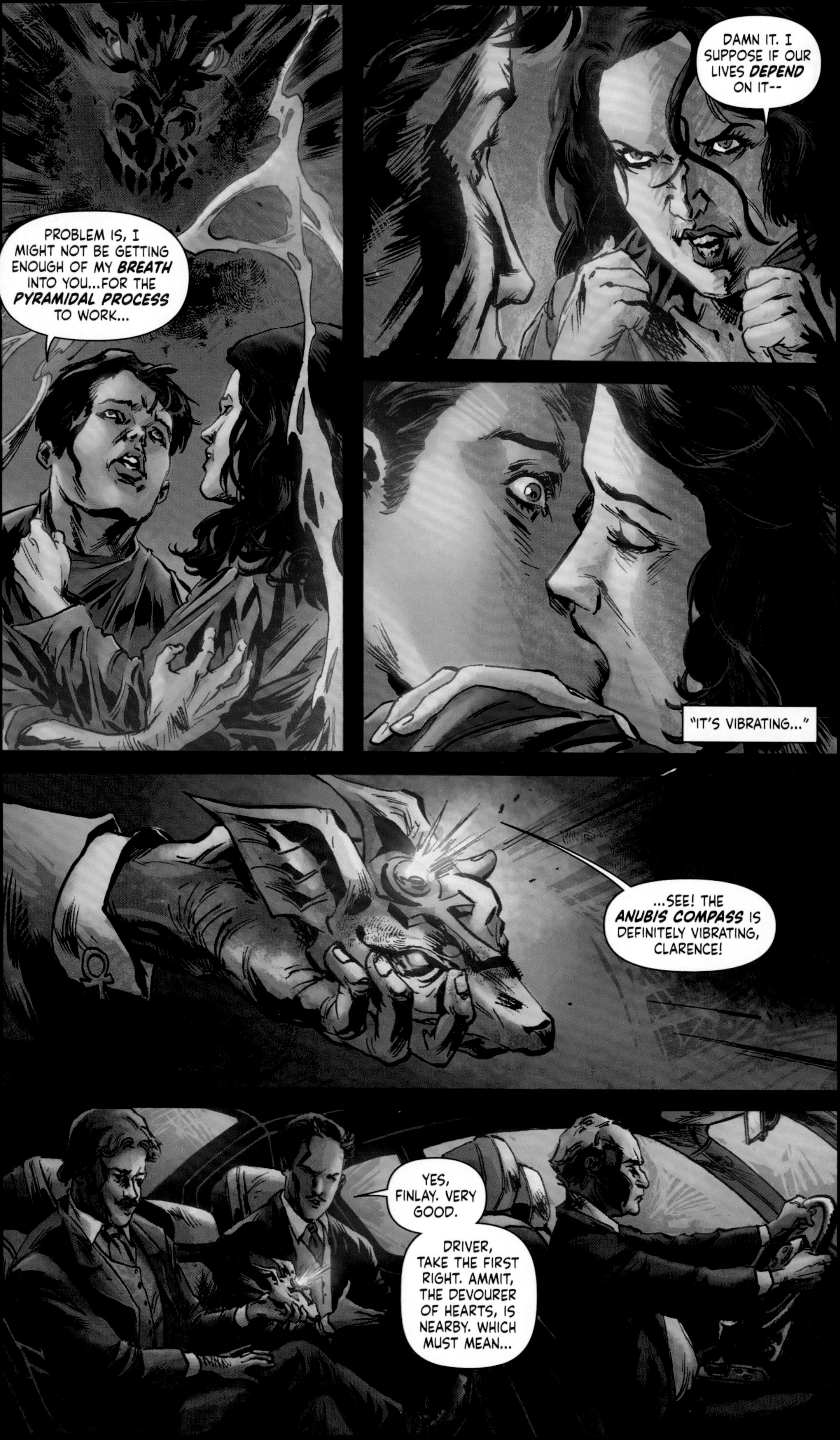
PROBLEM IS, I MIGHT NOT BE GETTING ENOUGH OF MY BREATH INTO YOU...FOR THE PYRAMIDAL PROCESS TO WORK...
DAMN IT. I SUPPOSE IF OUR LIVES DEPEND ON IT--
"IT'S VIBRATING..."
...SEE! THE ANUBIS COMPASS IS DEFINITELY VIBRATING, CLARENCE!
YES, FINLAY. VERY GOOD.
DRIVER, TAKE THE FIRST RIGHT. AMMIT, THE DEVOURER OF HEARTS, IS NEARBY. WHICH MUST MEAN...

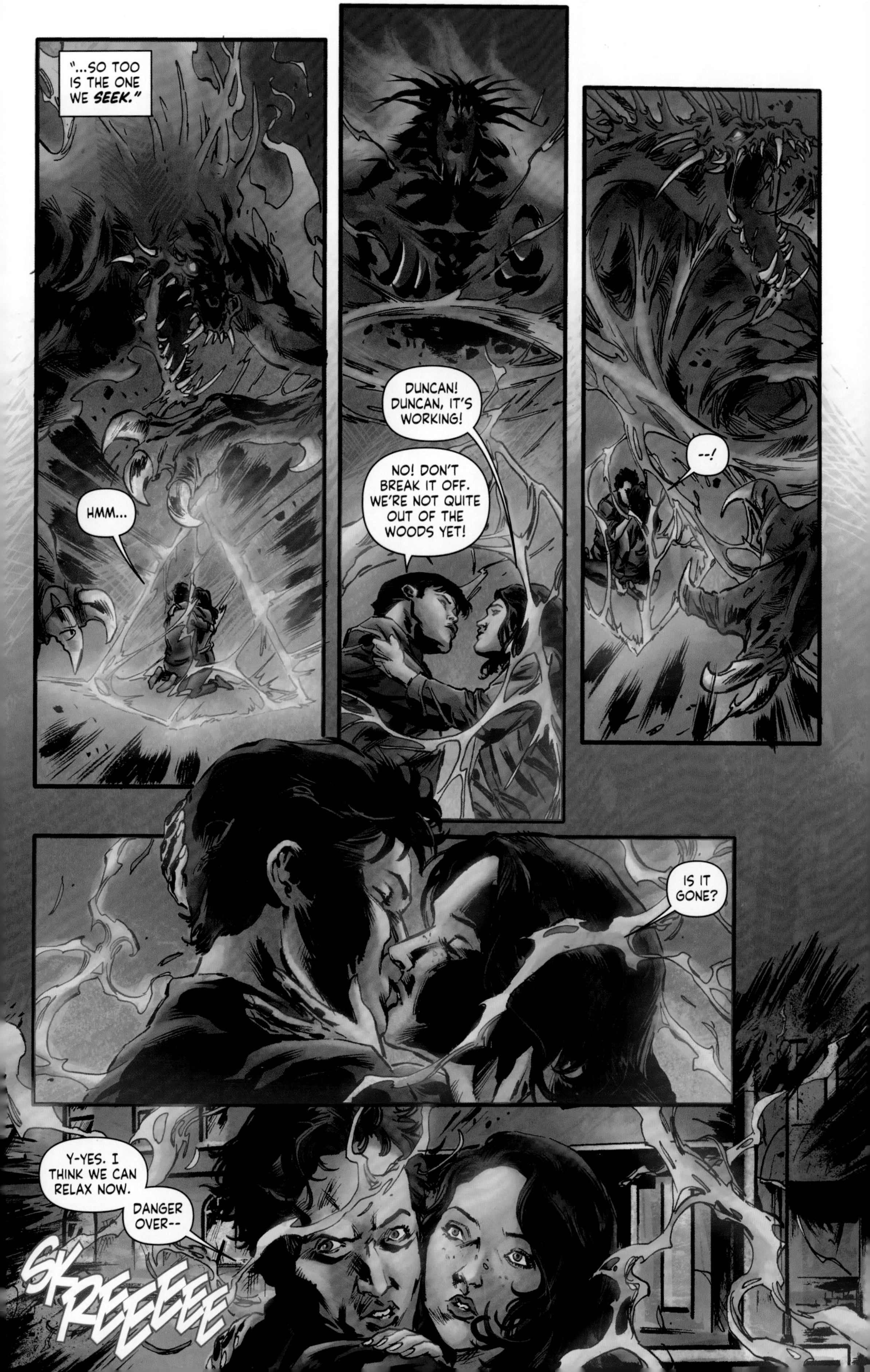
"...SO TOO IS THE ONE WE **SEEK.**"
HMM...
DUNCAN! DUNCAN, IT'S WORKING!
NO! DON'T BREAK IT OFF. WE'RE NOT QUITE OUT OF THE WOODS YET!
--!
IS IT GONE?
Y-YES. I THINK WE CAN RELAX NOW.
DANGER OVER--
SKREEEEEE

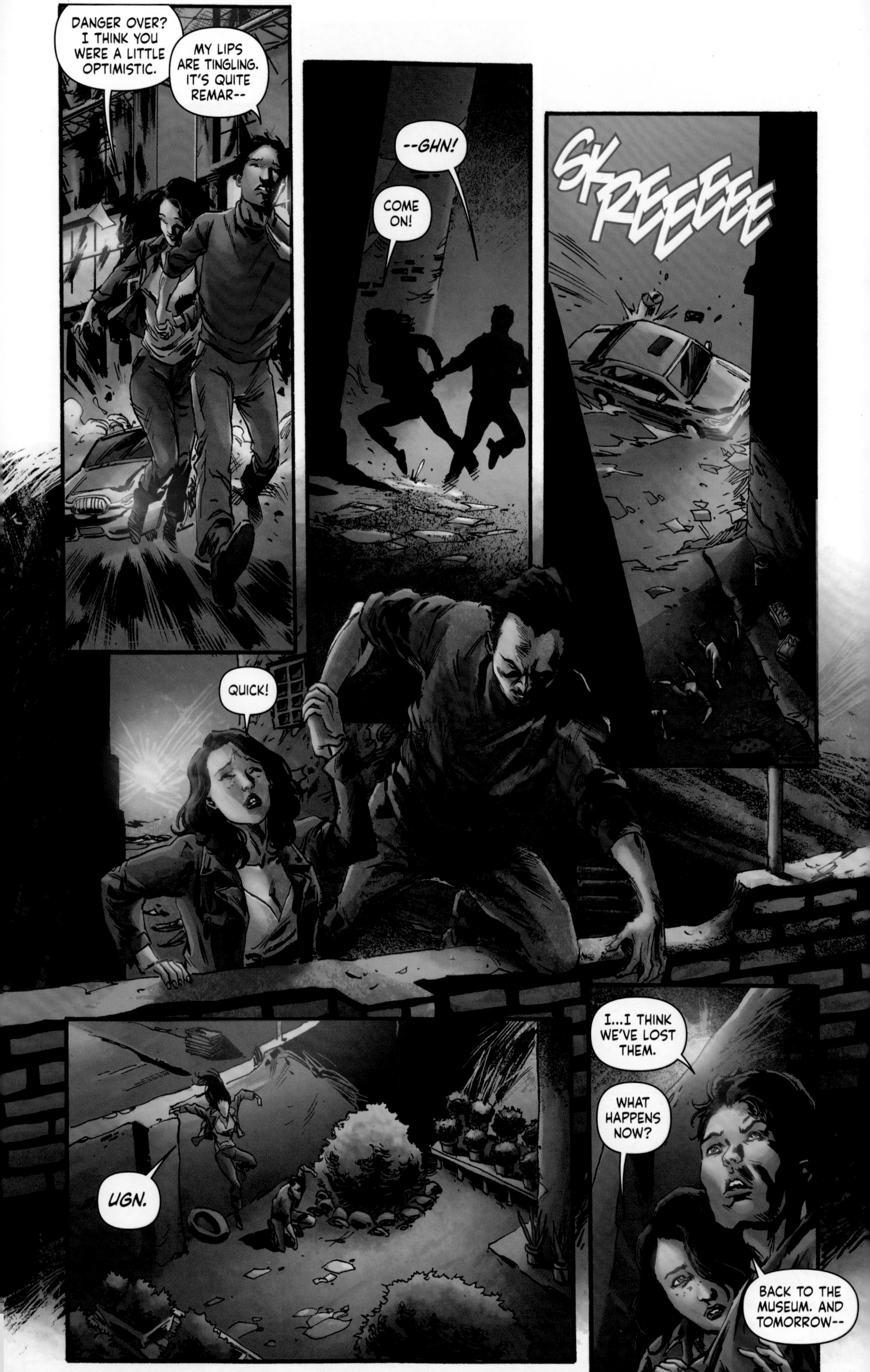
DANGER OVER? I THINK YOU WERE A LITTLE OPTIMISTIC.
MY LIPS ARE TINGLING. IT'S QUITE REMAR--
--GHN!
COME ON!
SKREEEEE
QUICK!
UGN.
I...I THINK WE'VE LOST THEM.
WHAT HAPPENS NOW?
BACK TO THE MUSEUM. AND TOMORROW--

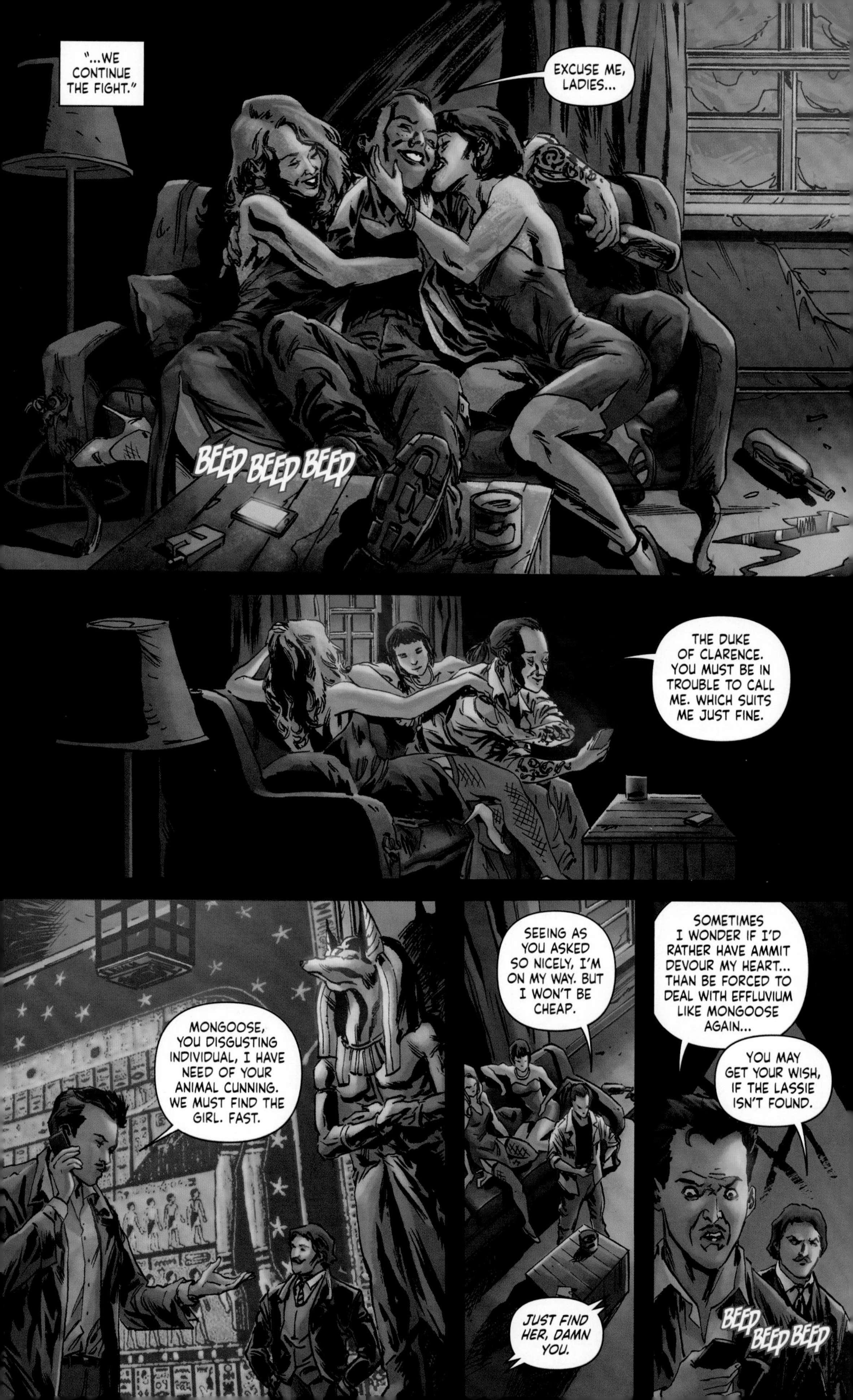
"...WE CONTINUE THE FIGHT."
EXCUSE ME, LADIES...
BEEP BEEP BEEP
THE DUKE OF CLARENCE. YOU MUST BE IN TROUBLE TO CALL ME. WHICH SUITS ME JUST FINE.
MONGOOSE, YOU DISGUSTING INDIVIDUAL, I HAVE NEED OF YOUR ANIMAL CUNNING. WE MUST FIND THE GIRL. FAST.
SEEING AS YOU ASKED SO NICELY, I'M ON MY WAY. BUT I WON'T BE CHEAP.
JUST FIND HER, DAMN YOU.
SOMETIMES I WONDER IF I'D RATHER HAVE AMMIT DEVOUR MY HEART... THAN BE FORCED TO DEAL WITH EFFLUVIUM LIKE MONGOOSE AGAIN...
YOU MAY GET YOUR WISH, IF THE LASSIE ISN'T FOUND.
BEEP BEEP BEEP

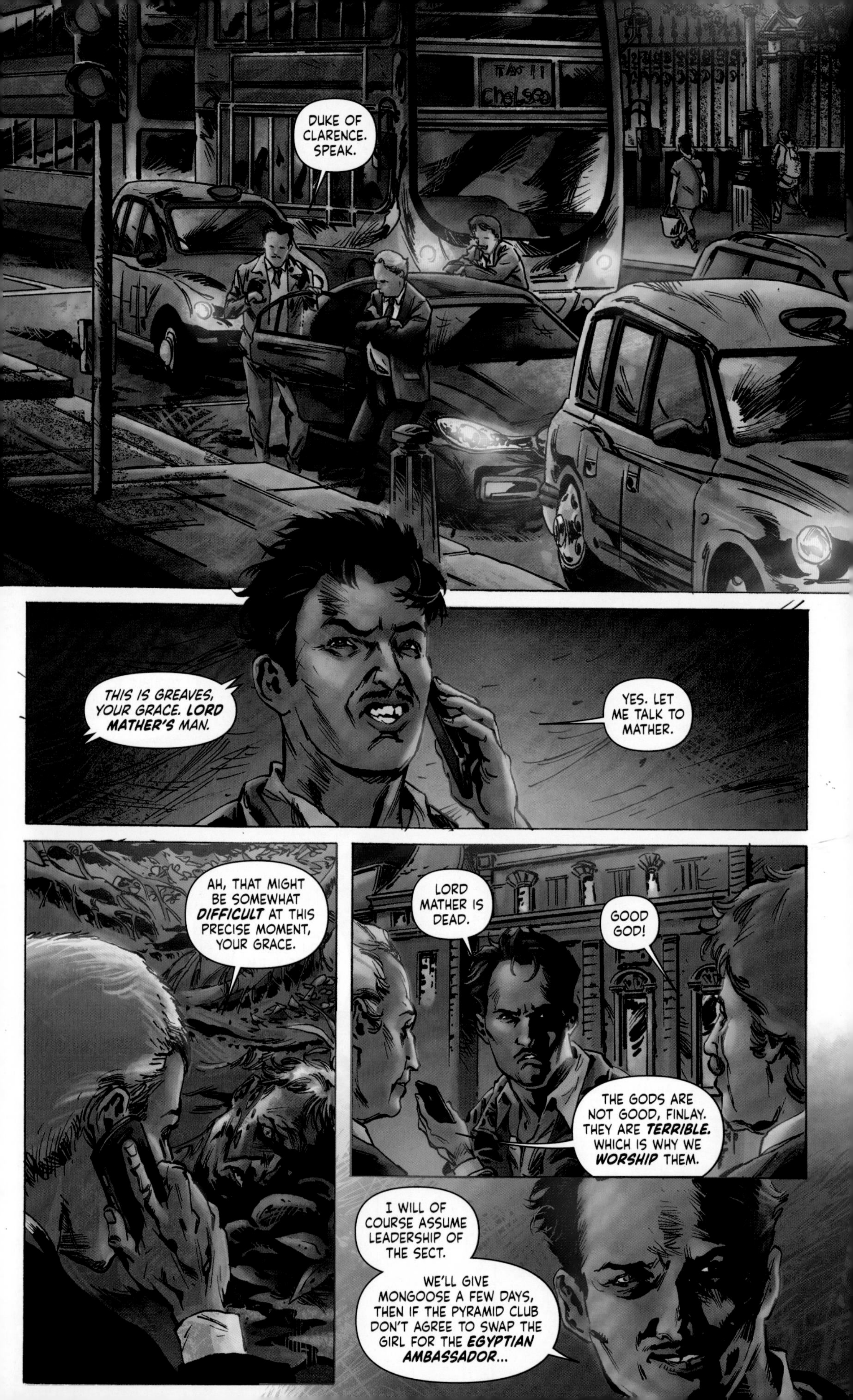
Chelsea
DUKE OF CLARENCE. SPEAK.
THIS IS GREAVES, YOUR GRACE. **LORD MATHER'S** MAN.
YES. LET ME TALK TO MATHER.
AH, THAT MIGHT BE SOMEWHAT ***DIFFICULT*** AT THIS PRECISE MOMENT, YOUR GRACE.
LORD MATHER IS DEAD.
GOOD GOD!
THE GODS ARE NOT GOOD, FINLAY. THEY ARE ***TERRIBLE.*** WHICH IS WHY WE ***WORSHIP*** THEM.
I WILL OF COURSE ASSUME LEADERSHIP OF THE SECT.
WE'LL GIVE MONGOOSE A FEW DAYS, THEN IF THE PYRAMID CLUB DON'T AGREE TO SWAP THE GIRL FOR THE ***EGYPTIAN AMBASSADOR***...

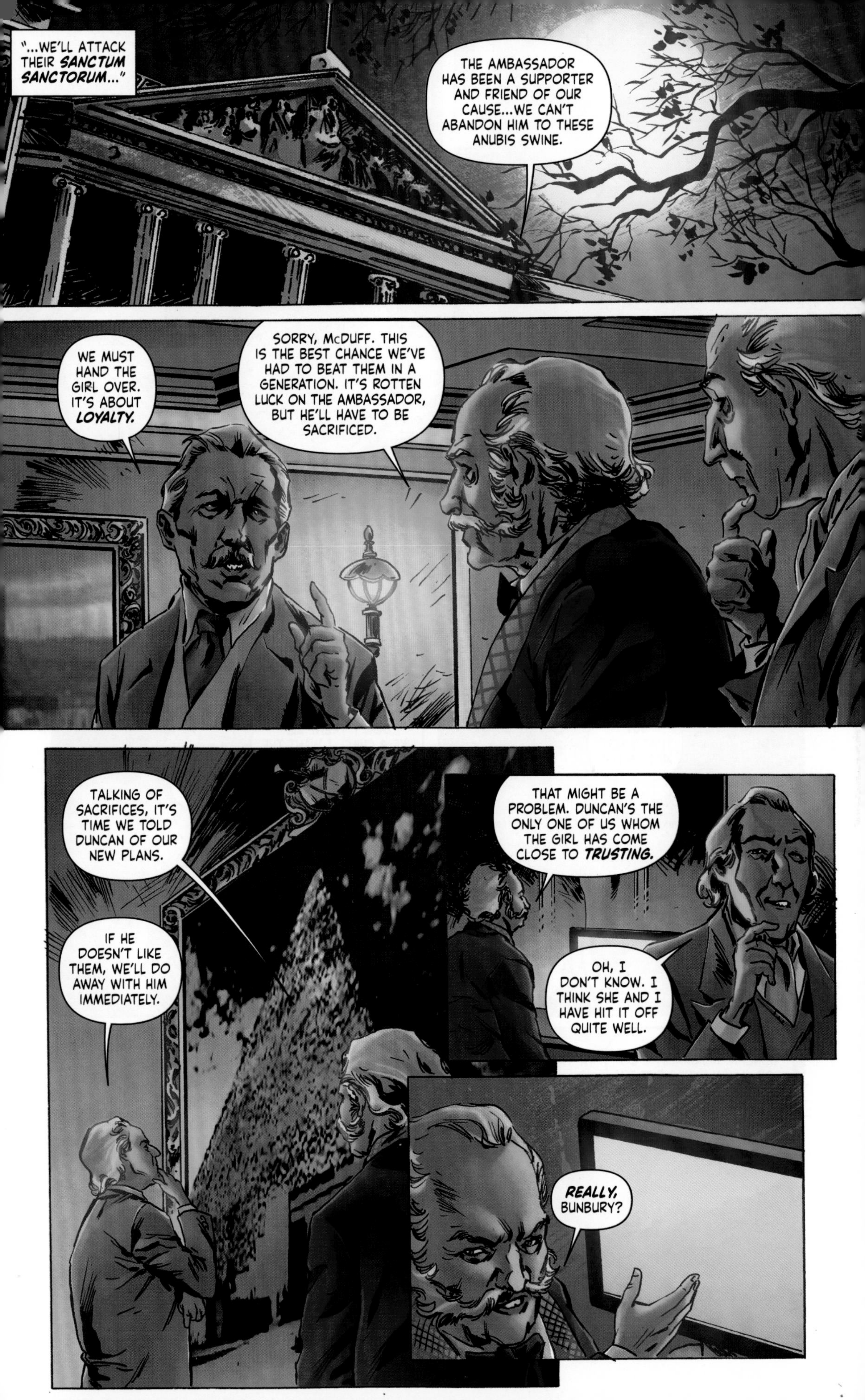
"...WE'LL ATTACK THEIR *SANCTUM SANCTORUM*..."
THE AMBASSADOR HAS BEEN A SUPPORTER AND FRIEND OF OUR CAUSE...WE CAN'T ABANDON HIM TO THESE ANUBIS SWINE.
WE MUST HAND THE GIRL OVER. IT'S ABOUT *LOYALTY.*
SORRY, McDUFF. THIS IS THE BEST CHANCE WE'VE HAD TO BEAT THEM IN A GENERATION. IT'S ROTTEN LUCK ON THE AMBASSADOR, BUT HE'LL HAVE TO BE SACRIFICED.
TALKING OF SACRIFICES, IT'S TIME WE TOLD DUNCAN OF OUR NEW PLANS.
IF HE DOESN'T LIKE THEM, WE'LL DO AWAY WITH HIM IMMEDIATELY.
THAT MIGHT BE A PROBLEM. DUNCAN'S THE ONLY ONE OF US WHOM THE GIRL HAS COME CLOSE TO *TRUSTING.*
OH, I DON'T KNOW. I THINK SHE AND I HAVE HIT IT OFF QUITE WELL.
REALLY, BUNBURY?

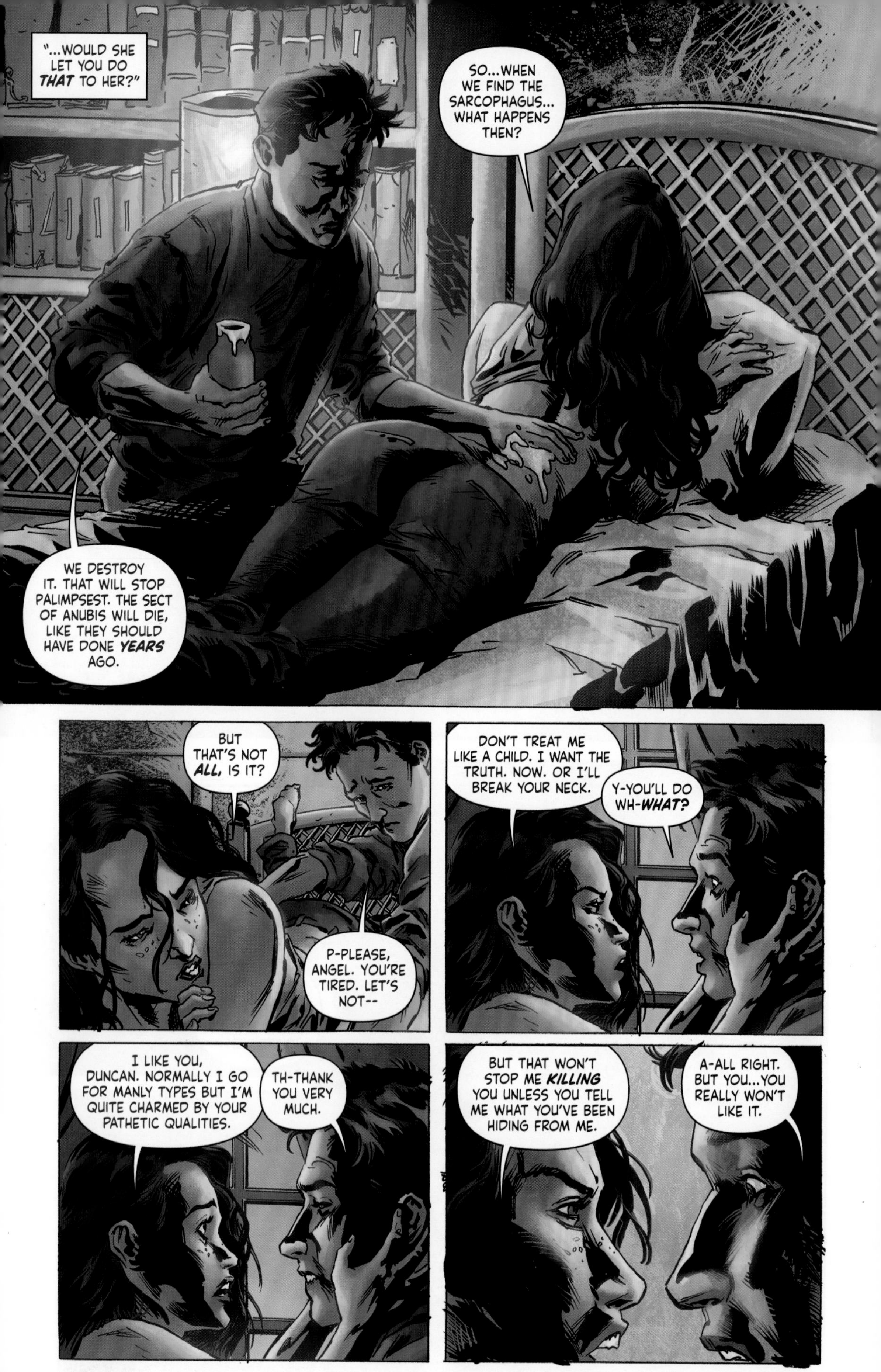
"...WOULD SHE LET YOU DO *THAT* TO HER?"
SO...WHEN WE FIND THE SARCOPHAGUS... WHAT HAPPENS THEN?
WE DESTROY IT. THAT WILL STOP PALIMPSEST. THE SECT OF ANUBIS WILL DIE, LIKE THEY SHOULD HAVE DONE *YEARS* AGO.
BUT THAT'S NOT *ALL,* IS IT?
P-PLEASE, ANGEL. YOU'RE TIRED. LET'S NOT--
DON'T TREAT ME LIKE A CHILD. I WANT THE TRUTH. NOW. OR I'LL BREAK YOUR NECK.
Y-YOU'LL DO WH-*WHAT?*
I LIKE YOU, DUNCAN. NORMALLY I GO FOR MANLY TYPES BUT I'M QUITE CHARMED BY YOUR PATHETIC QUALITIES.
TH-THANK YOU VERY MUCH.
BUT THAT WON'T STOP ME *KILLING* YOU UNLESS YOU TELL ME WHAT YOU'VE BEEN HIDING FROM ME.
A-ALL RIGHT. BUT YOU...YOU REALLY WON'T LIKE IT.

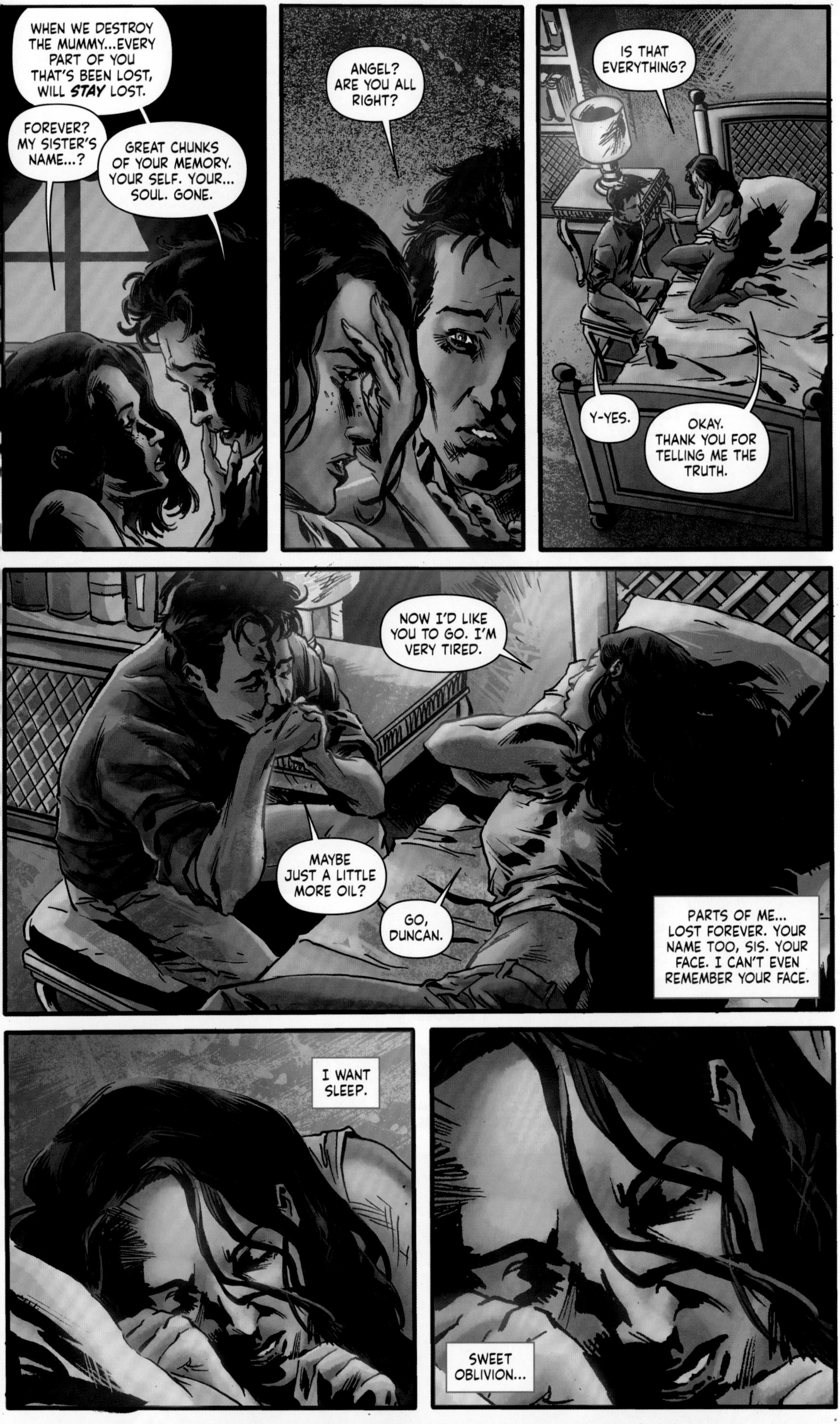
WHEN WE DESTROY THE MUMMY...EVERY PART OF YOU THAT'S BEEN LOST, WILL STAY LOST.
FOREVER? MY SISTER'S NAME...?
GREAT CHUNKS OF YOUR MEMORY. YOUR SELF. YOUR... SOUL. GONE.
ANGEL? ARE YOU ALL RIGHT?
IS THAT EVERYTHING?
Y-YES.
OKAY. THANK YOU FOR TELLING ME THE TRUTH.
NOW I'D LIKE YOU TO GO. I'M VERY TIRED.
MAYBE JUST A LITTLE MORE OIL?
GO, DUNCAN.
PARTS OF ME... LOST FOREVER. YOUR NAME TOO, SIS. YOUR FACE. I CAN'T EVEN REMEMBER YOUR FACE.
I WANT SLEEP.
SWEET OBLIVION...

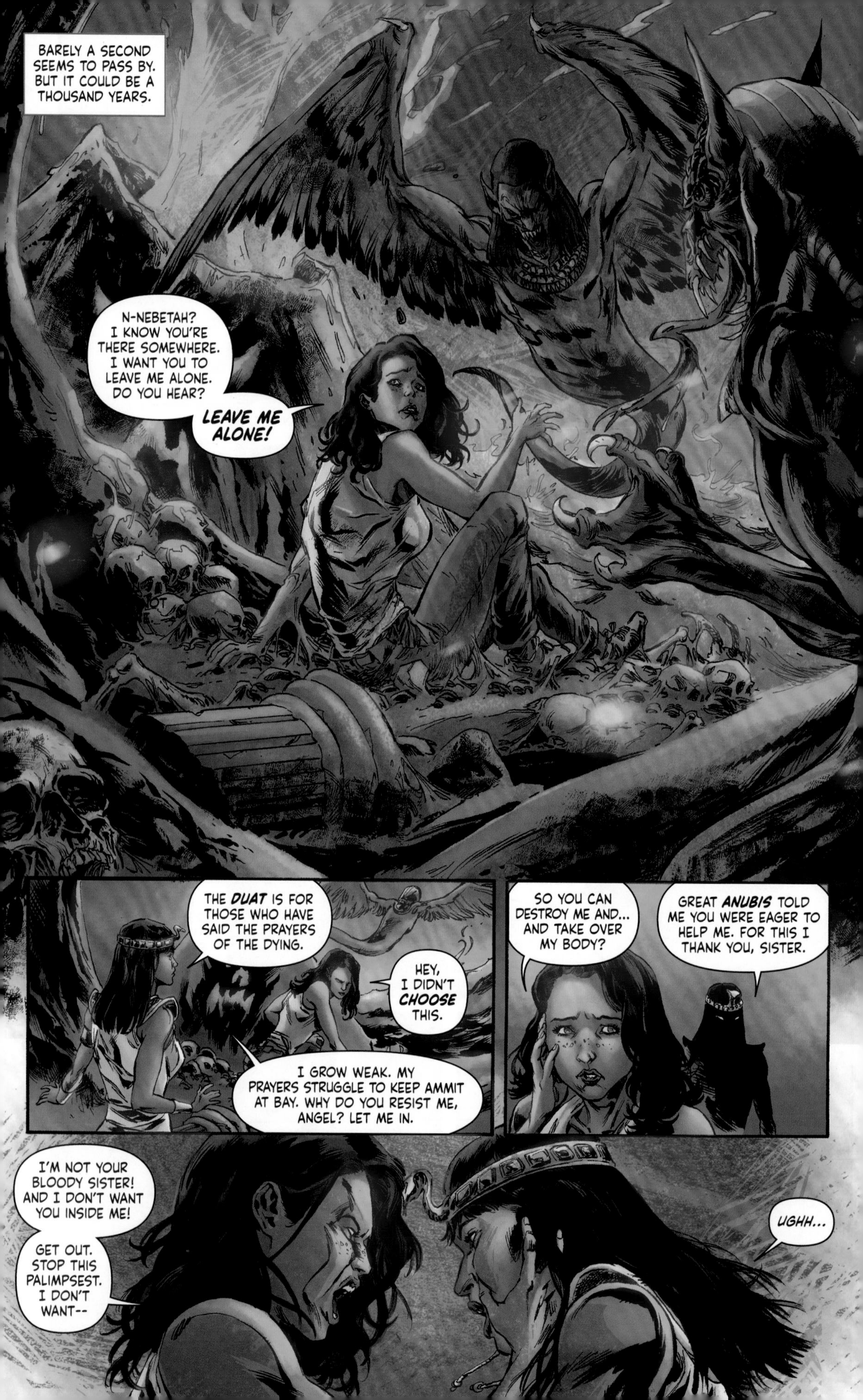
BARELY A SECOND SEEMS TO PASS BY. BUT IT COULD BE A THOUSAND YEARS.
N-NEBETAH? I KNOW YOU'RE THERE SOMEWHERE. I WANT YOU TO LEAVE ME ALONE. DO YOU HEAR?
LEAVE ME ALONE!
THE DUAT IS FOR THOSE WHO HAVE SAID THE PRAYERS OF THE DYING.
HEY, I DIDN'T CHOOSE THIS.
I GROW WEAK. MY PRAYERS STRUGGLE TO KEEP AMMIT AT BAY. WHY DO YOU RESIST ME, ANGEL? LET ME IN.
SO YOU CAN DESTROY ME AND... AND TAKE OVER MY BODY?
GREAT ANUBIS TOLD ME YOU WERE EAGER TO HELP ME. FOR THIS I THANK YOU, SISTER.
I'M NOT YOUR BLOODY SISTER! AND I DON'T WANT YOU INSIDE ME!
GET OUT. STOP THIS PALIMPSEST. I DON'T WANT--
UGHH...

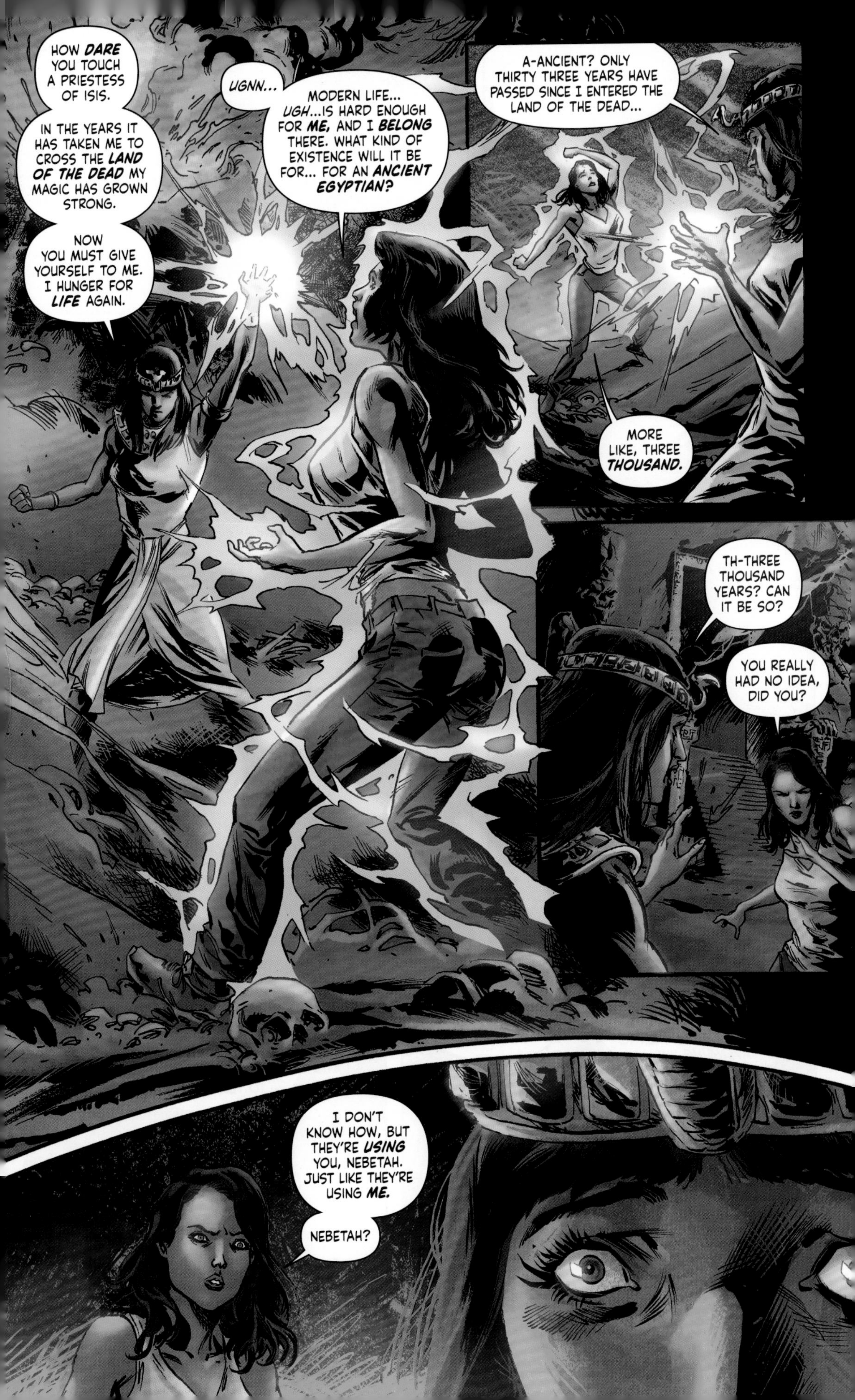
HOW DARE YOU TOUCH A PRIESTESS OF ISIS.
IN THE YEARS IT HAS TAKEN ME TO CROSS THE LAND OF THE DEAD MY MAGIC HAS GROWN STRONG.
NOW YOU MUST GIVE YOURSELF TO ME. I HUNGER FOR LIFE AGAIN.
UGNN...
MODERN LIFE... UGH...IS HARD ENOUGH FOR ME, AND I BELONG THERE. WHAT KIND OF EXISTENCE WILL IT BE FOR... FOR AN ANCIENT EGYPTIAN?
A-ANCIENT? ONLY THIRTY THREE YEARS HAVE PASSED SINCE I ENTERED THE LAND OF THE DEAD...
MORE LIKE, THREE THOUSAND.
TH-THREE THOUSAND YEARS? CAN IT BE SO?
YOU REALLY HAD NO IDEA, DID YOU?
I DON'T KNOW HOW, BUT THEY'RE USING YOU, NEBETAH. JUST LIKE THEY'RE USING ME.
NEBETAH?

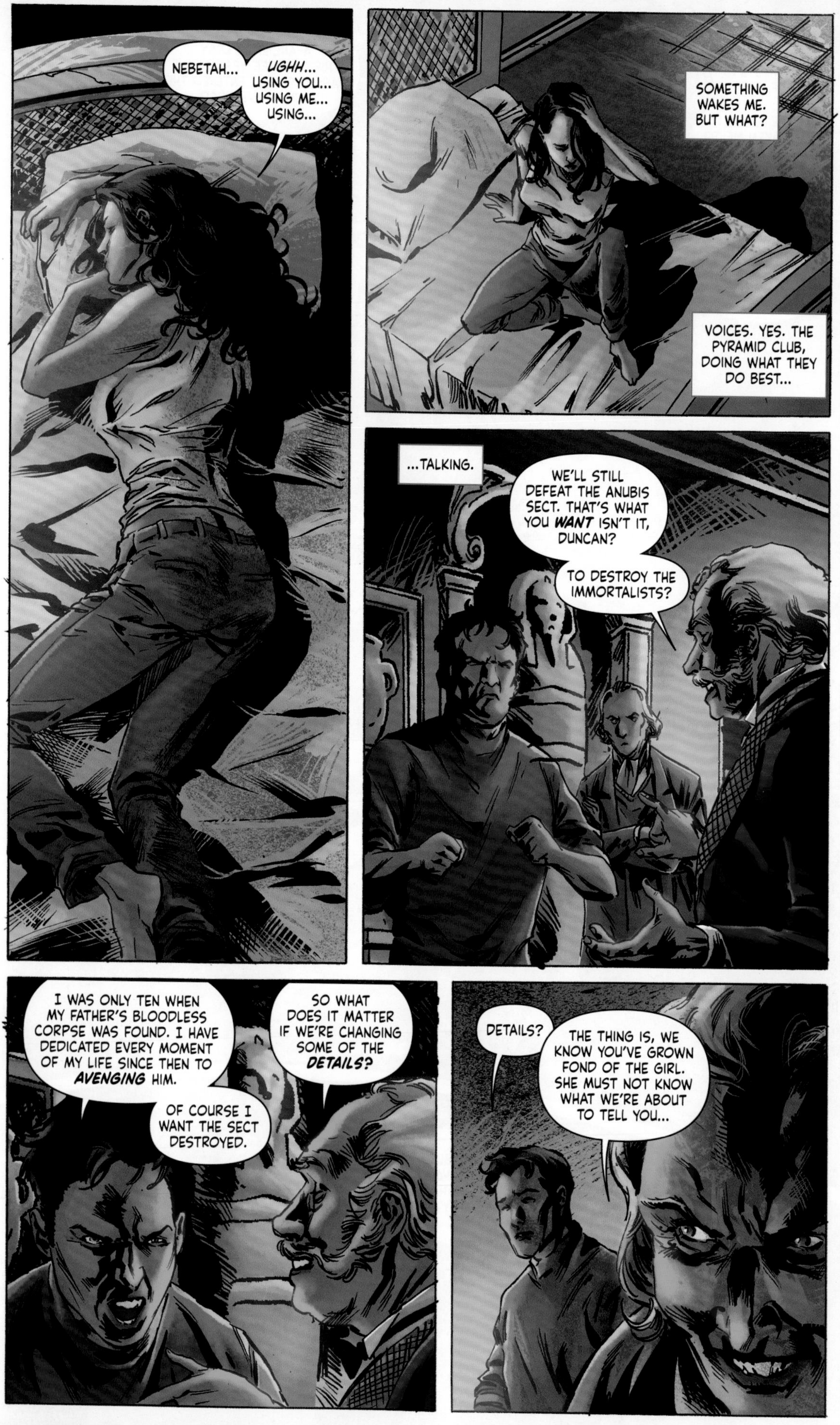
NEBETAH...
UGHH... USING YOU... USING ME... USING...
SOMETHING WAKES ME. BUT WHAT?
VOICES. YES. THE PYRAMID CLUB, DOING WHAT THEY DO BEST...
...TALKING.
WE'LL STILL DEFEAT THE ANUBIS SECT. THAT'S WHAT YOU WANT ISN'T IT, DUNCAN?
TO DESTROY THE IMMORTALISTS?
I WAS ONLY TEN WHEN MY FATHER'S BLOODLESS CORPSE WAS FOUND. I HAVE DEDICATED EVERY MOMENT OF MY LIFE SINCE THEN TO AVENGING HIM.
OF COURSE I WANT THE SECT DESTROYED.
SO WHAT DOES IT MATTER IF WE'RE CHANGING SOME OF THE DETAILS?
DETAILS?
THE THING IS, WE KNOW YOU'VE GROWN FOND OF THE GIRL. SHE MUST NOT KNOW WHAT WE'RE ABOUT TO TELL YOU...

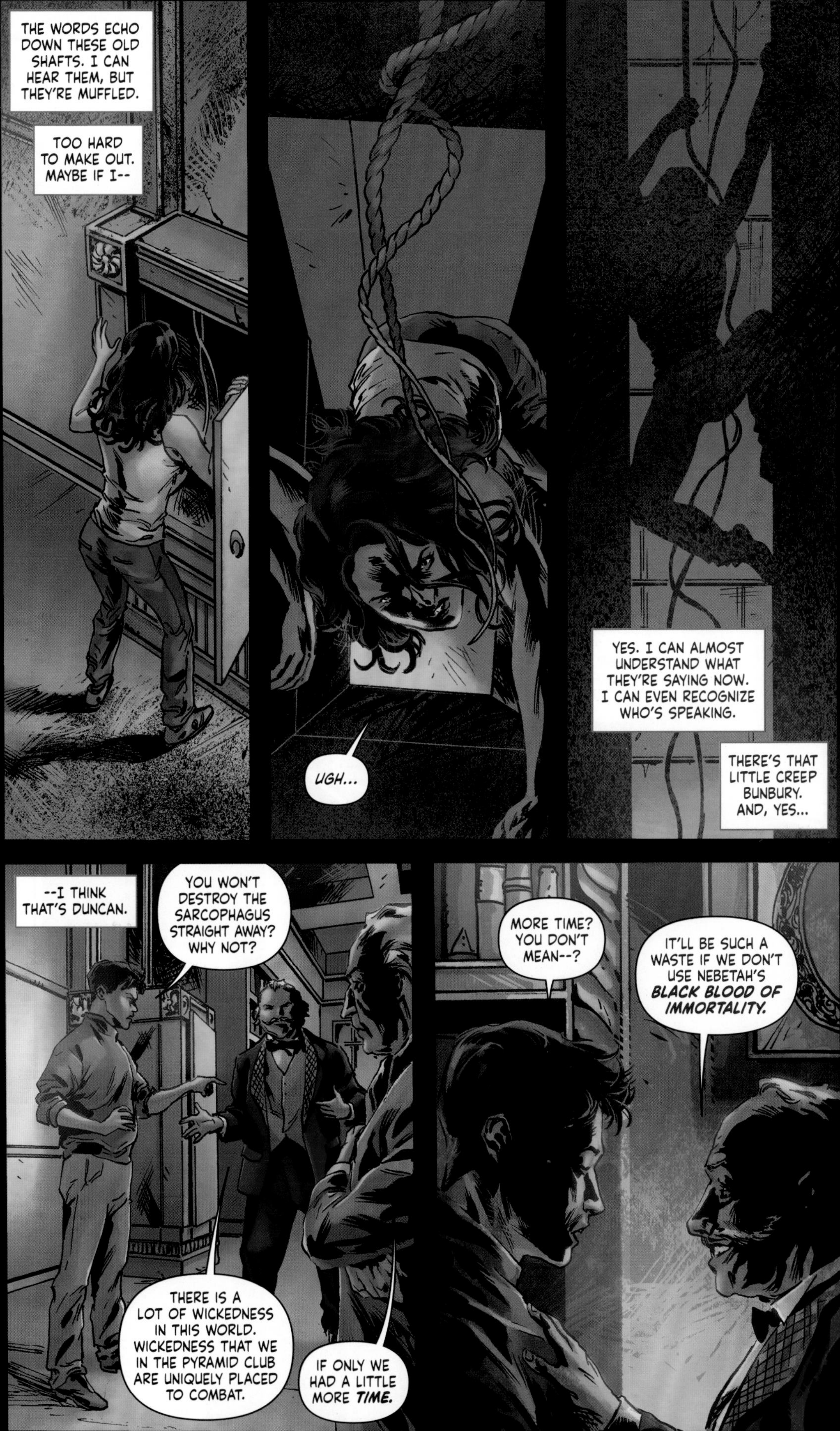
THE WORDS ECHO DOWN THESE OLD SHAFTS. I CAN HEAR THEM, BUT THEY'RE MUFFLED.
TOO HARD TO MAKE OUT. MAYBE IF I--
UGH...
YES. I CAN ALMOST UNDERSTAND WHAT THEY'RE SAYING NOW. I CAN EVEN RECOGNIZE WHO'S SPEAKING.
THERE'S THAT LITTLE CREEP BUNBURY. AND, YES...
--I THINK THAT'S DUNCAN.
YOU WON'T DESTROY THE SARCOPHAGUS STRAIGHT AWAY? WHY NOT?
THERE IS A LOT OF WICKEDNESS IN THIS WORLD. WICKEDNESS THAT WE IN THE PYRAMID CLUB ARE UNIQUELY PLACED TO COMBAT.
IF ONLY WE HAD A LITTLE MORE *TIME.*
MORE TIME? YOU DON'T MEAN--?
IT'LL BE SUCH A WASTE IF WE DON'T USE NEBETAH'S ***BLACK BLOOD OF IMMORTALITY.***

THINK WHAT GOOD WE CAN DO, WITH ANOTHER THIRTY-THREE YEARS.

YOU FOOLS! THIS IS HOW IT BEGINS. SOON YOU'LL BE AS ADDICTED TO IMMORTALITY AS THE ANUBIS SECT.

WE'LL JUST HAVE TO TAKE THAT CHANCE.

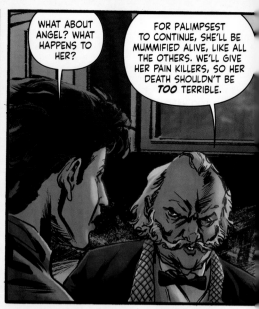

WHAT ABOUT ANGEL? WHAT HAPPENS TO HER?

FOR PALIMPSEST TO CONTINUE, SHE'LL BE MUMMIFIED ALIVE, LIKE ALL THE OTHERS. WE'LL GIVE HER PAIN KILLERS, SO HER DEATH SHOULDN'T BE TOO TERRIBLE.

NOT TOO TERRIBLE? HER BRAINS WILL BE PULLED OUT OF HER NOSE!

HER ORGANS WILL BE TORN FROM HER BODY AND STUFFED IN CANOPIC JARS!

I KNEW IT.

I KNEW I SHOULDN'T HAVE TRUSTED THEM.

BUT IF THEY THINK THEY'RE GOING TO STUFF AN IRON HOOK UP THIS GIRL'S NOSE THEY'RE MISTAKEN.

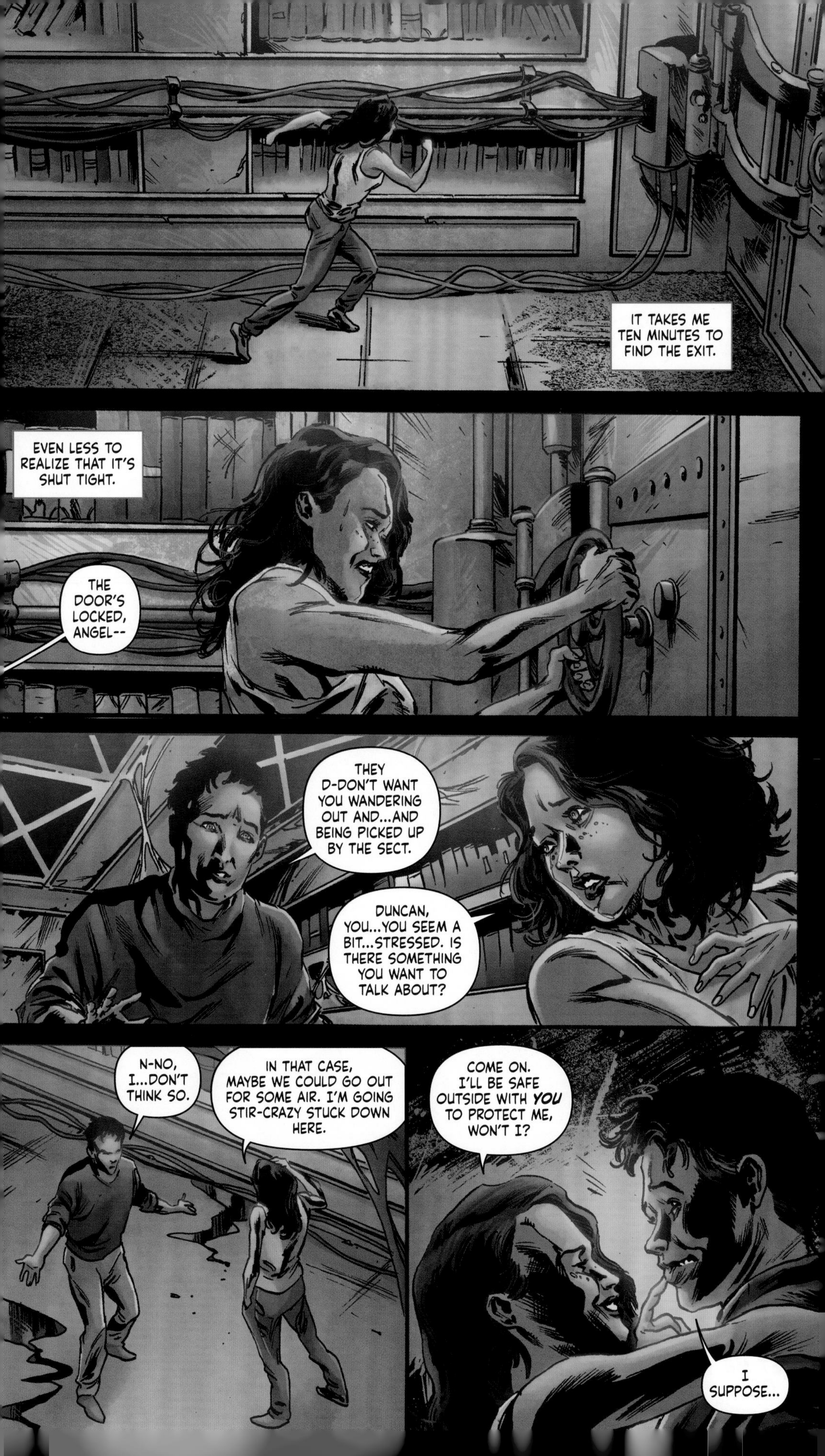
IT TAKES ME TEN MINUTES TO FIND THE EXIT.
EVEN LESS TO REALIZE THAT IT'S SHUT TIGHT.
THE DOOR'S LOCKED, ANGEL--
THEY D-DON'T WANT YOU WANDERING OUT AND...AND BEING PICKED UP BY THE SECT.
DUNCAN, YOU...YOU SEEM A BIT...STRESSED. IS THERE SOMETHING YOU WANT TO TALK ABOUT?
N-NO, I...DON'T THINK SO.
IN THAT CASE, MAYBE WE COULD GO OUT FOR SOME AIR. I'M GOING STIR-CRAZY STUCK DOWN HERE.
COME ON. I'LL BE SAFE OUTSIDE WITH *YOU* TO PROTECT ME, WON'T I?
I SUPPOSE...

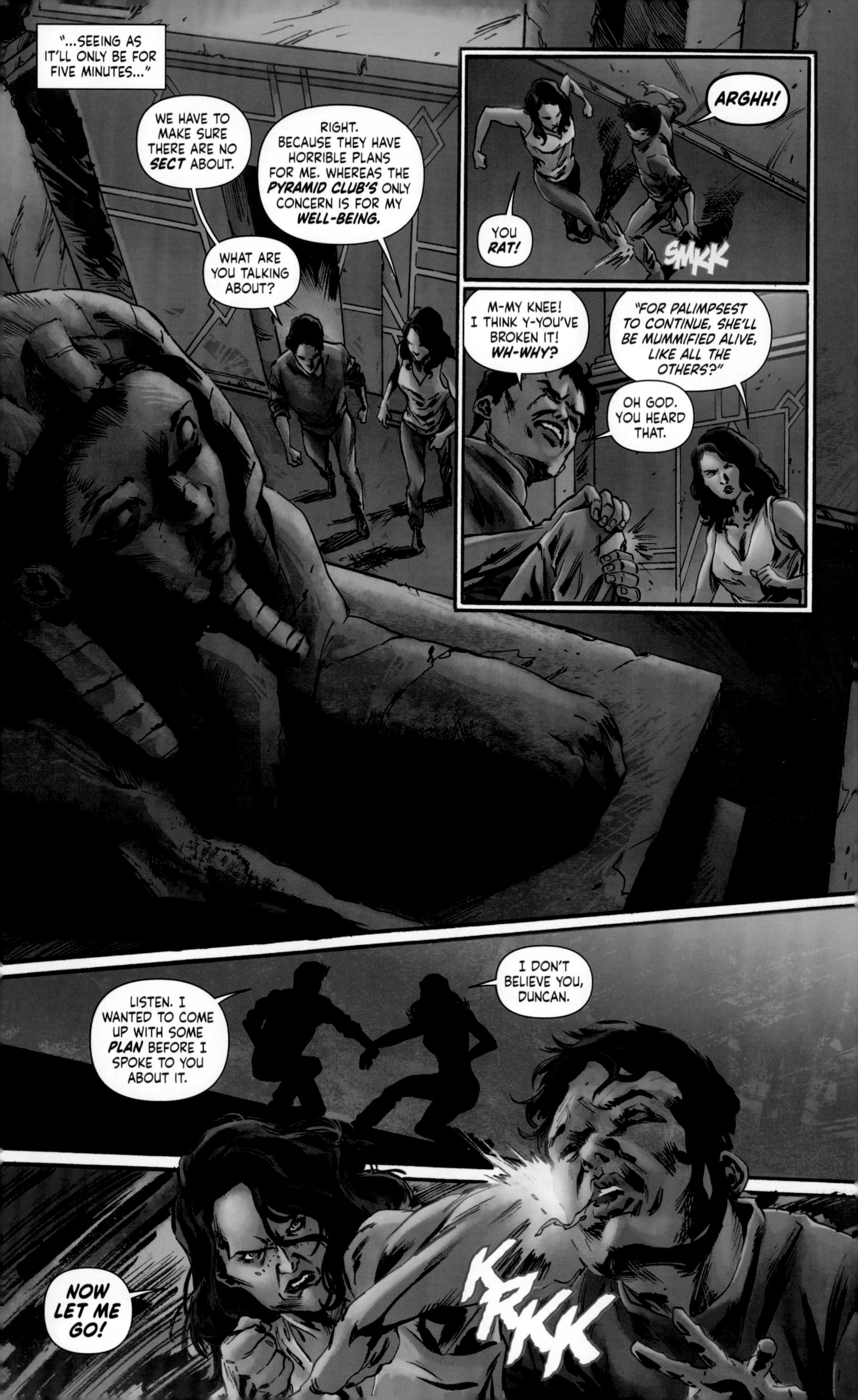
"...SEEING AS IT'LL ONLY BE FOR FIVE MINUTES..."
WE HAVE TO MAKE SURE THERE ARE NO SECT ABOUT.
RIGHT. BECAUSE THEY HAVE HORRIBLE PLANS FOR ME. WHEREAS THE PYRAMID CLUB'S ONLY CONCERN IS FOR MY WELL-BEING.
WHAT ARE YOU TALKING ABOUT?
ARGHH!
YOU RAT!
SMKK
M-MY KNEE! I THINK Y-YOU'VE BROKEN IT! WH-WHY?
"FOR PALIMPSEST TO CONTINUE, SHE'LL BE MUMMIFIED ALIVE, LIKE ALL THE OTHERS?"
OH GOD. YOU HEARD THAT.
LISTEN. I WANTED TO COME UP WITH SOME PLAN BEFORE I SPOKE TO YOU ABOUT IT.
I DON'T BELIEVE YOU, DUNCAN.
NOW LET ME GO!
KRKK

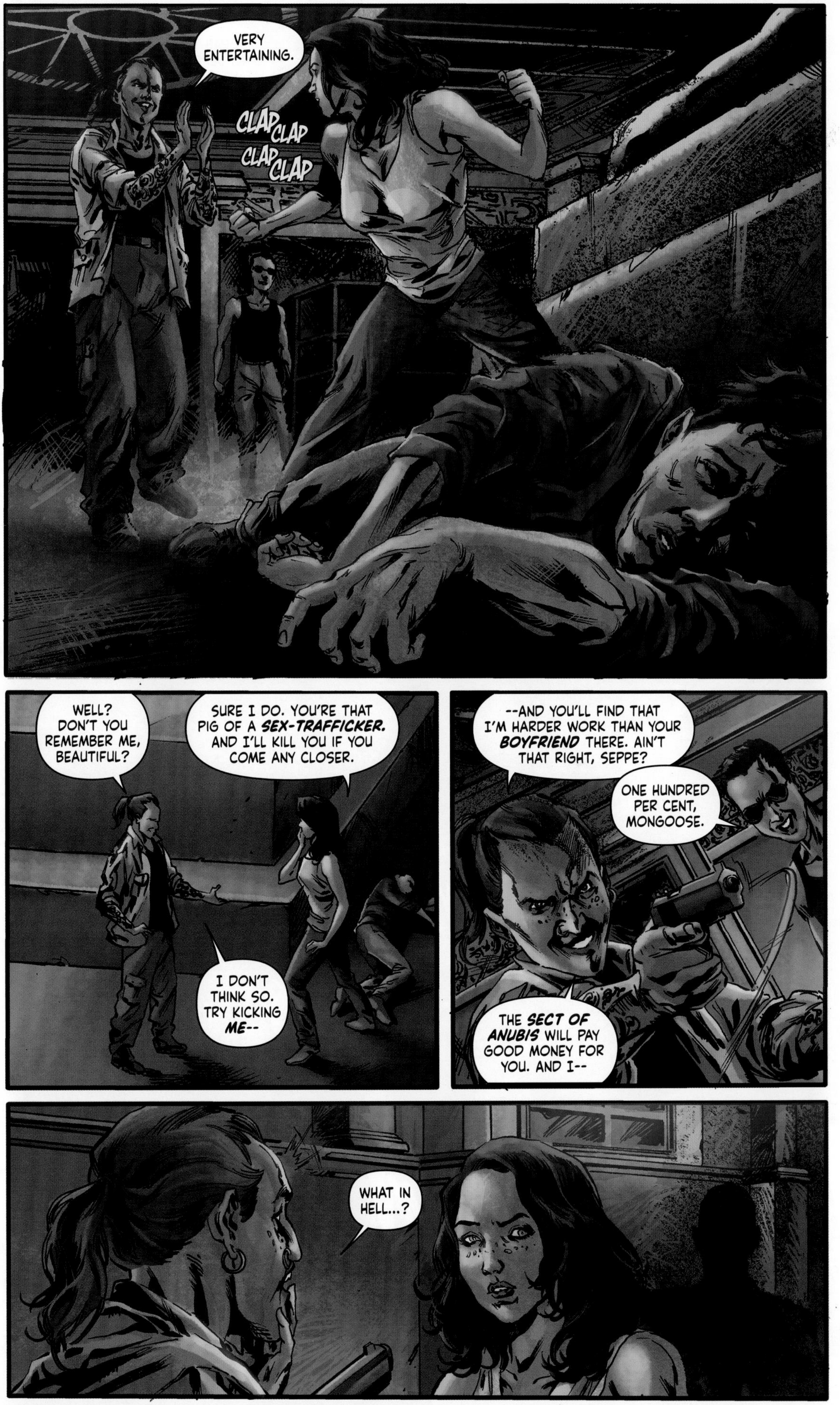
VERY ENTERTAINING.
CLAP CLAP CLAP CLAP
WELL? DON'T YOU REMEMBER ME, BEAUTIFUL?
SURE I DO. YOU'RE THAT PIG OF A SEX-TRAFFICKER. AND I'LL KILL YOU IF YOU COME ANY CLOSER.
I DON'T THINK SO. TRY KICKING ME--
--AND YOU'LL FIND THAT I'M HARDER WORK THAN YOUR BOYFRIEND THERE. AIN'T THAT RIGHT, SEPPE?
ONE HUNDRED PER CENT, MONGOOSE.
THE SECT OF ANUBIS WILL PAY GOOD MONEY FOR YOU. AND I--
WHAT IN HELL...?

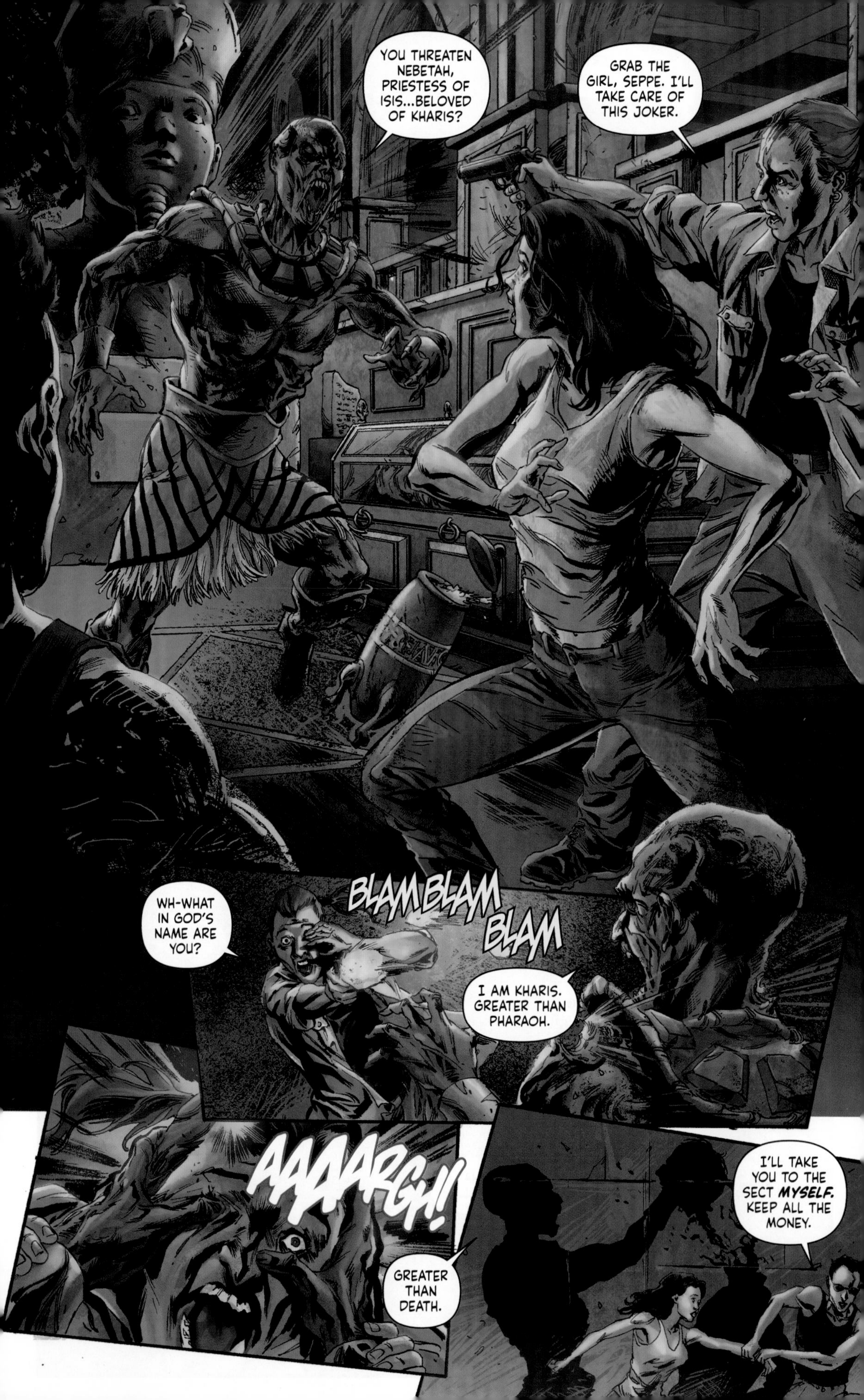
YOU THREATEN NEBETAH, PRIESTESS OF ISIS...BELOVED OF KHARIS?
GRAB THE GIRL, SEPPE. I'LL TAKE CARE OF THIS JOKER.
WH-WHAT IN GOD'S NAME ARE YOU?
BLAM BLAM BLAM
I AM KHARIS. GREATER THAN PHARAOH.
AAAARGH!!
GREATER THAN DEATH.
I'LL TAKE YOU TO THE SECT **MYSELF.** KEEP ALL THE MONEY.

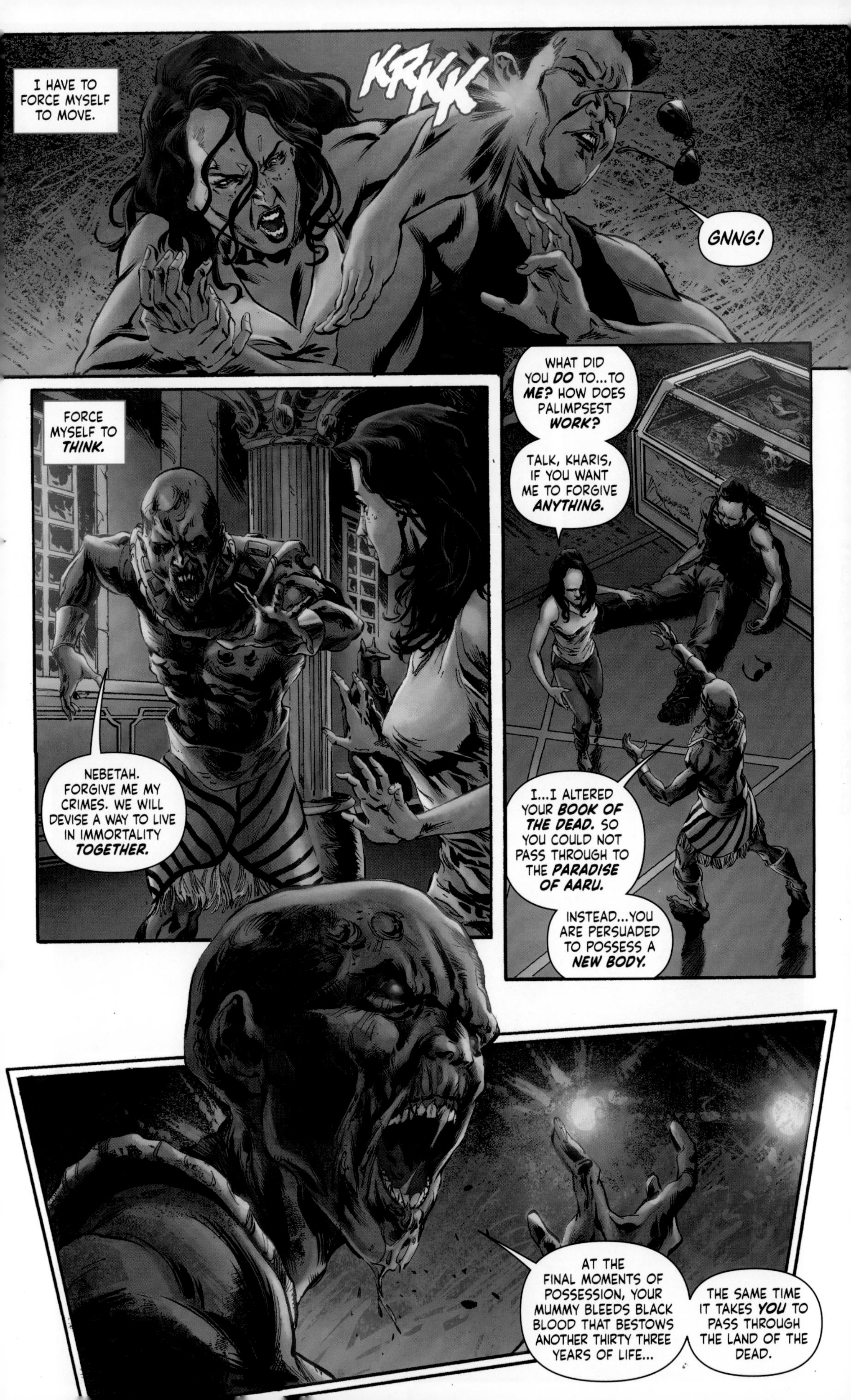
I HAVE TO FORCE MYSELF TO MOVE.
KRKK
GNNG!
FORCE MYSELF TO THINK.
NEBETAH. FORGIVE ME MY CRIMES. WE WILL DEVISE A WAY TO LIVE IN IMMORTALITY TOGETHER.
WHAT DID YOU DO TO...TO ME? HOW DOES PALIMPSEST WORK?
TALK, KHARIS, IF YOU WANT ME TO FORGIVE ANYTHING.
I...I ALTERED YOUR BOOK OF THE DEAD. SO YOU COULD NOT PASS THROUGH TO THE PARADISE OF AARU.
INSTEAD...YOU ARE PERSUADED TO POSSESS A NEW BODY.
AT THE FINAL MOMENTS OF POSSESSION, YOUR MUMMY BLEEDS BLACK BLOOD THAT BESTOWS ANOTHER THIRTY THREE YEARS OF LIFE...
THE SAME TIME IT TAKES YOU TO PASS THROUGH THE LAND OF THE DEAD.

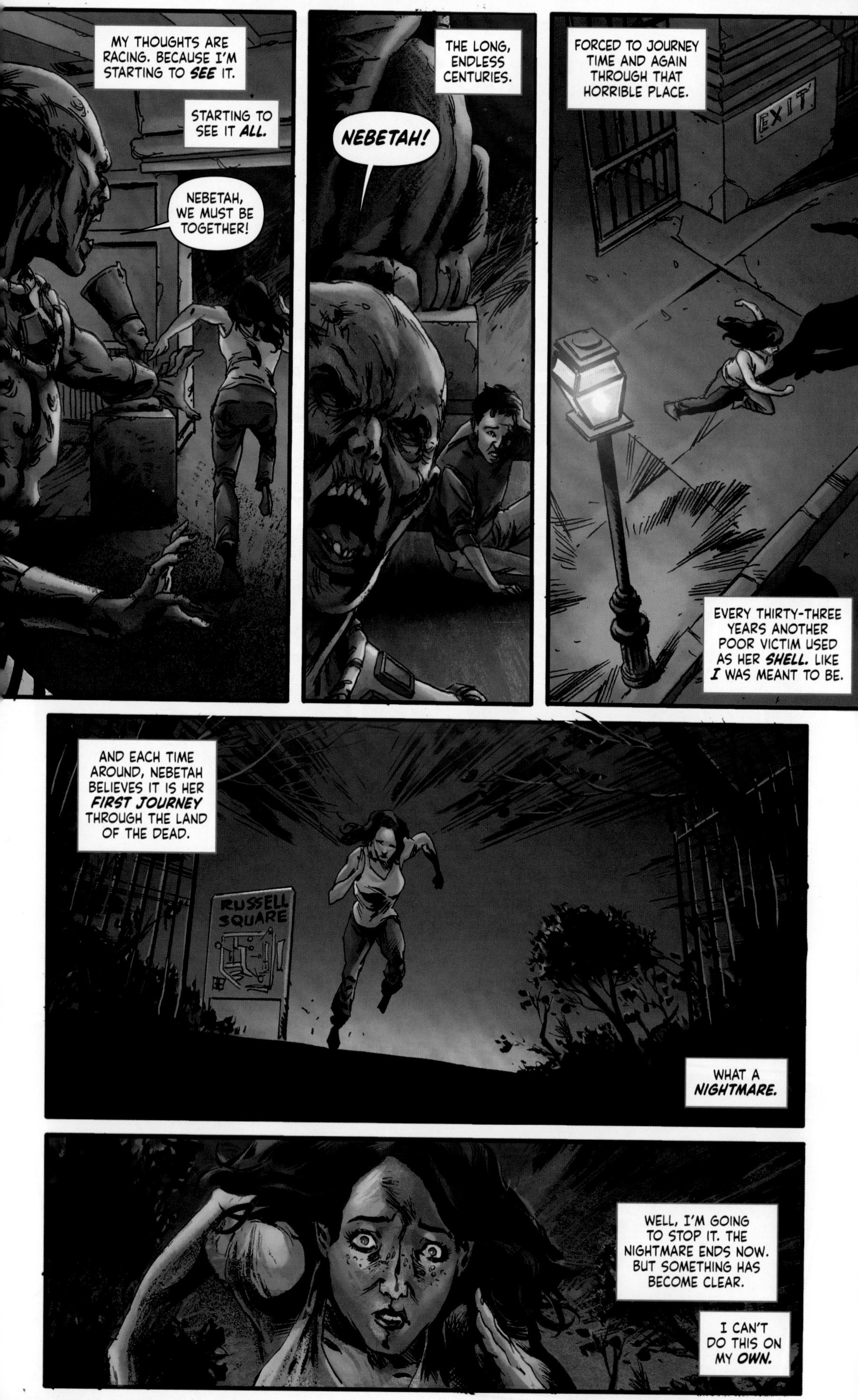
MY THOUGHTS ARE RACING. BECAUSE I'M STARTING TO SEE IT.
STARTING TO SEE IT ALL.
NEBETAH, WE MUST BE TOGETHER!
THE LONG, ENDLESS CENTURIES.
NEBETAH!
FORCED TO JOURNEY TIME AND AGAIN THROUGH THAT HORRIBLE PLACE.
EXIT
EVERY THIRTY-THREE YEARS ANOTHER POOR VICTIM USED AS HER SHELL. LIKE I WAS MEANT TO BE.
AND EACH TIME AROUND, NEBETAH BELIEVES IT IS HER FIRST JOURNEY THROUGH THE LAND OF THE DEAD.
RUSSELL SQUARE
WHAT A NIGHTMARE.
WELL, I'M GOING TO STOP IT. THE NIGHTMARE ENDS NOW. BUT SOMETHING HAS BECOME CLEAR.
I CAN'T DO THIS ON MY OWN.

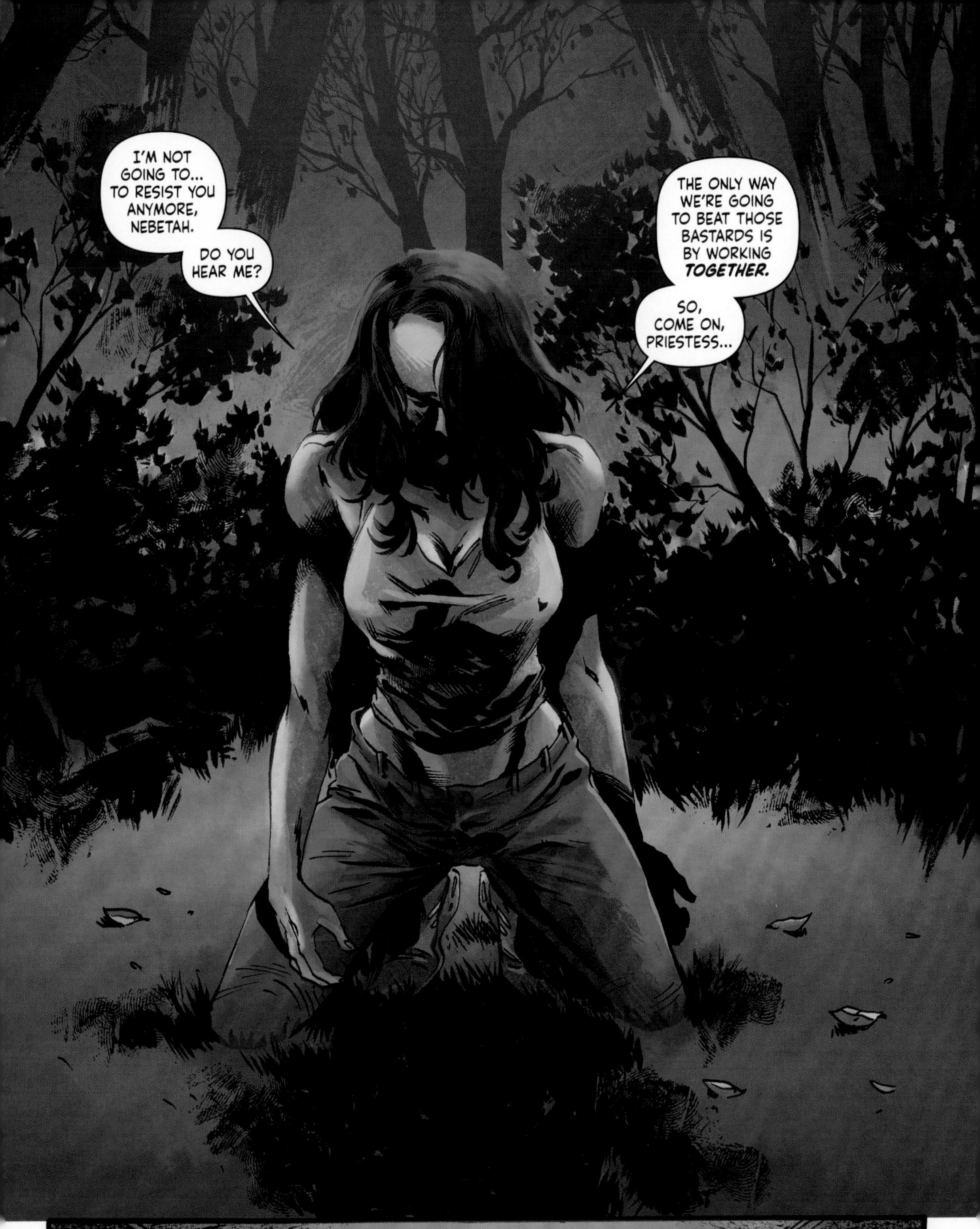
I'M NOT GOING TO... TO RESIST YOU ANYMORE, NEBETAH.
DO YOU HEAR ME?
THE ONLY WAY WE'RE GOING TO BEAT THOSE BASTARDS IS BY WORKING ***TOGETHER.***
SO, COME ON, PRIESTESS...

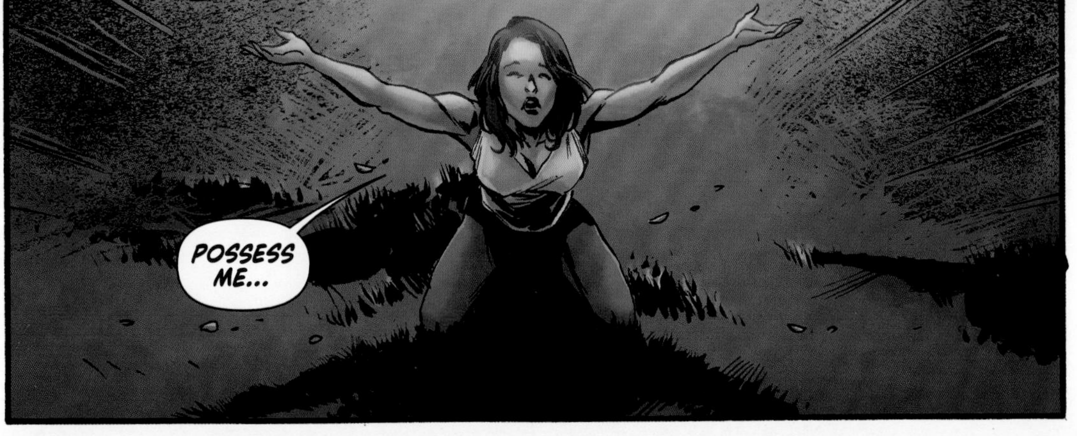
POSSESS ME...

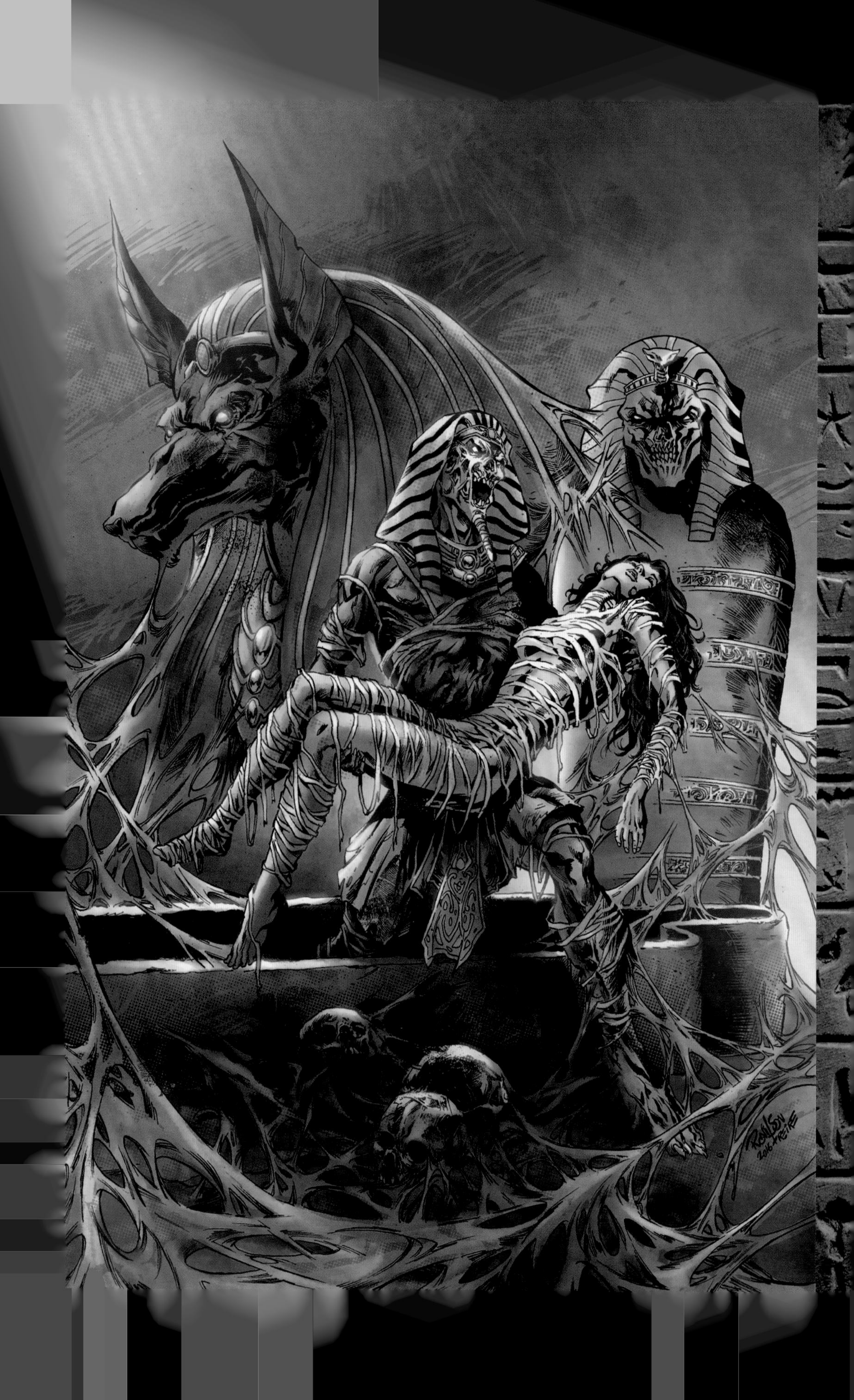

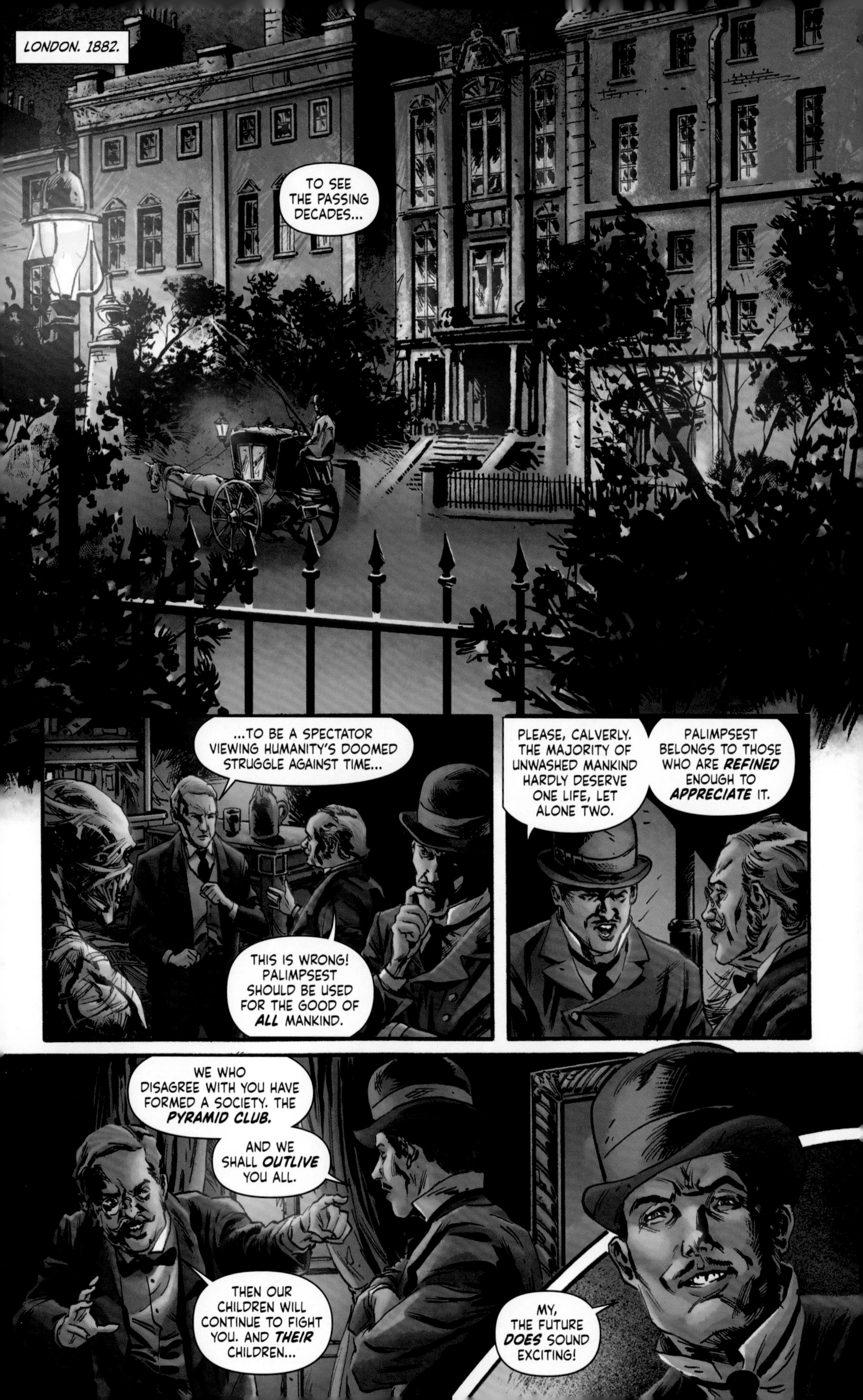
LONDON. 1882.
TO SEE THE PASSING DECADES...
...TO BE A SPECTATOR VIEWING HUMANITY'S DOOMED STRUGGLE AGAINST TIME...
THIS IS WRONG! PALIMPSEST SHOULD BE USED FOR THE GOOD OF ALL MANKIND.
PLEASE, CALVERLY. THE MAJORITY OF UNWASHED MANKIND HARDLY DESERVE ONE LIFE, LET ALONE TWO.
PALIMPSEST BELONGS TO THOSE WHO ARE REFINED ENOUGH TO APPRECIATE IT.
WE WHO DISAGREE WITH YOU HAVE FORMED A SOCIETY. THE PYRAMID CLUB.
AND WE SHALL OUTLIVE YOU ALL.
THEN OUR CHILDREN WILL CONTINUE TO FIGHT YOU. AND THEIR CHILDREN...
MY, THE FUTURE DOES SOUND EXCITING!

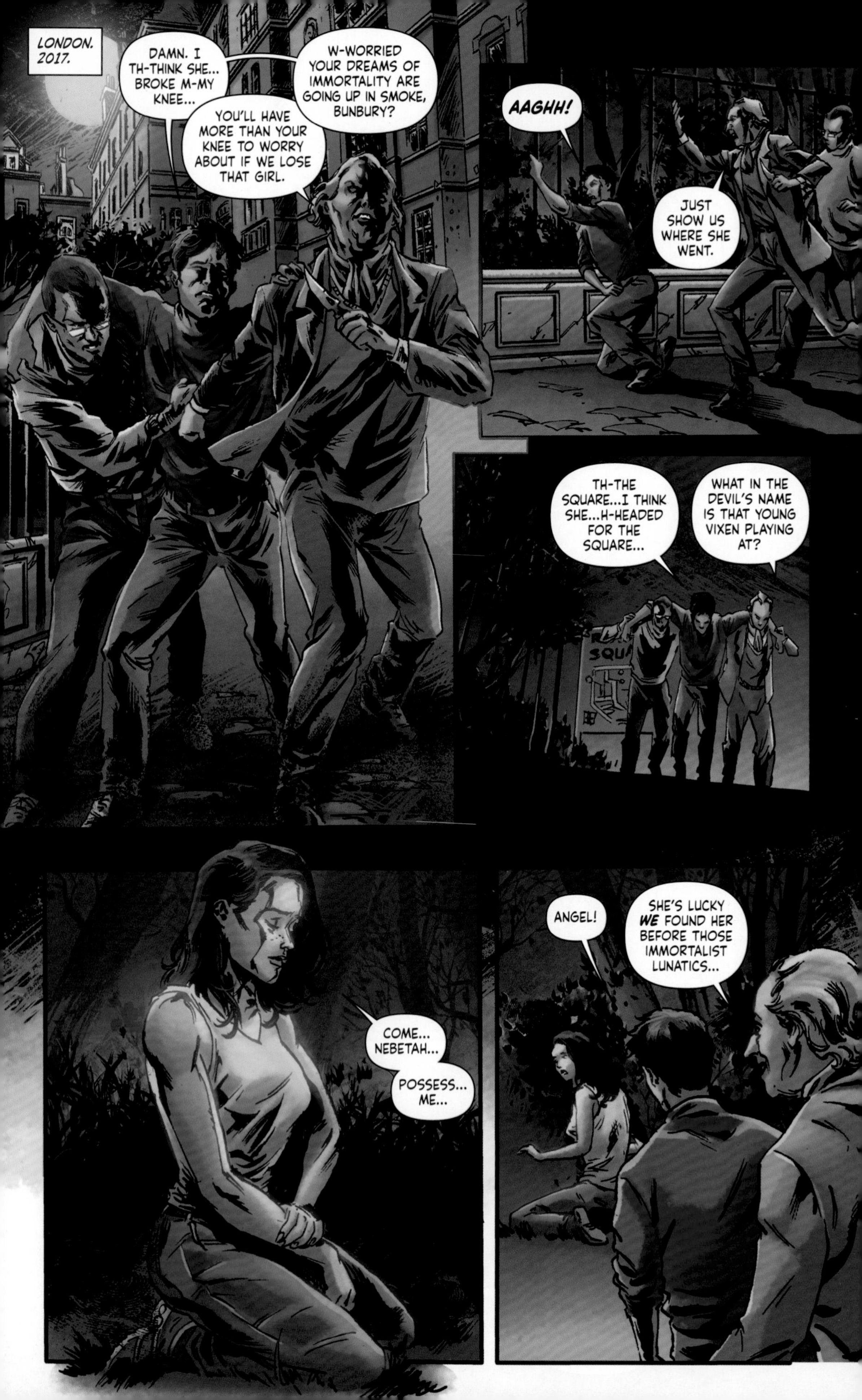
LONDON. 2017.
DAMN. I TH-THINK SHE... BROKE M-MY KNEE...
W-WORRIED YOUR DREAMS OF IMMORTALITY ARE GOING UP IN SMOKE, BUNBURY?
YOU'LL HAVE MORE THAN YOUR KNEE TO WORRY ABOUT IF WE LOSE THAT GIRL.
AAGHH!
JUST SHOW US WHERE SHE WENT.
TH-THE SQUARE...I THINK SHE...H-HEADED FOR THE SQUARE...
WHAT IN THE DEVIL'S NAME IS THAT YOUNG VIXEN PLAYING AT?
COME... NEBETAH...
POSSESS... ME...
ANGEL!
SHE'S LUCKY WE FOUND HER BEFORE THOSE IMMORTALIST LUNATICS...

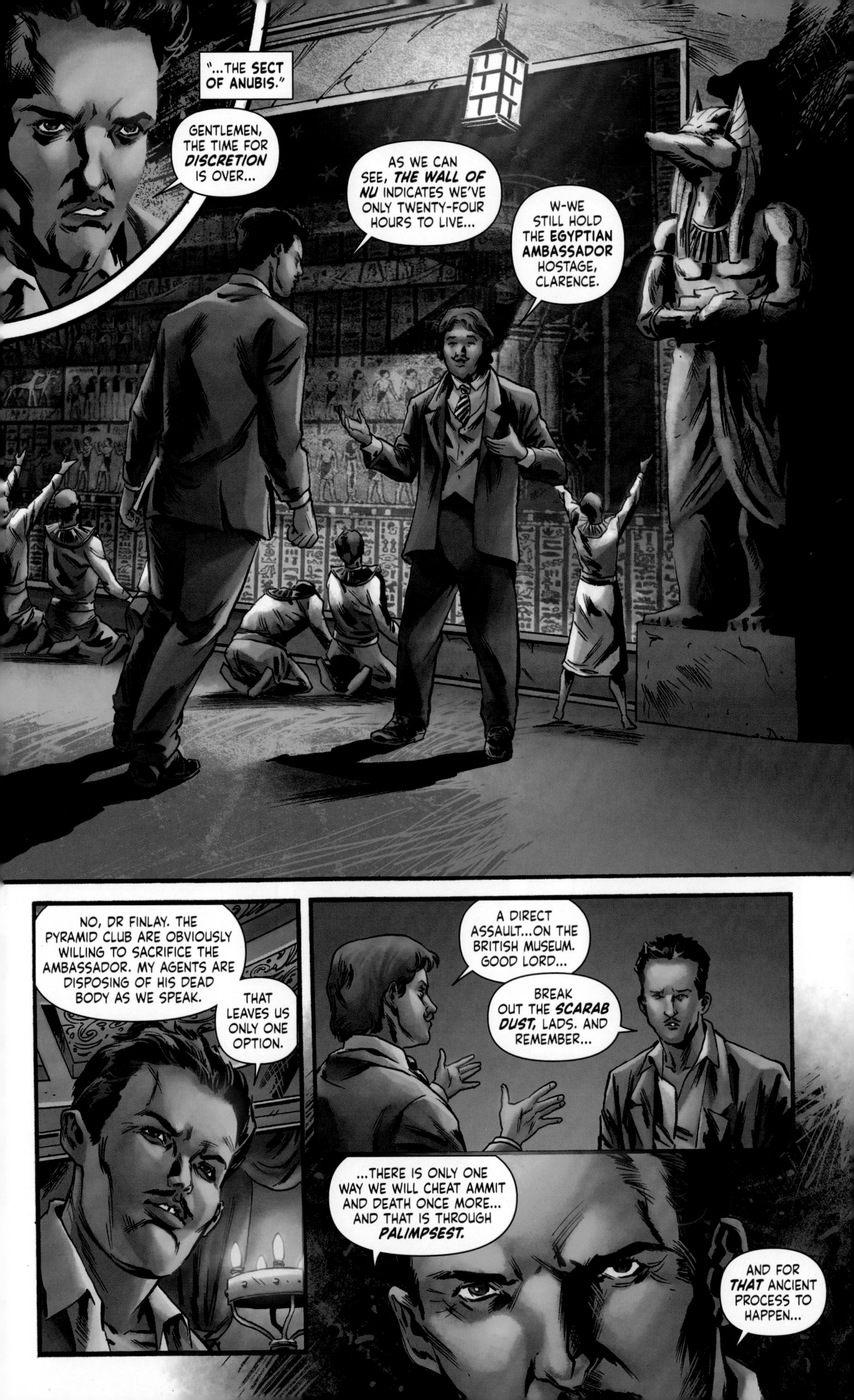
"...THE SECT OF ANUBIS."
GENTLEMEN, THE TIME FOR DISCRETION IS OVER...
AS WE CAN SEE, THE WALL OF NU INDICATES WE'VE ONLY TWENTY-FOUR HOURS TO LIVE...
W-WE STILL HOLD THE EGYPTIAN AMBASSADOR HOSTAGE, CLARENCE.
NO, DR FINLAY. THE PYRAMID CLUB ARE OBVIOUSLY WILLING TO SACRIFICE THE AMBASSADOR. MY AGENTS ARE DISPOSING OF HIS DEAD BODY AS WE SPEAK.
THAT LEAVES US ONLY ONE OPTION.
A DIRECT ASSAULT...ON THE BRITISH MUSEUM. GOOD LORD...
BREAK OUT THE SCARAB DUST, LADS. AND REMEMBER...
...THERE IS ONLY ONE WAY WE WILL CHEAT AMMIT AND DEATH ONCE MORE... AND THAT IS THROUGH PALIMPSEST.
AND FOR THAT ANCIENT PROCESS TO HAPPEN...

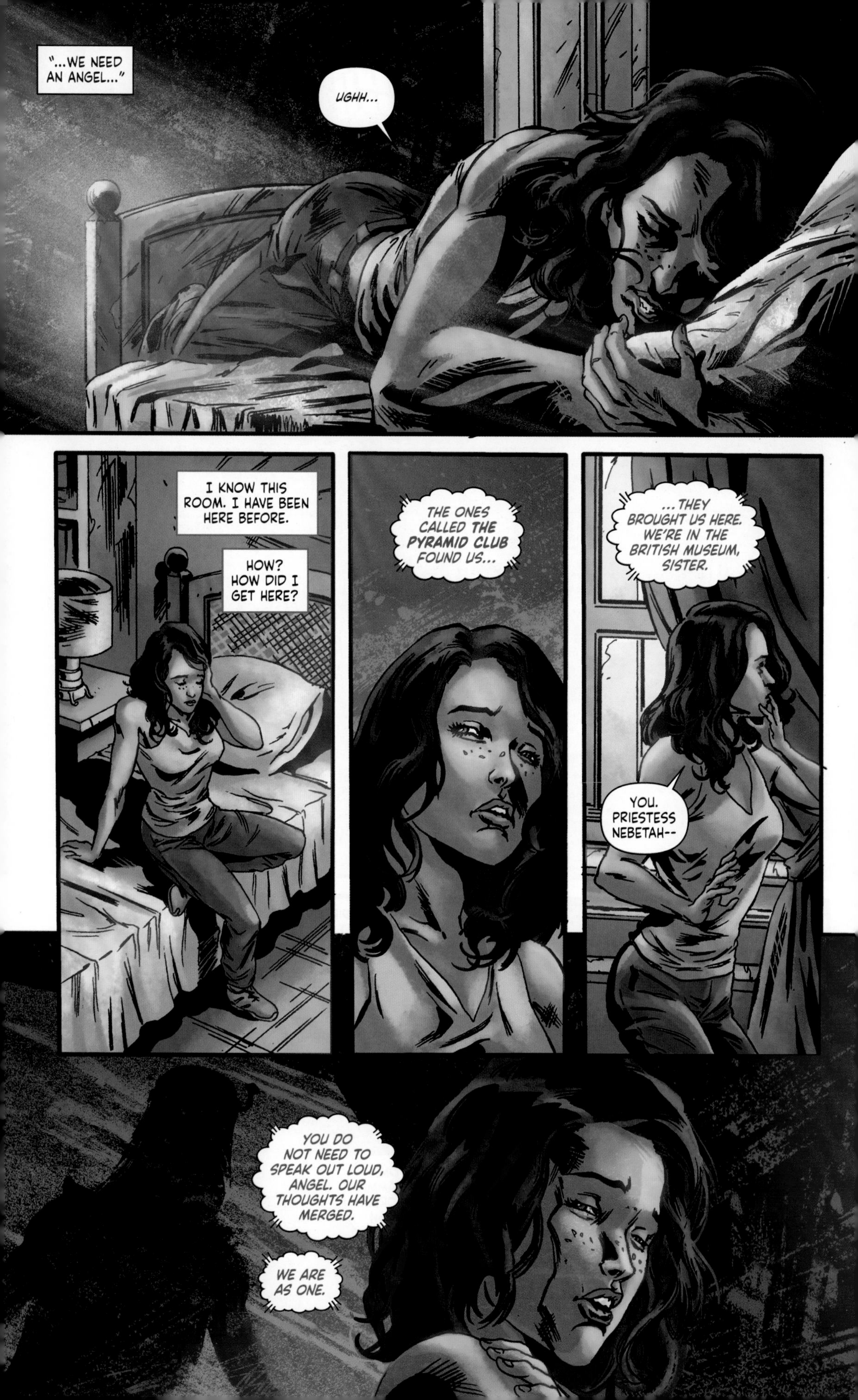
"...WE NEED AN ANGEL..."
UGHH...
I KNOW THIS ROOM. I HAVE BEEN HERE BEFORE.
HOW? HOW DID I GET HERE?
THE ONES CALLED **THE PYRAMID CLUB** FOUND US...
...THEY BROUGHT US HERE. WE'RE IN THE BRITISH MUSEUM, SISTER.
YOU. PRIESTESS NEBETAH--
YOU DO NOT NEED TO SPEAK OUT LOUD, ANGEL. OUR THOUGHTS HAVE MERGED.
WE ARE AS ONE.

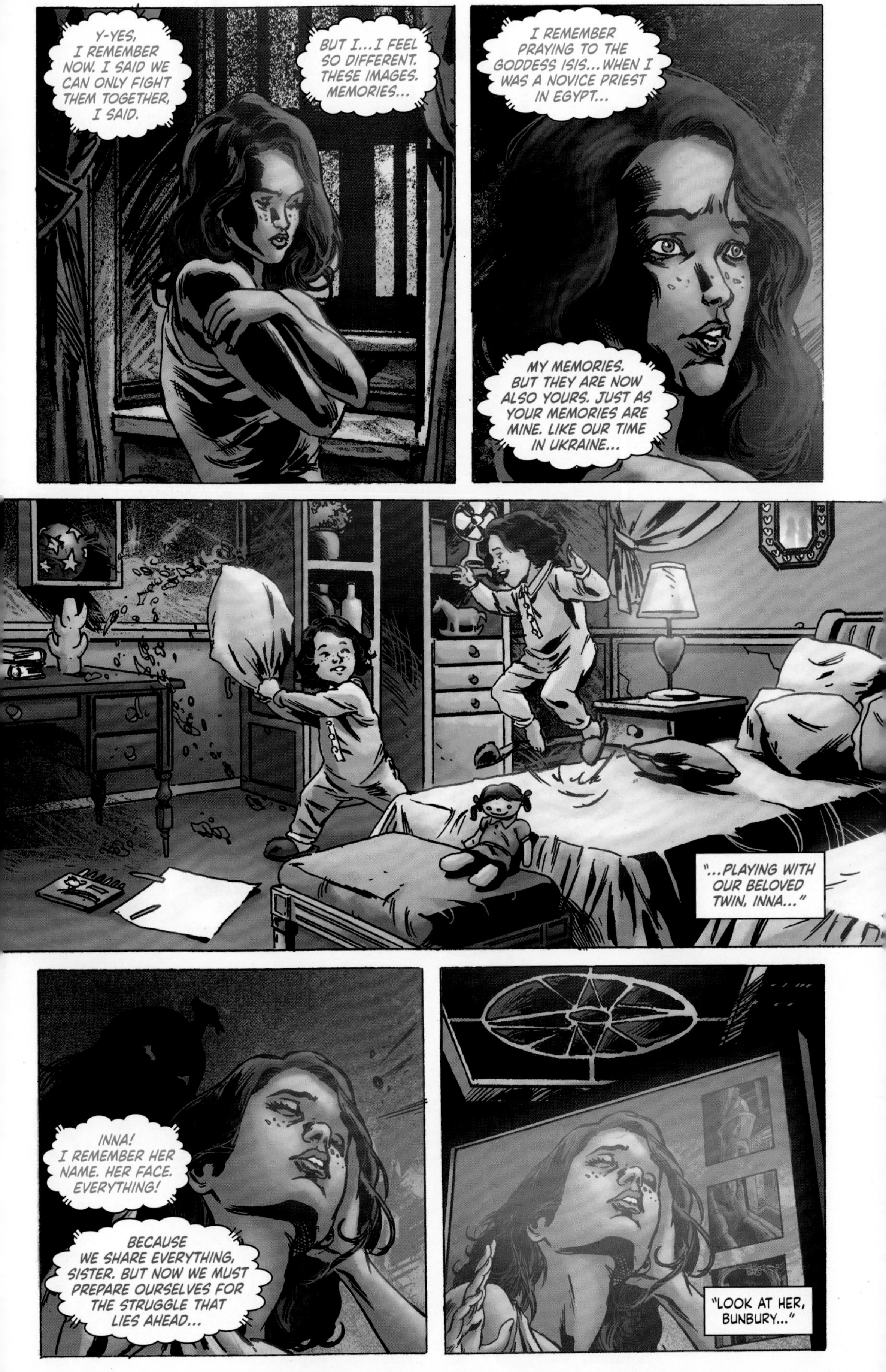
Y-YES, I REMEMBER NOW. I SAID WE CAN ONLY FIGHT THEM TOGETHER, I SAID.
BUT I...I FEEL SO DIFFERENT. THESE IMAGES. MEMORIES...
I REMEMBER PRAYING TO THE GODDESS ISIS...WHEN I WAS A NOVICE PRIEST IN EGYPT...
MY MEMORIES. BUT THEY ARE NOW ALSO YOURS. JUST AS YOUR MEMORIES ARE MINE. LIKE OUR TIME IN UKRAINE...
"...PLAYING WITH OUR BELOVED TWIN, INNA..."
INNA! I REMEMBER HER NAME. HER FACE. EVERYTHING!
BECAUSE WE SHARE EVERYTHING, SISTER. BUT NOW WE MUST PREPARE OURSELVES FOR THE STRUGGLE THAT LIES AHEAD...
"LOOK AT HER, BUNBURY..."

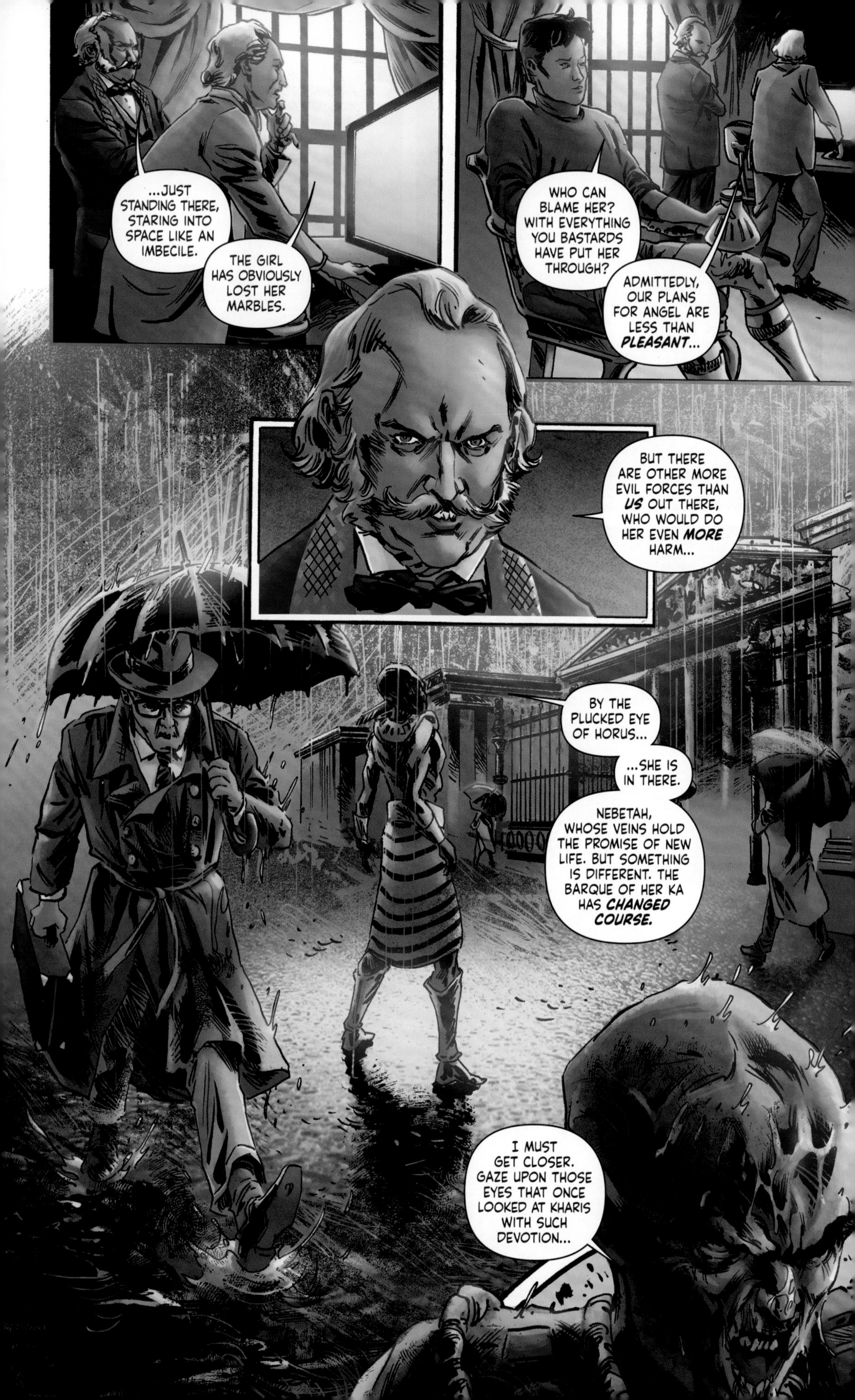
...JUST STANDING THERE, STARING INTO SPACE LIKE AN IMBECILE.
THE GIRL HAS OBVIOUSLY LOST HER MARBLES.
WHO CAN BLAME HER? WITH EVERYTHING YOU BASTARDS HAVE PUT HER THROUGH?
ADMITTEDLY, OUR PLANS FOR ANGEL ARE LESS THAN *PLEASANT*...
BUT THERE ARE OTHER MORE EVIL FORCES THAN *US* OUT THERE, WHO WOULD DO HER EVEN *MORE* HARM...
BY THE PLUCKED EYE OF HORUS...
...SHE IS IN THERE.
NEBETAH, WHOSE VEINS HOLD THE PROMISE OF NEW LIFE. BUT SOMETHING IS DIFFERENT. THE BARQUE OF HER KA HAS *CHANGED COURSE.*
I MUST GET CLOSER. GAZE UPON THOSE EYES THAT ONCE LOOKED AT KHARIS WITH SUCH DEVOTION...

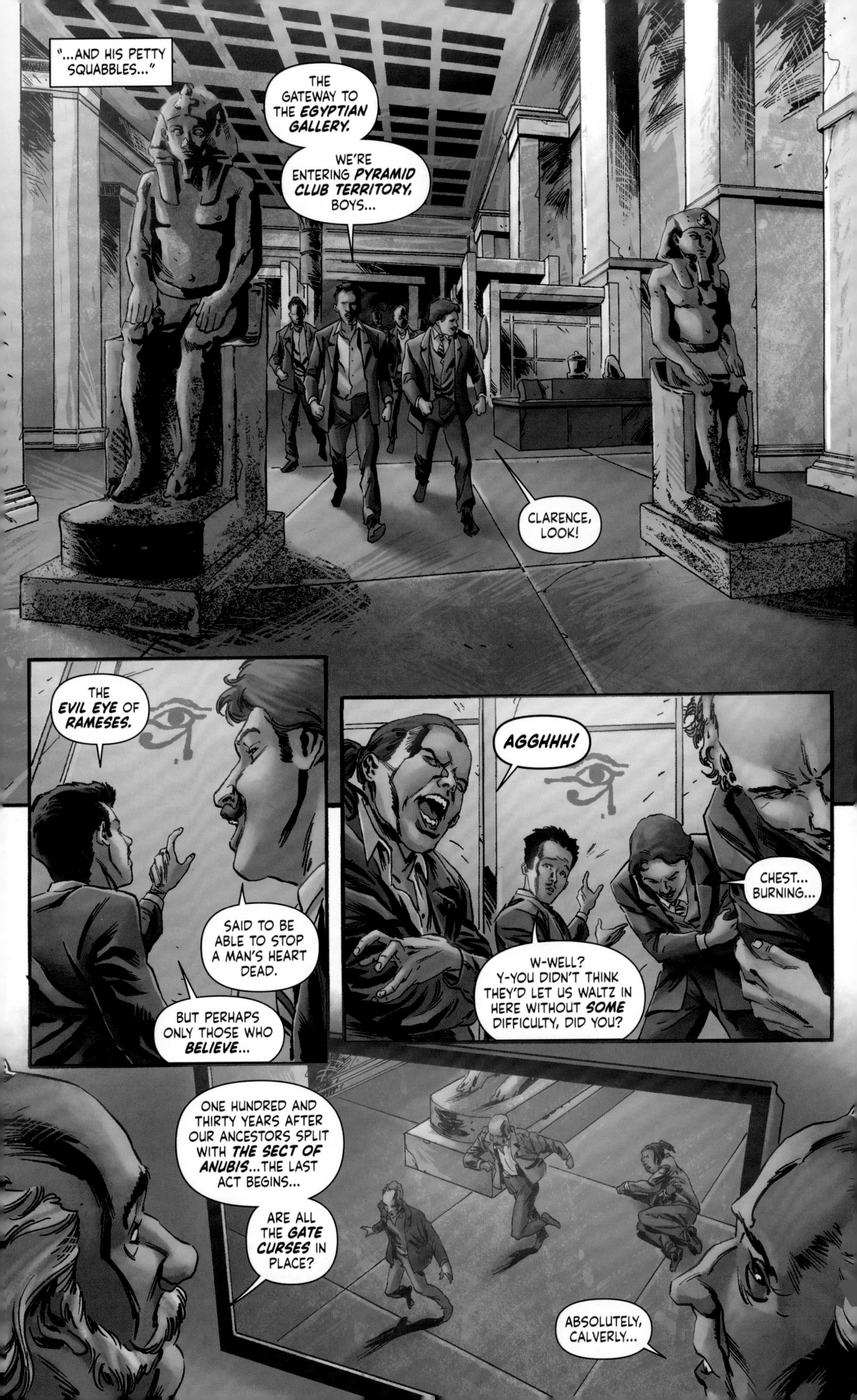
"...AND HIS PETTY SQUABBLES..."
THE GATEWAY TO THE EGYPTIAN GALLERY.
WE'RE ENTERING PYRAMID CLUB TERRITORY, BOYS...
CLARENCE, LOOK!
THE EVIL EYE OF RAMESES.
SAID TO BE ABLE TO STOP A MAN'S HEART DEAD.
BUT PERHAPS ONLY THOSE WHO BELIEVE...
AGGHHH!
CHEST... BURNING...
W-WELL? Y-YOU DIDN'T THINK THEY'D LET US WALTZ IN HERE WITHOUT SOME DIFFICULTY, DID YOU?
ONE HUNDRED AND THIRTY YEARS AFTER OUR ANCESTORS SPLIT WITH THE SECT OF ANUBIS...THE LAST ACT BEGINS...
ARE ALL THE GATE CURSES IN PLACE?
ABSOLUTELY, CALVERLY...

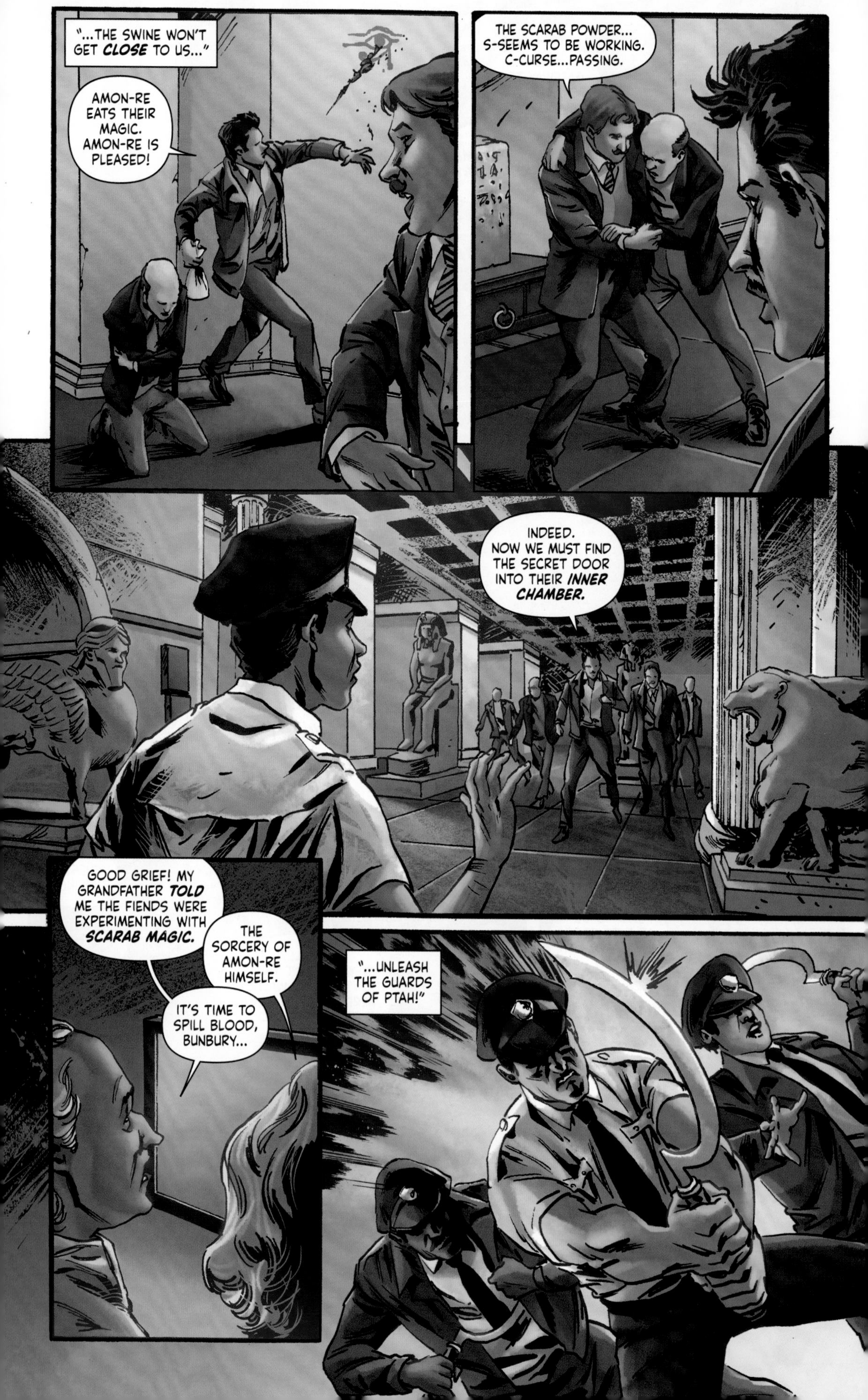
"...THE SWINE WON'T GET *CLOSE* TO US..."
AMON-RE EATS THEIR MAGIC. AMON-RE IS PLEASED!
THE SCARAB POWDER... S-SEEMS TO BE WORKING. C-CURSE...PASSING.
INDEED. NOW WE MUST FIND THE SECRET DOOR INTO THEIR *INNER CHAMBER.*
GOOD GRIEF! MY GRANDFATHER *TOLD* ME THE FIENDS WERE EXPERIMENTING WITH *SCARAB MAGIC.*
THE SORCERY OF AMON-RE HIMSELF.
IT'S TIME TO SPILL BLOOD, BUNBURY...
"...UNLEASH THE GUARDS OF PTAH!"

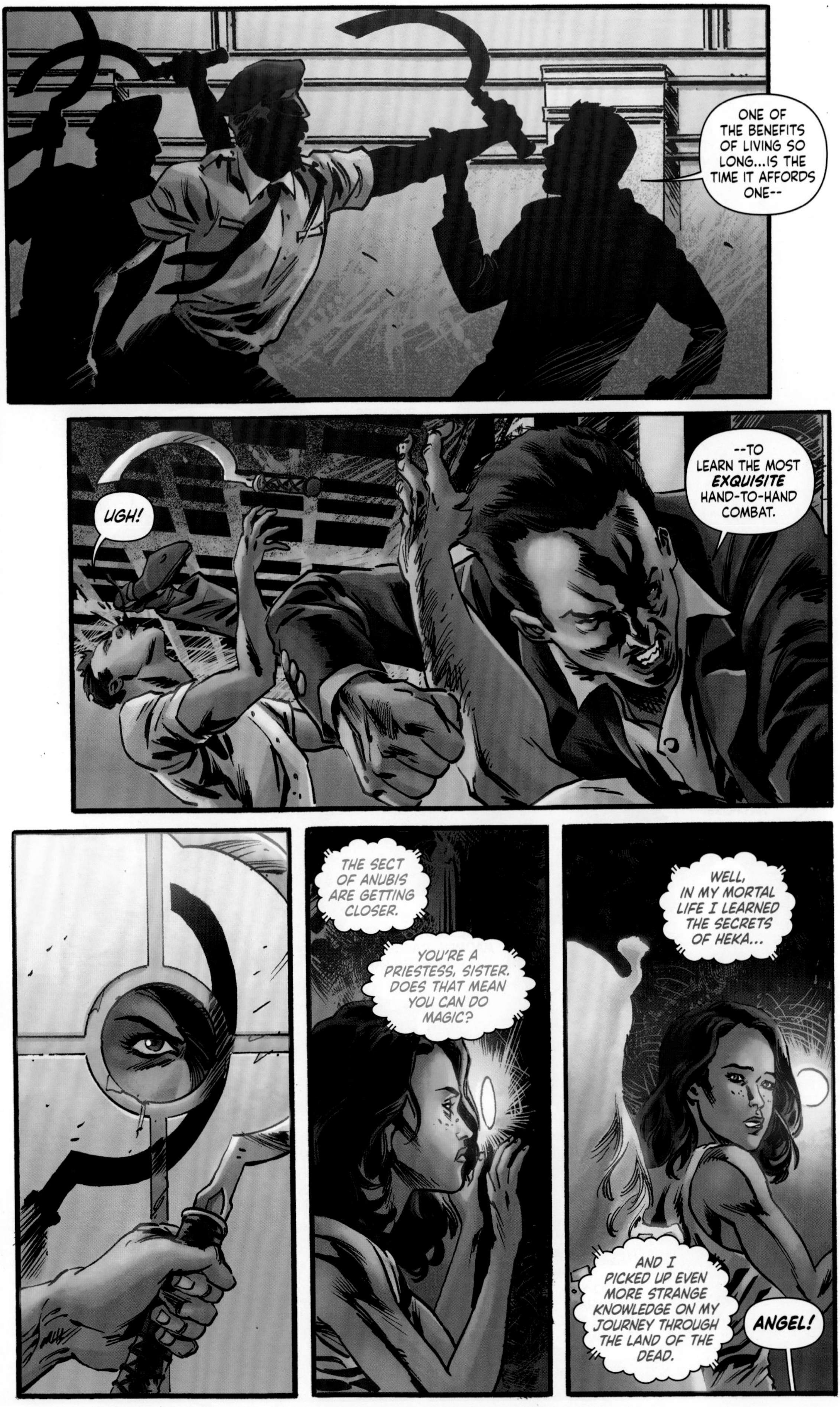

ONE OF THE BENEFITS OF LIVING SO LONG...IS THE TIME IT AFFORDS ONE--
UGH!
--TO LEARN THE MOST EXQUISITE HAND-TO-HAND COMBAT.
THE SECT OF ANUBIS ARE GETTING CLOSER.
YOU'RE A PRIESTESS, SISTER. DOES THAT MEAN YOU CAN DO MAGIC?
WELL, IN MY MORTAL LIFE I LEARNED THE SECRETS OF HEKA...
AND I PICKED UP EVEN MORE STRANGE KNOWLEDGE ON MY JOURNEY THROUGH THE LAND OF THE DEAD.
ANGEL!

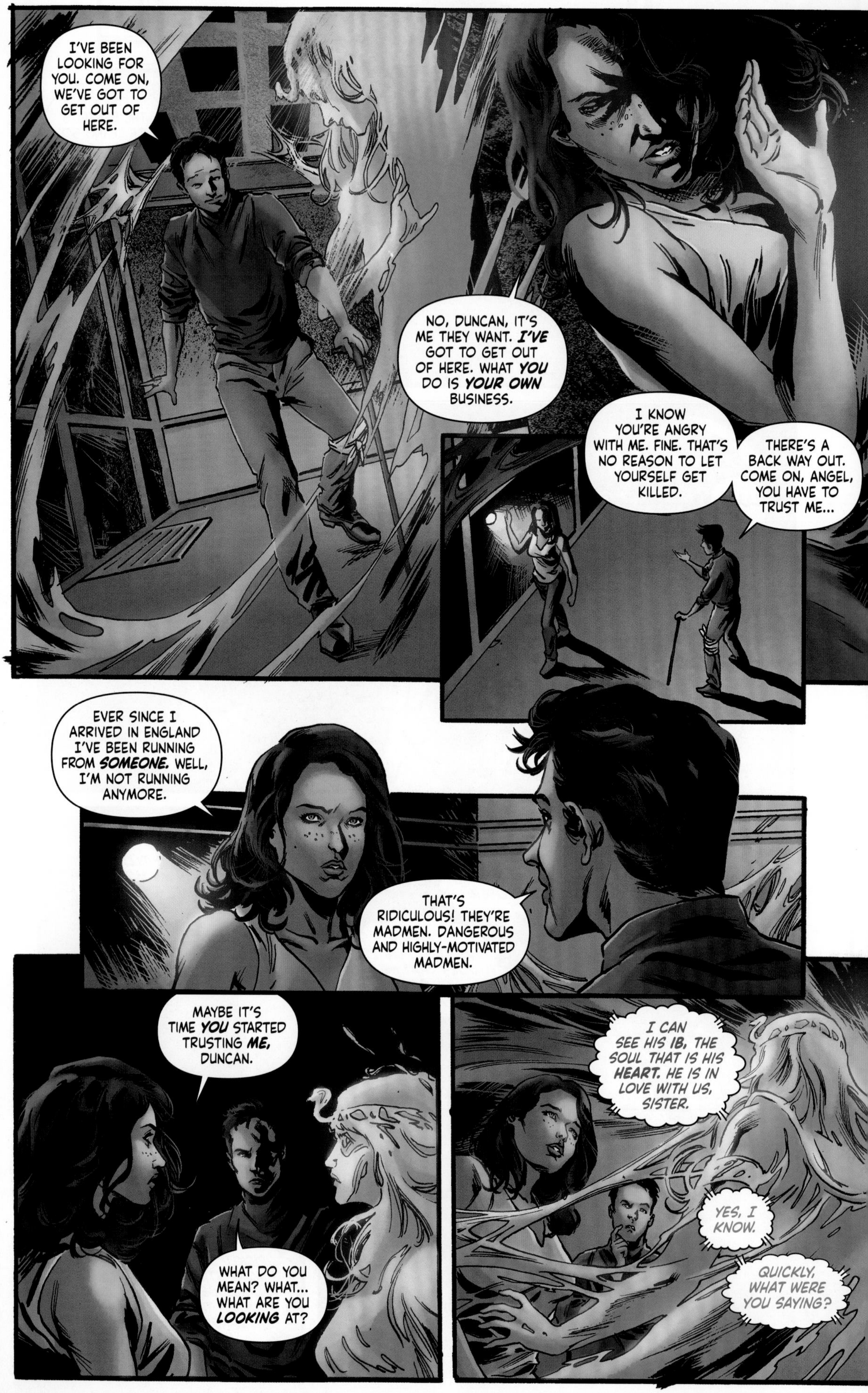
I'VE BEEN LOOKING FOR YOU. COME ON, WE'VE GOT TO GET OUT OF HERE.
NO, DUNCAN, IT'S ME THEY WANT. I'VE GOT TO GET OUT OF HERE. WHAT YOU DO IS YOUR OWN BUSINESS.
I KNOW YOU'RE ANGRY WITH ME. FINE. THAT'S NO REASON TO LET YOURSELF GET KILLED.
THERE'S A BACK WAY OUT. COME ON, ANGEL, YOU HAVE TO TRUST ME...
EVER SINCE I ARRIVED IN ENGLAND I'VE BEEN RUNNING FROM SOMEONE. WELL, I'M NOT RUNNING ANYMORE.
THAT'S RIDICULOUS! THEY'RE MADMEN. DANGEROUS AND HIGHLY-MOTIVATED MADMEN.
MAYBE IT'S TIME YOU STARTED TRUSTING ME, DUNCAN.
WHAT DO YOU MEAN? WHAT... WHAT ARE YOU LOOKING AT?
I CAN SEE HIS IB, THE SOUL THAT IS HIS HEART. HE IS IN LOVE WITH US, SISTER.
YES, I KNOW.
QUICKLY, WHAT WERE YOU SAYING?

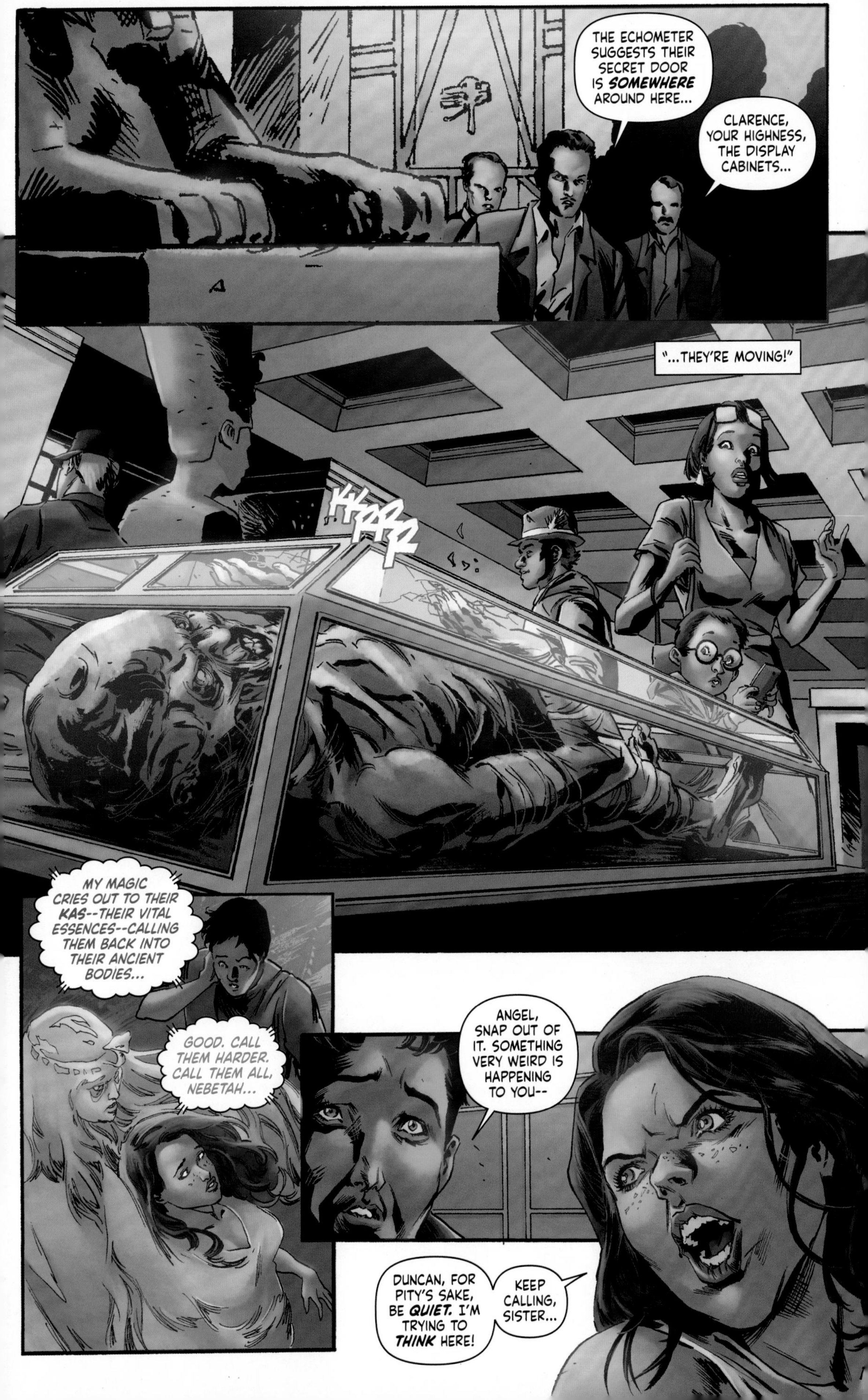

THE ECHOMETER SUGGESTS THEIR SECRET DOOR IS *SOMEWHERE* AROUND HERE...
CLARENCE, YOUR HIGHNESS, THE DISPLAY CABINETS...
"...THEY'RE MOVING!"
KKRRR
MY MAGIC CRIES OUT TO THEIR *KAS*--THEIR VITAL ESSENCES--CALLING THEM BACK INTO THEIR ANCIENT BODIES...
GOOD. CALL THEM HARDER. CALL THEM ALL, NEBETAH...
ANGEL, SNAP OUT OF IT. SOMETHING VERY WEIRD IS HAPPENING TO YOU--
DUNCAN, FOR PITY'S SAKE, BE *QUIET.* I'M TRYING TO *THINK* HERE!
KEEP CALLING, SISTER...

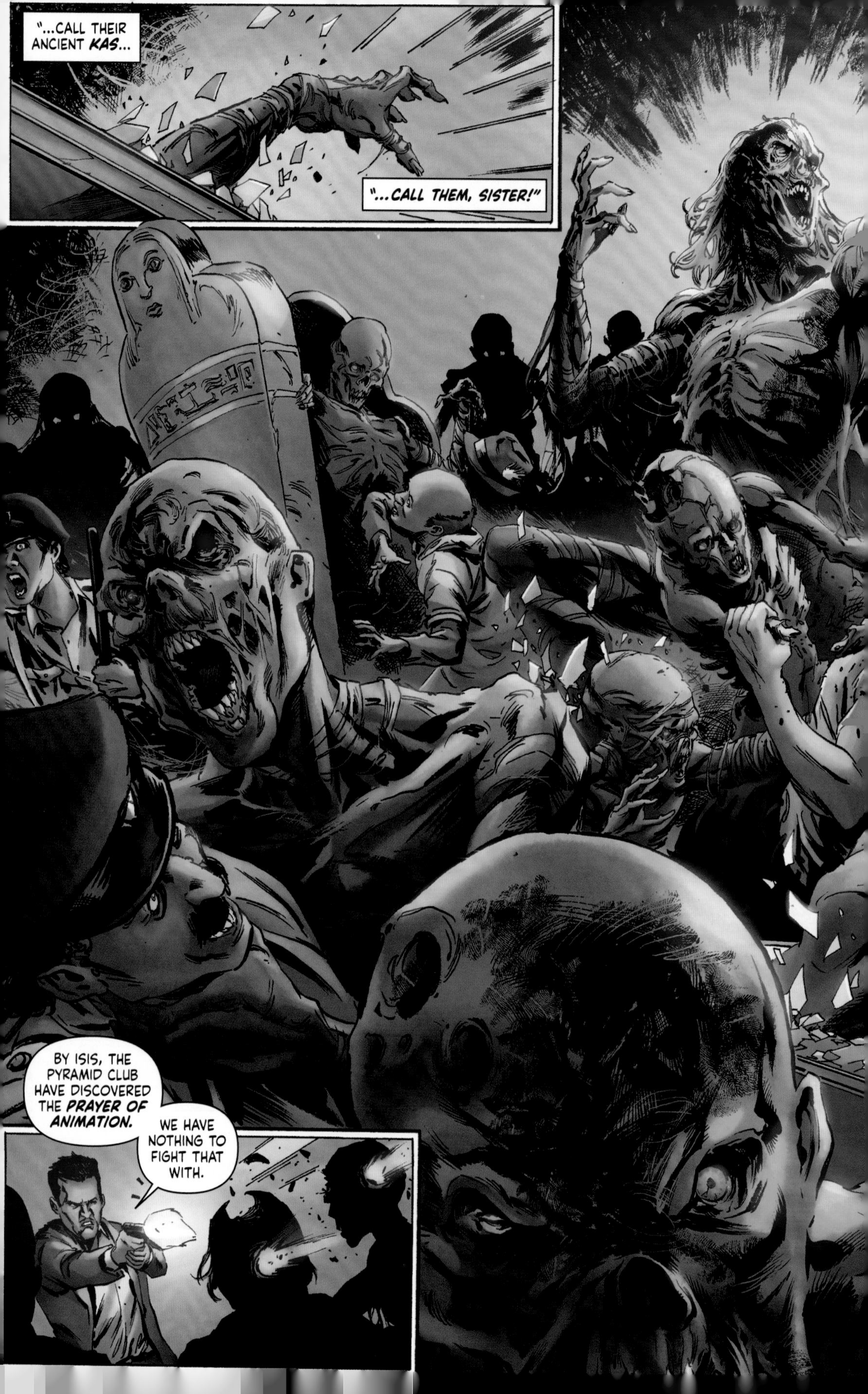
"...CALL THEIR ANCIENT KAS...
"...CALL THEM, SISTER!"
BY ISIS, THE PYRAMID CLUB HAVE DISCOVERED THE PRAYER OF ANIMATION.
WE HAVE NOTHING TO FIGHT THAT WITH.

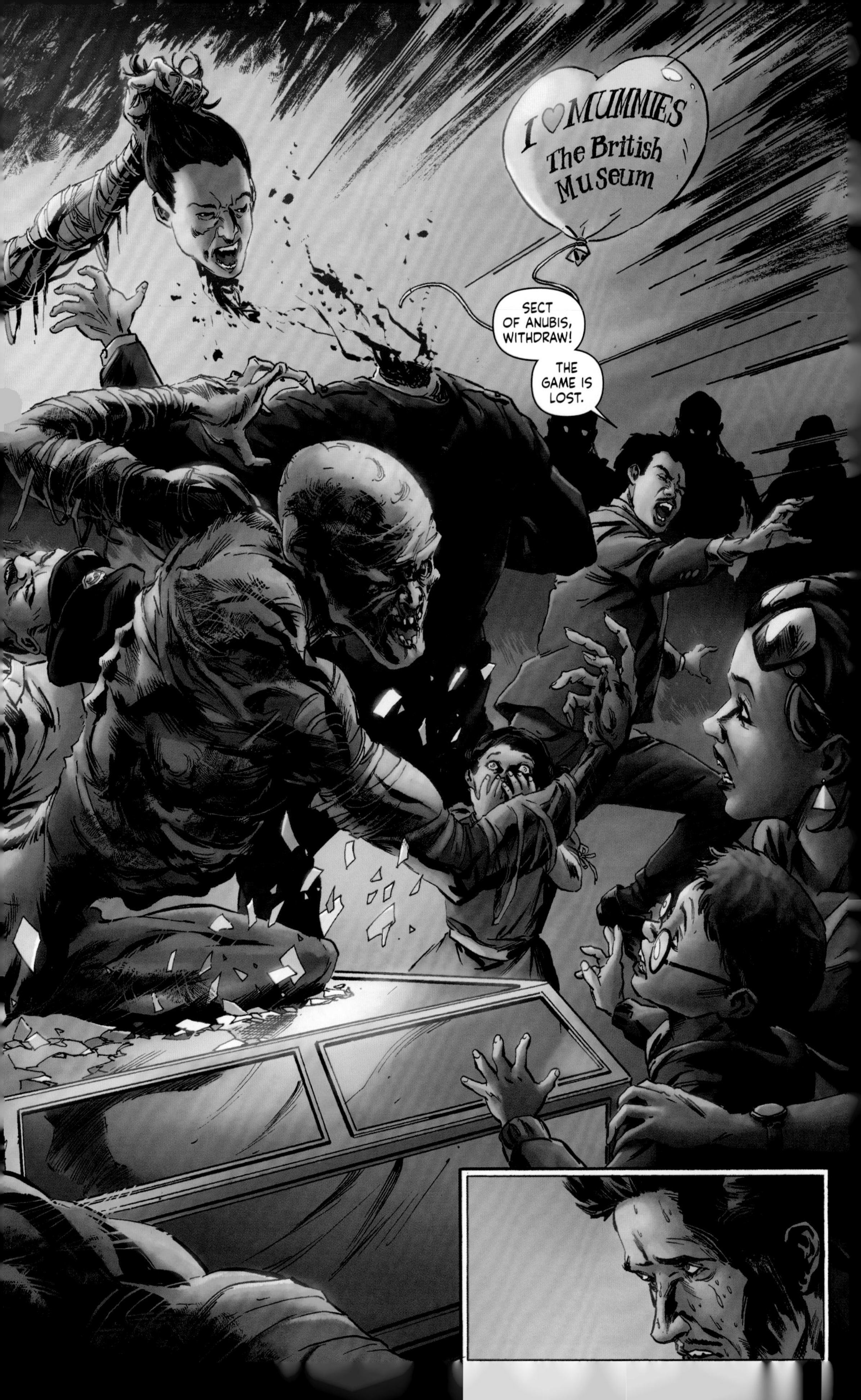
I ♡ MUMMIES
The British Museum
SECT OF ANUBIS, WITHDRAW!
THE GAME IS LOST.

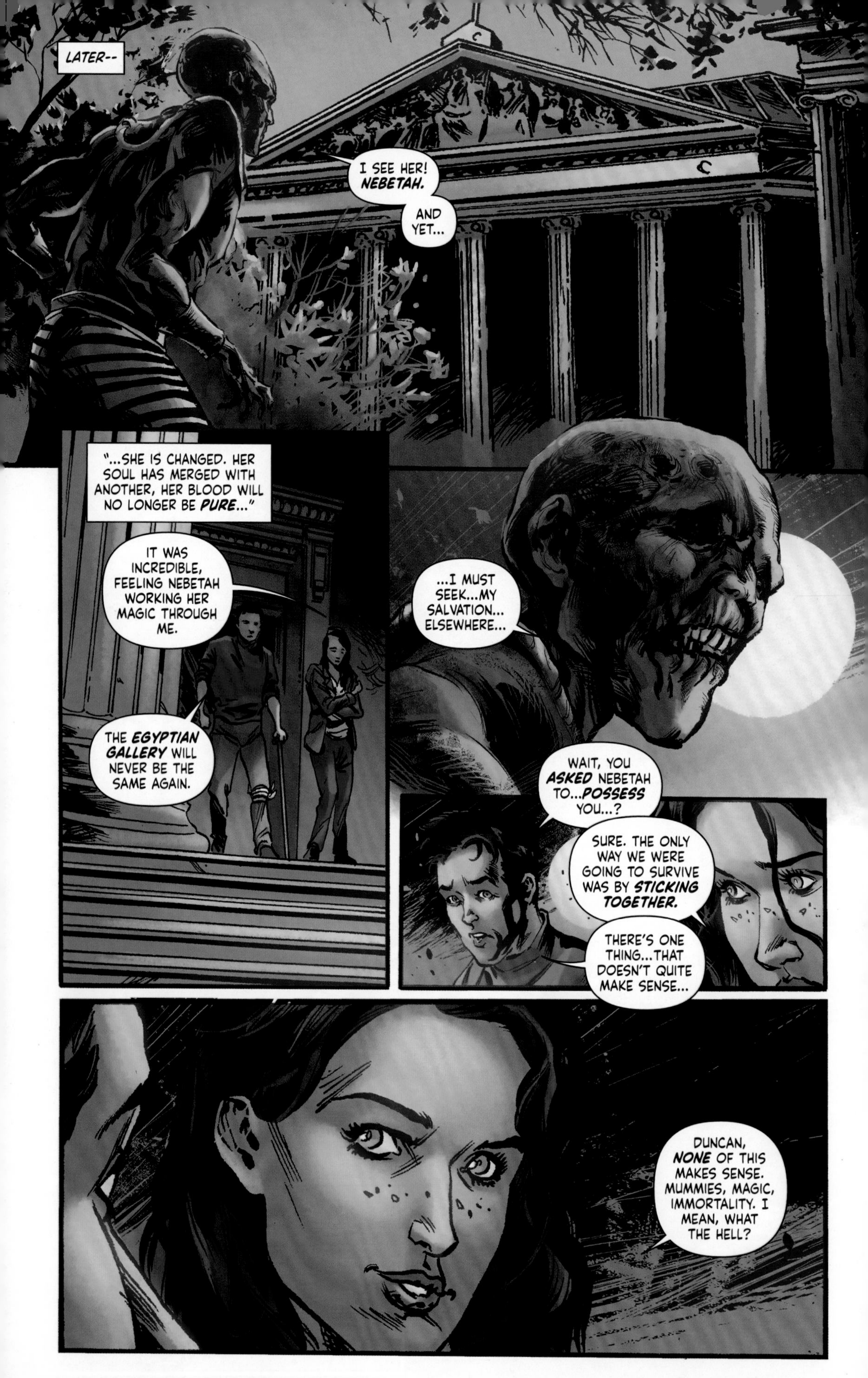

LATER--
I SEE HER! NEBETAH.
AND YET...
"...SHE IS CHANGED. HER SOUL HAS MERGED WITH ANOTHER, HER BLOOD WILL NO LONGER BE PURE..."
...I MUST SEEK...MY SALVATION... ELSEWHERE...
IT WAS INCREDIBLE, FEELING NEBETAH WORKING HER MAGIC THROUGH ME.
THE EGYPTIAN GALLERY WILL NEVER BE THE SAME AGAIN.
WAIT, YOU ASKED NEBETAH TO...POSSESS YOU...?
SURE. THE ONLY WAY WE WERE GOING TO SURVIVE WAS BY STICKING TOGETHER.
THERE'S ONE THING...THAT DOESN'T QUITE MAKE SENSE...
DUNCAN, NONE OF THIS MAKES SENSE. MUMMIES, MAGIC, IMMORTALITY. I MEAN, WHAT THE HELL?

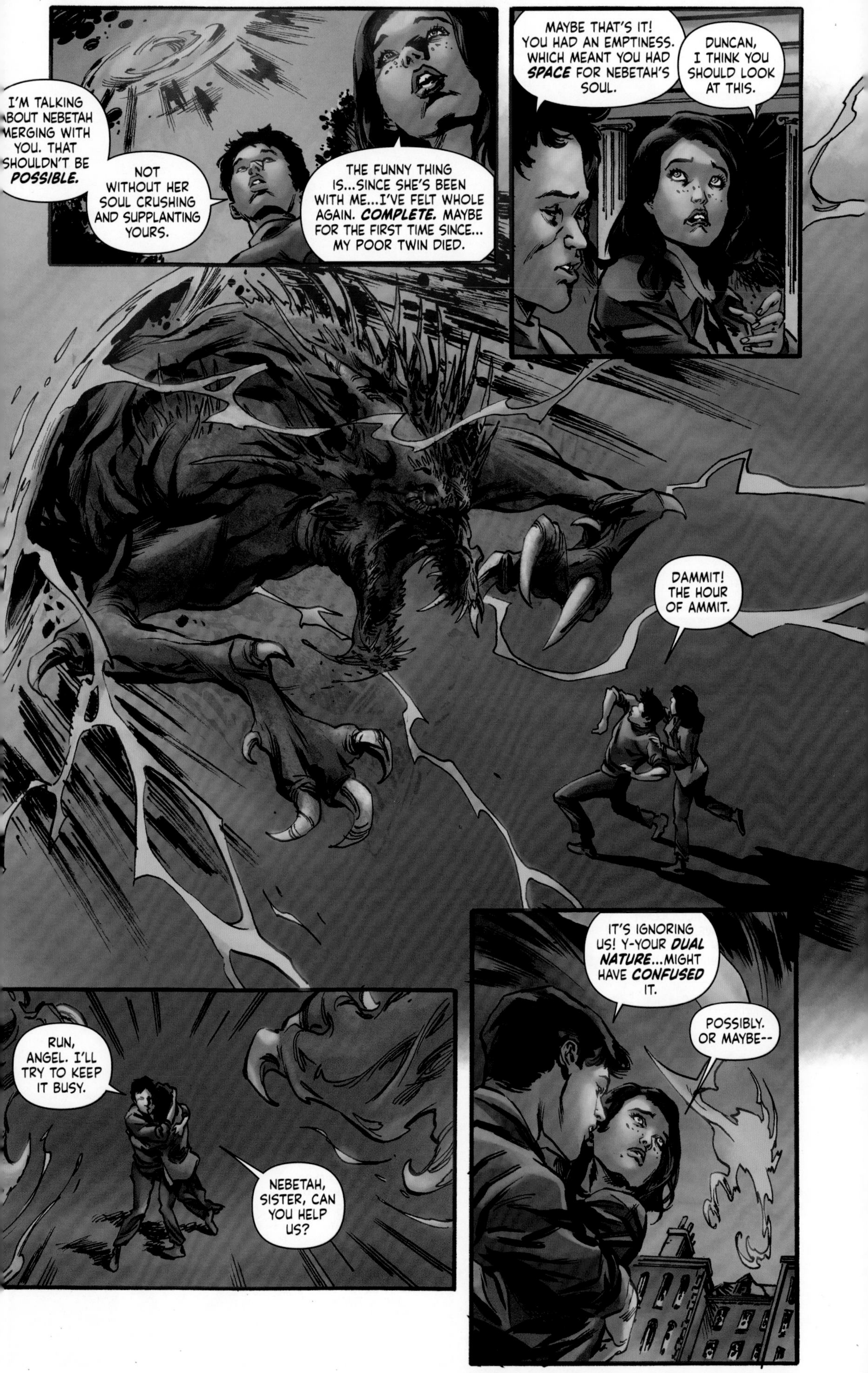
I'M TALKING ABOUT NEBETAH MERGING WITH YOU. THAT SHOULDN'T BE **POSSIBLE.**
NOT WITHOUT HER SOUL CRUSHING AND SUPPLANTING YOURS.
THE FUNNY THING IS...SINCE SHE'S BEEN WITH ME...I'VE FELT WHOLE AGAIN. **COMPLETE.** MAYBE FOR THE FIRST TIME SINCE... MY POOR TWIN DIED.
MAYBE THAT'S IT! YOU HAD AN EMPTINESS. WHICH MEANT YOU HAD **SPACE** FOR NEBETAH'S SOUL.
DUNCAN, I THINK YOU SHOULD LOOK AT THIS.
DAMMIT! THE HOUR OF AMMIT.
RUN, ANGEL. I'LL TRY TO KEEP IT BUSY.
NEBETAH, SISTER, CAN YOU HELP US?
IT'S IGNORING US! Y-YOUR **DUAL NATURE**...MIGHT HAVE **CONFUSED** IT.
POSSIBLY. OR MAYBE--

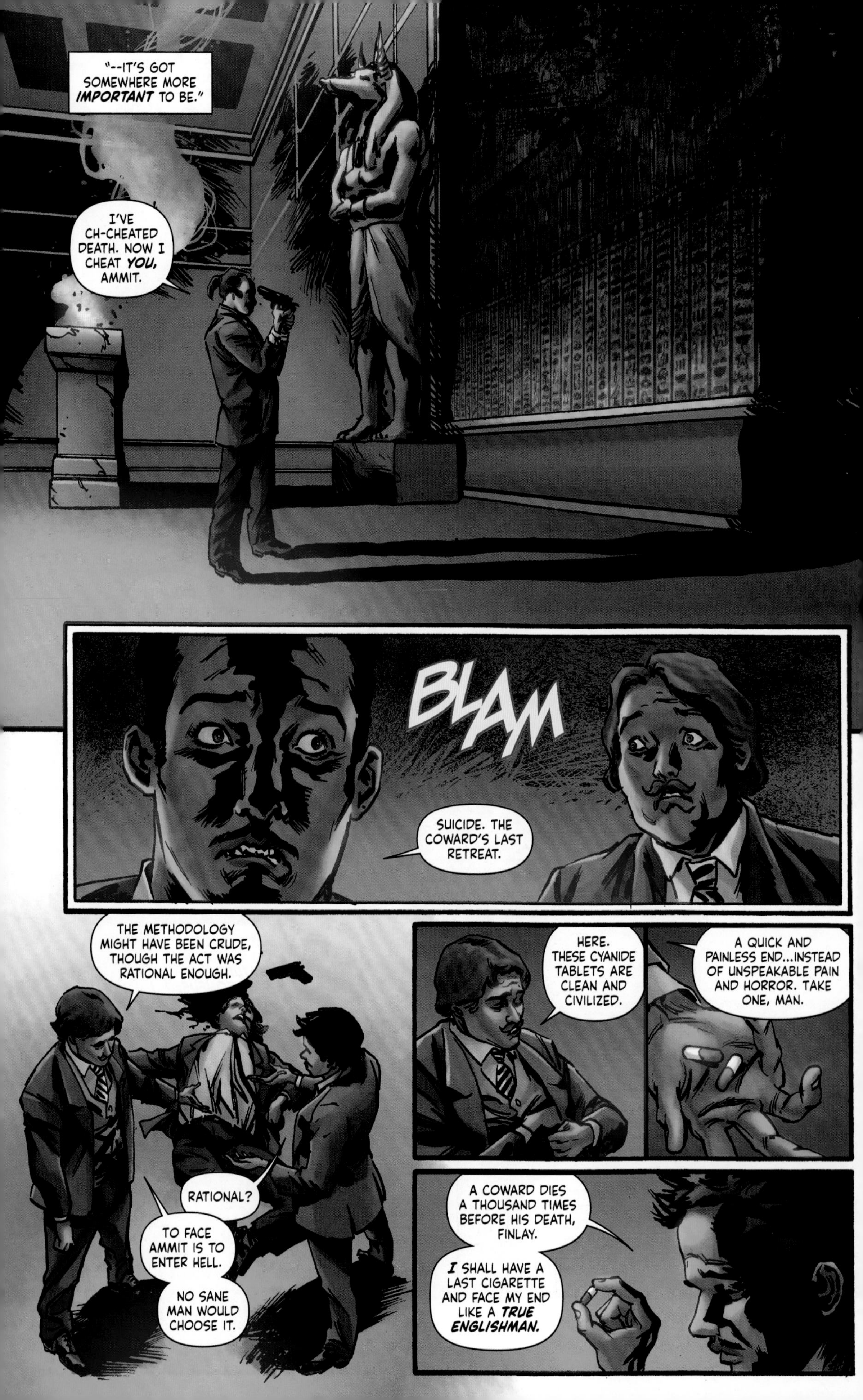
"--IT'S GOT SOMEWHERE MORE *IMPORTANT* TO BE."
I'VE CH-CHEATED DEATH. NOW I CHEAT *YOU,* AMMIT.
BLAM
SUICIDE. THE COWARD'S LAST RETREAT.
THE METHODOLOGY MIGHT HAVE BEEN CRUDE, THOUGH THE ACT WAS RATIONAL ENOUGH.
RATIONAL?
TO FACE AMMIT IS TO ENTER HELL.
NO SANE MAN WOULD CHOOSE IT.
HERE. THESE CYANIDE TABLETS ARE CLEAN AND CIVILIZED.
A QUICK AND PAINLESS END...INSTEAD OF UNSPEAKABLE PAIN AND HORROR. TAKE ONE, MAN.
A COWARD DIES A THOUSAND TIMES BEFORE HIS DEATH, FINLAY.
I SHALL HAVE A LAST CIGARETTE AND FACE MY END LIKE A ***TRUE ENGLISHMAN.***

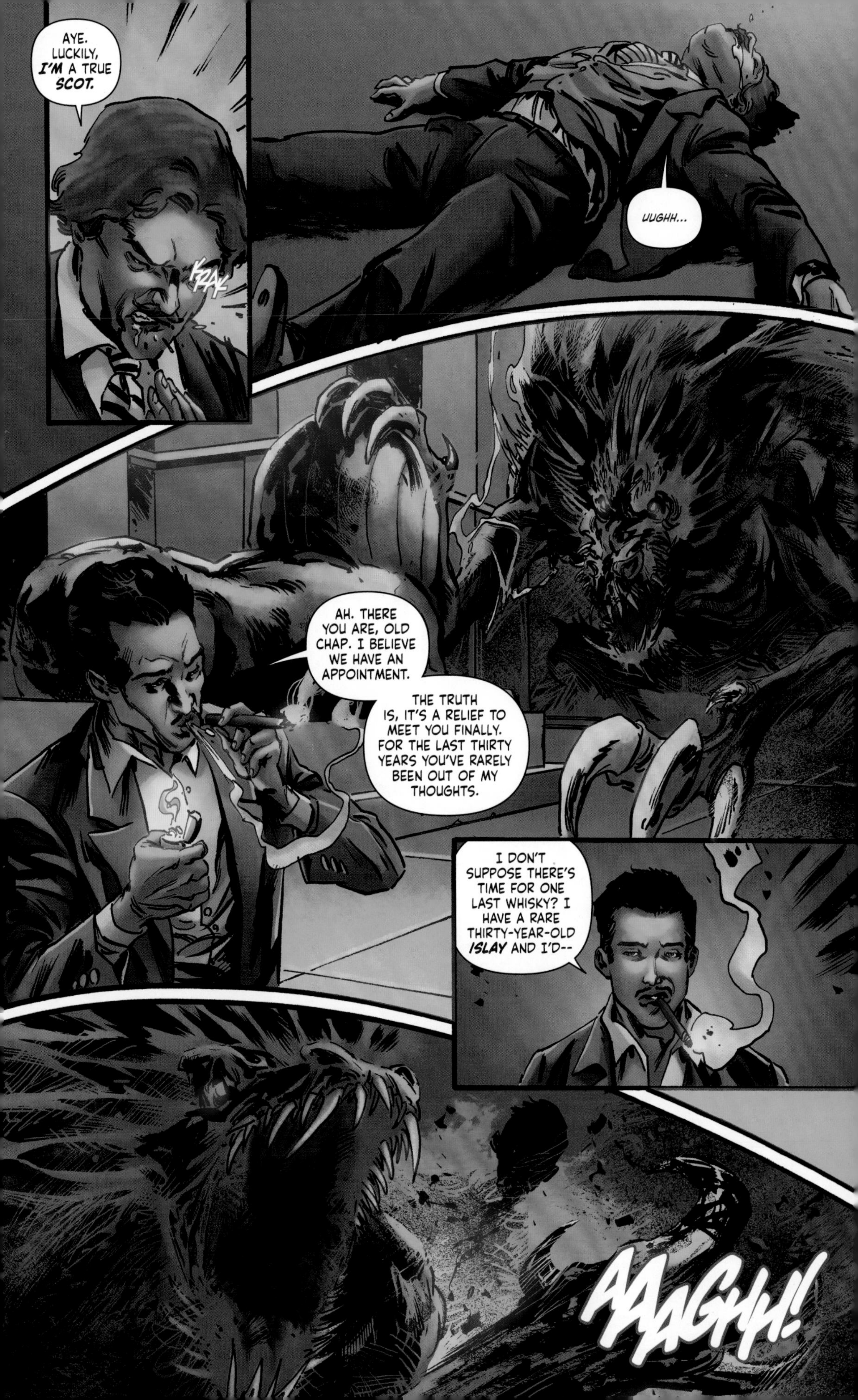
AYE. LUCKILY, I'M A TRUE SCOT.
KRAK
UUGHH...
AH. THERE YOU ARE, OLD CHAP. I BELIEVE WE HAVE AN APPOINTMENT.
THE TRUTH IS, IT'S A RELIEF TO MEET YOU FINALLY. FOR THE LAST THIRTY YEARS YOU'VE RARELY BEEN OUT OF MY THOUGHTS.
I DON'T SUPPOSE THERE'S TIME FOR ONE LAST WHISKY? I HAVE A RARE THIRTY-YEAR-OLD ISLAY AND I'D--
AAAAGHH!

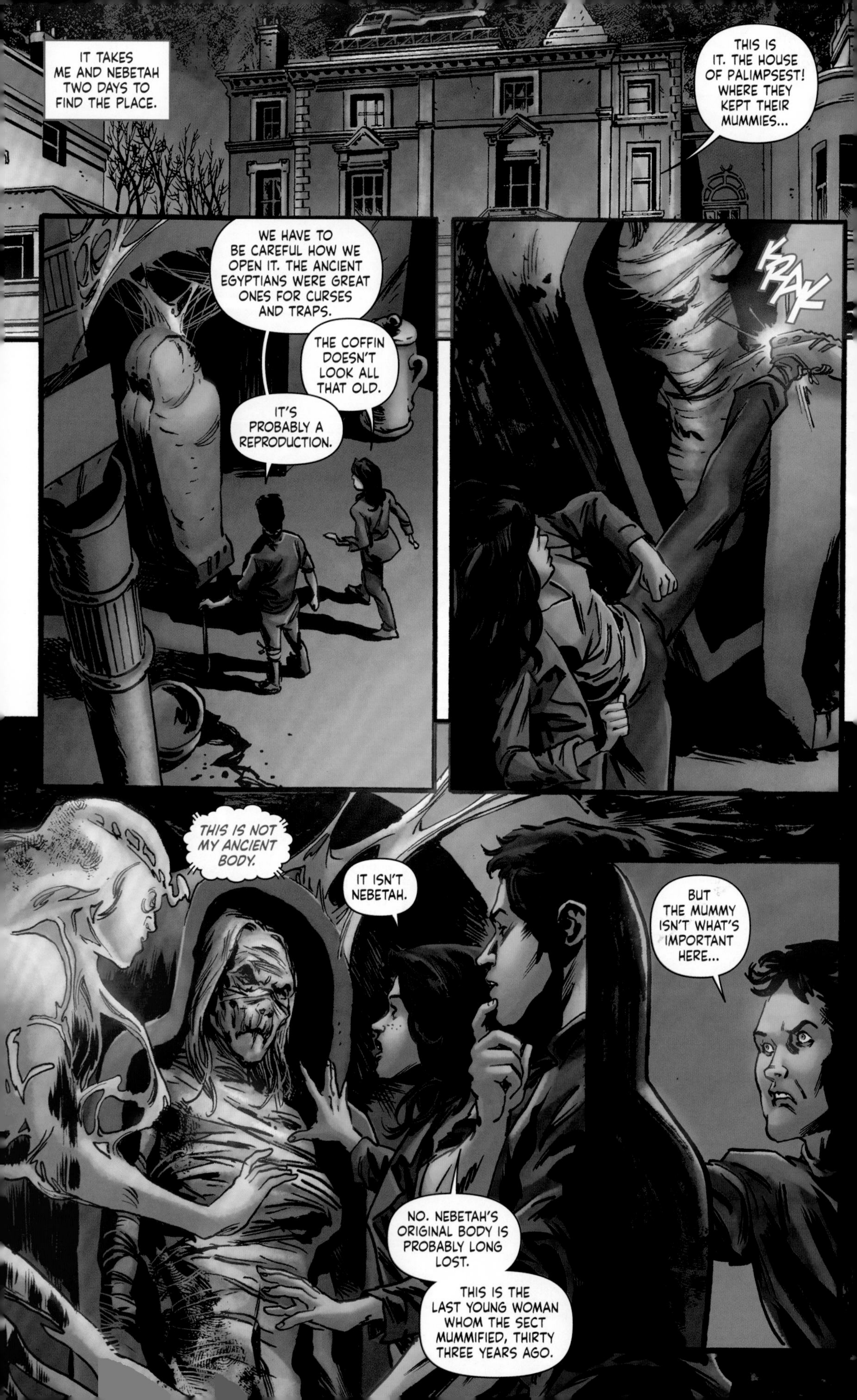
IT TAKES ME AND NEBETAH TWO DAYS TO FIND THE PLACE.
THIS IS IT. THE HOUSE OF PALIMPSEST! WHERE THEY KEPT THEIR MUMMIES...
WE HAVE TO BE CAREFUL HOW WE OPEN IT. THE ANCIENT EGYPTIANS WERE GREAT ONES FOR CURSES AND TRAPS.
THE COFFIN DOESN'T LOOK ALL THAT OLD.
IT'S PROBABLY A REPRODUCTION.
KRAK
THIS IS NOT MY ANCIENT BODY.
IT ISN'T NEBETAH.
BUT THE MUMMY ISN'T WHAT'S IMPORTANT HERE...
NO. NEBETAH'S ORIGINAL BODY IS PROBABLY LONG LOST.
THIS IS THE LAST YOUNG WOMAN WHOM THE SECT MUMMIFIED, THIRTY THREE YEARS AGO.

IT'S *THIS*. NEBETAH'S *BOOK OF THE DEAD.*

IN MY DAY IT WAS KNOWN AS THE *BOOK OF COMING FORTH BY DAY...*

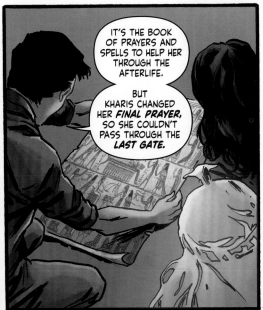

IT'S THE BOOK OF PRAYERS AND SPELLS TO HELP HER THROUGH THE AFTERLIFE.

BUT KHARIS CHANGED HER *FINAL PRAYER*, SO SHE COULDN'T PASS THROUGH THE *LAST GATE.*

IT IS TRUE. MY PRAYER DID NOT WORK.

IS THERE ANYTHING THAT CAN BE DONE, IN CASE NEBETAH WANTS TO LEAVE ME AND PASS THROUGH THE LAND OF THE DEAD?

I SHOULD BE ABLE TO ADAPT THE TEXT.

REALLY? HOW?

I'M A TRAINED EGYPTOLOGIST. WE HAVE OUR WAYS.

BEEP BEEP

WELL, WELL.

GUESS WHO'S ANXIOUS TO SEE *YOU?*

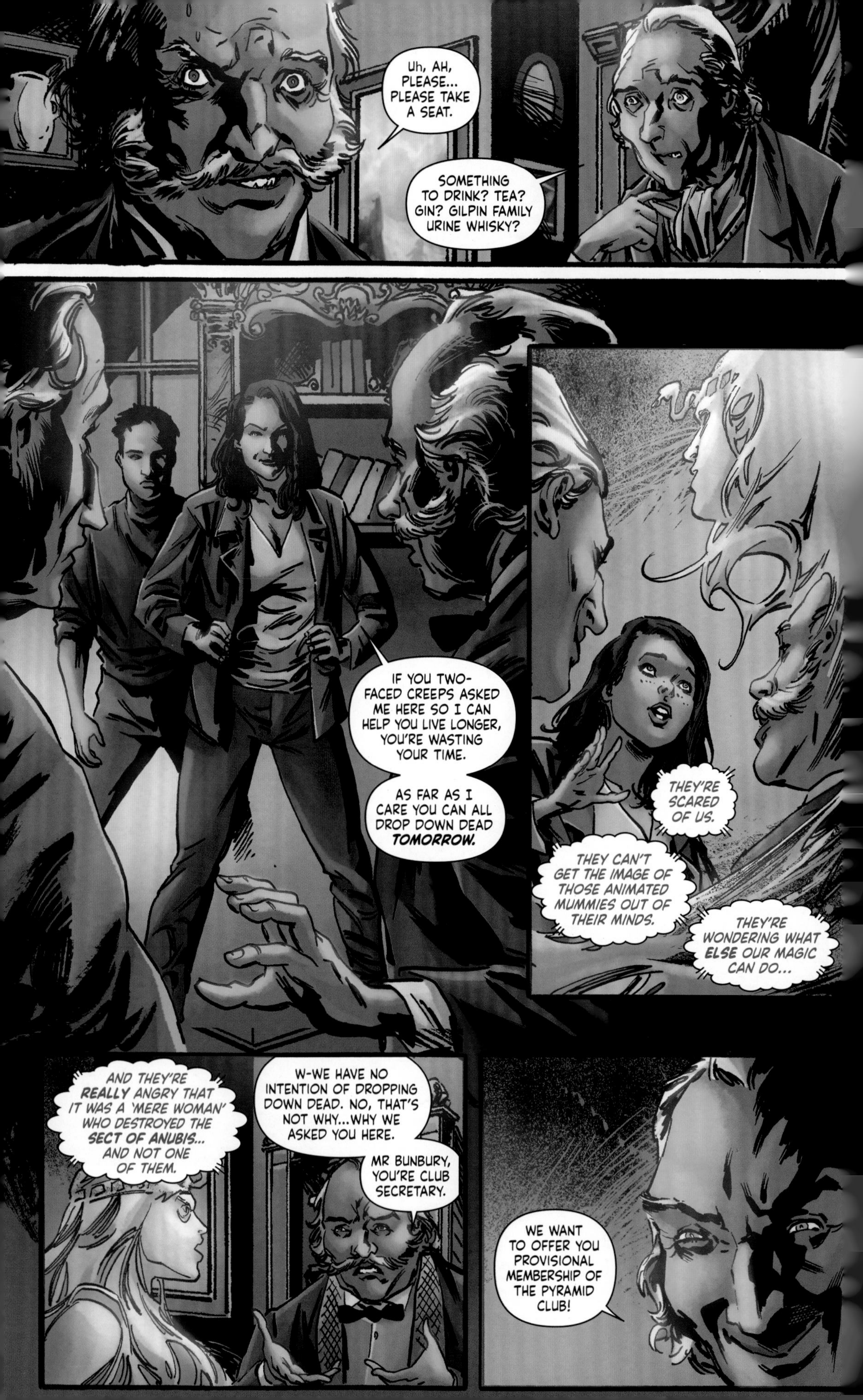
UH, AH, PLEASE... PLEASE TAKE A SEAT.
SOMETHING TO DRINK? TEA? GIN? GILPIN FAMILY URINE WHISKY?
IF YOU TWO-FACED CREEPS ASKED ME HERE SO I CAN HELP YOU LIVE LONGER, YOU'RE WASTING YOUR TIME.
AS FAR AS I CARE YOU CAN ALL DROP DOWN DEAD **TOMORROW.**
THEY'RE SCARED OF US.
THEY CAN'T GET THE IMAGE OF THOSE ANIMATED MUMMIES OUT OF THEIR MINDS.
*THEY'RE WONDERING WHAT **ELSE** OUR MAGIC CAN DO...*
*AND THEY'RE **REALLY** ANGRY THAT IT WAS A 'MERE WOMAN' WHO DESTROYED THE **SECT OF ANUBIS...** AND NOT ONE OF THEM.*
W-WE HAVE NO INTENTION OF DROPPING DOWN DEAD. NO, THAT'S NOT WHY...WHY WE ASKED YOU HERE.
MR BUNBURY, YOU'RE CLUB SECRETARY.
WE WANT TO OFFER YOU PROVISIONAL MEMBERSHIP OF THE PYRAMID CLUB!

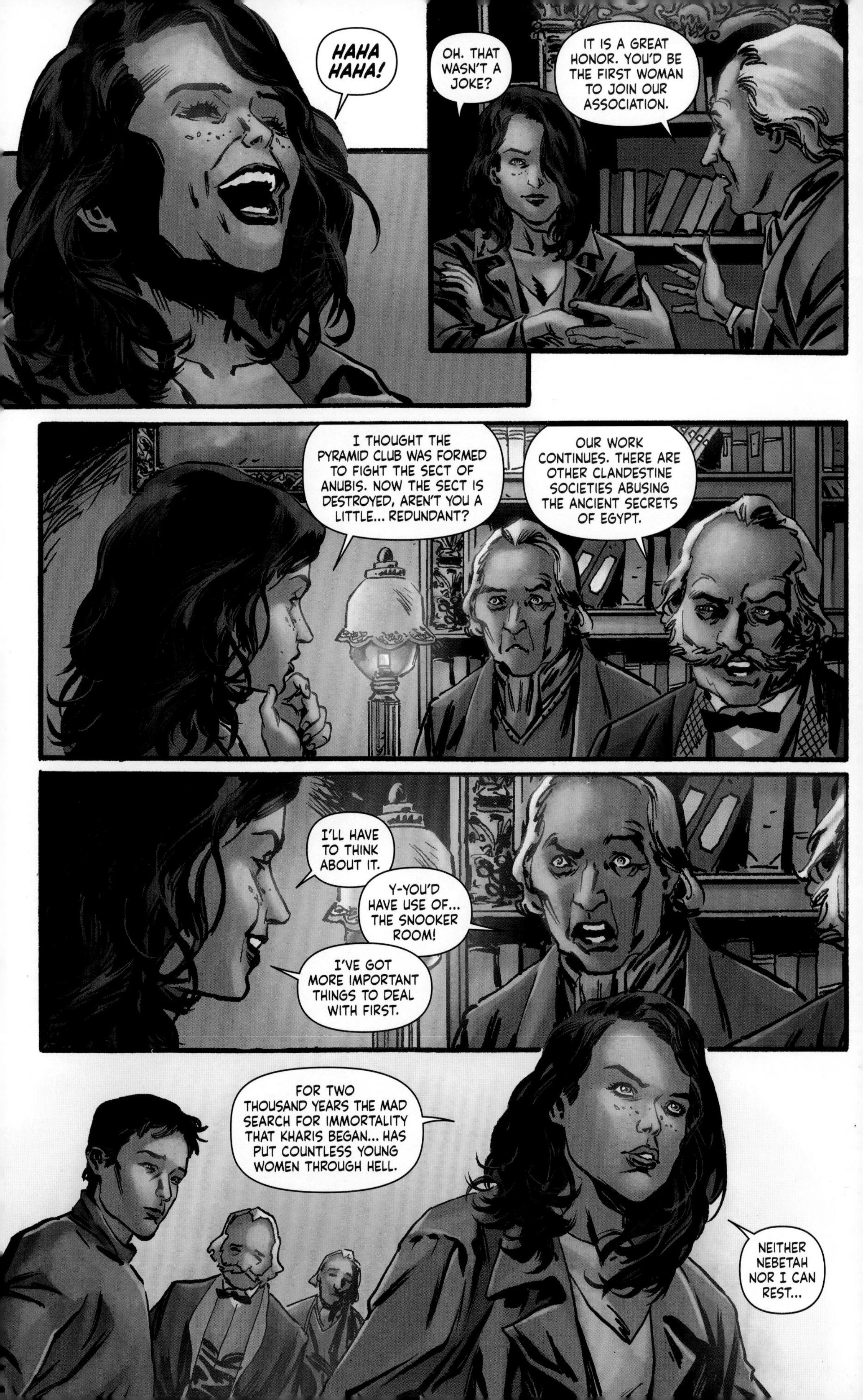
HAHA HAHA!
OH. THAT WASN'T A JOKE?
IT IS A GREAT HONOR. YOU'D BE THE FIRST WOMAN TO JOIN OUR ASSOCIATION.
I THOUGHT THE PYRAMID CLUB WAS FORMED TO FIGHT THE SECT OF ANUBIS. NOW THE SECT IS DESTROYED, AREN'T YOU A LITTLE... REDUNDANT?
OUR WORK CONTINUES. THERE ARE OTHER CLANDESTINE SOCIETIES ABUSING THE ANCIENT SECRETS OF EGYPT.
I'LL HAVE TO THINK ABOUT IT.
Y-YOU'D HAVE USE OF... THE SNOOKER ROOM!
I'VE GOT MORE IMPORTANT THINGS TO DEAL WITH FIRST.
FOR TWO THOUSAND YEARS THE MAD SEARCH FOR IMMORTALITY THAT KHARIS BEGAN... HAS PUT COUNTLESS YOUNG WOMEN THROUGH HELL.
NEITHER NEBETAH NOR I CAN REST...

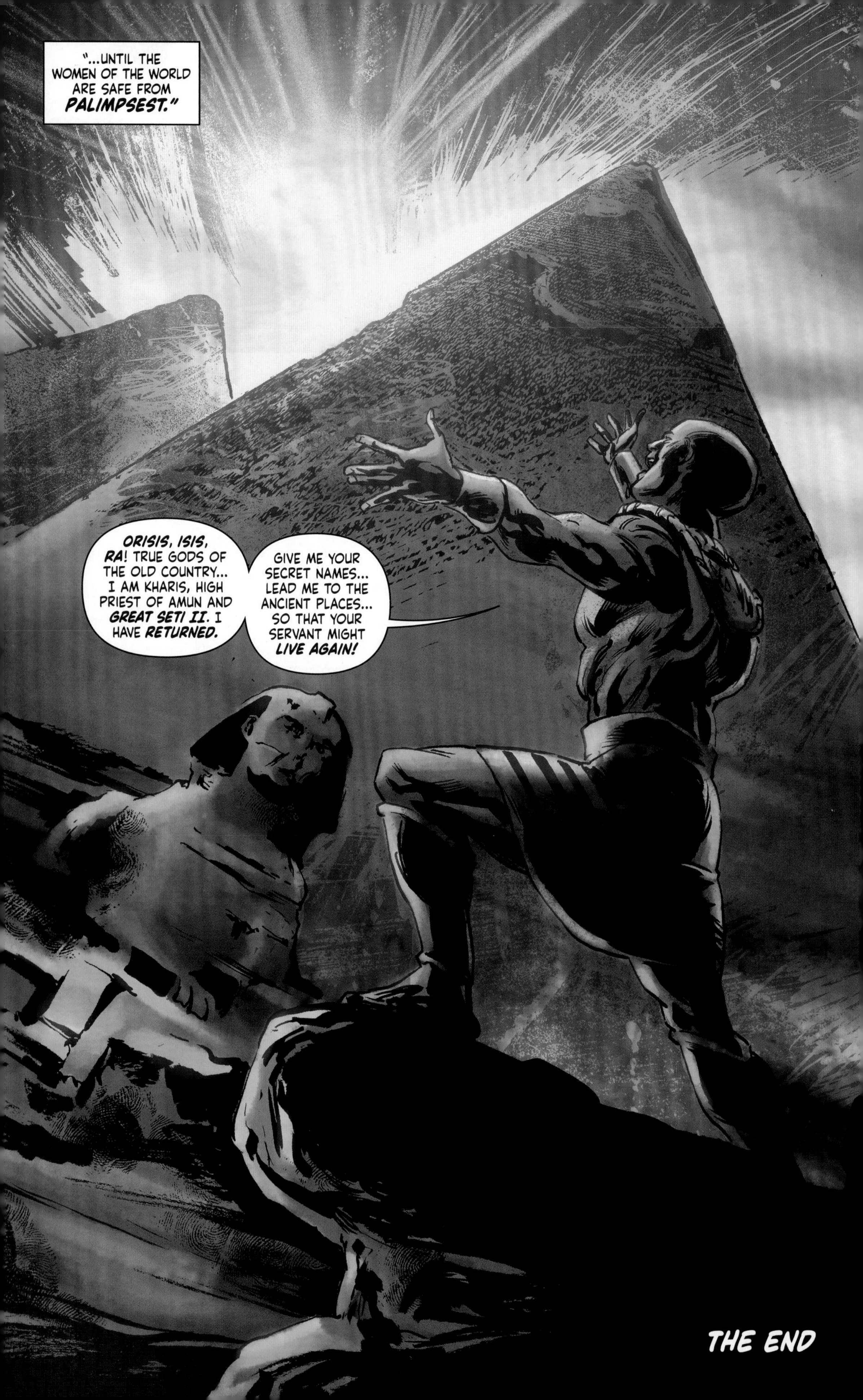
"...UNTIL THE WOMEN OF THE WORLD ARE SAFE FROM PALIMPSEST."
ORISIS, ISIS, RA! TRUE GODS OF THE OLD COUNTRY... I AM KHARIS, HIGH PRIEST OF AMUN AND GREAT SETI II. I HAVE RETURNED.
GIVE ME YOUR SECRET NAMES... LEAD ME TO THE ANCIENT PLACES... SO THAT YOUR SERVANT MIGHT LIVE AGAIN!
THE END

COVER GALLERY

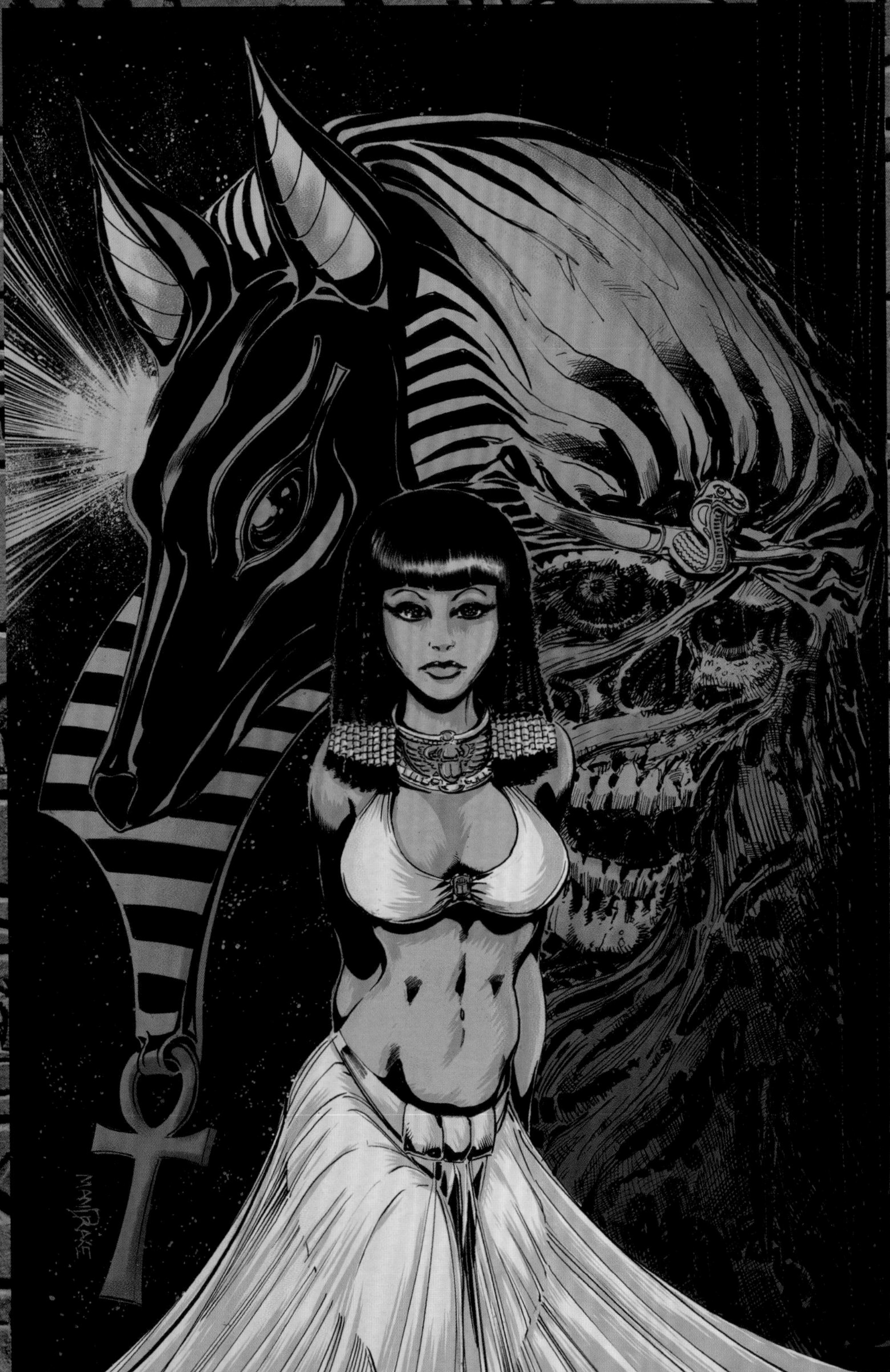
MANDRAKE

Issue One - Cover B
Tom Mandrake

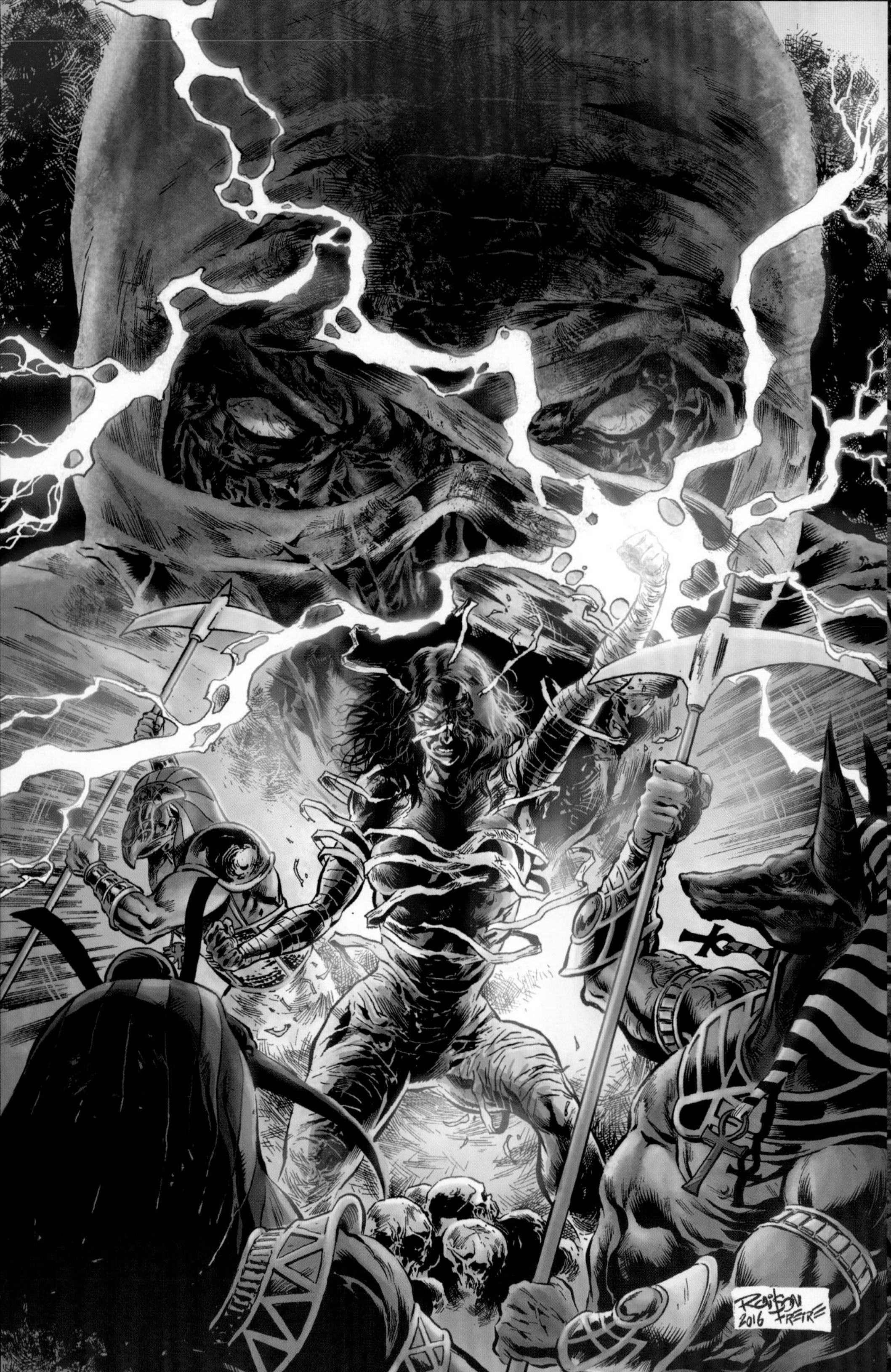

Issue One - Cover C
Ronilson Friere

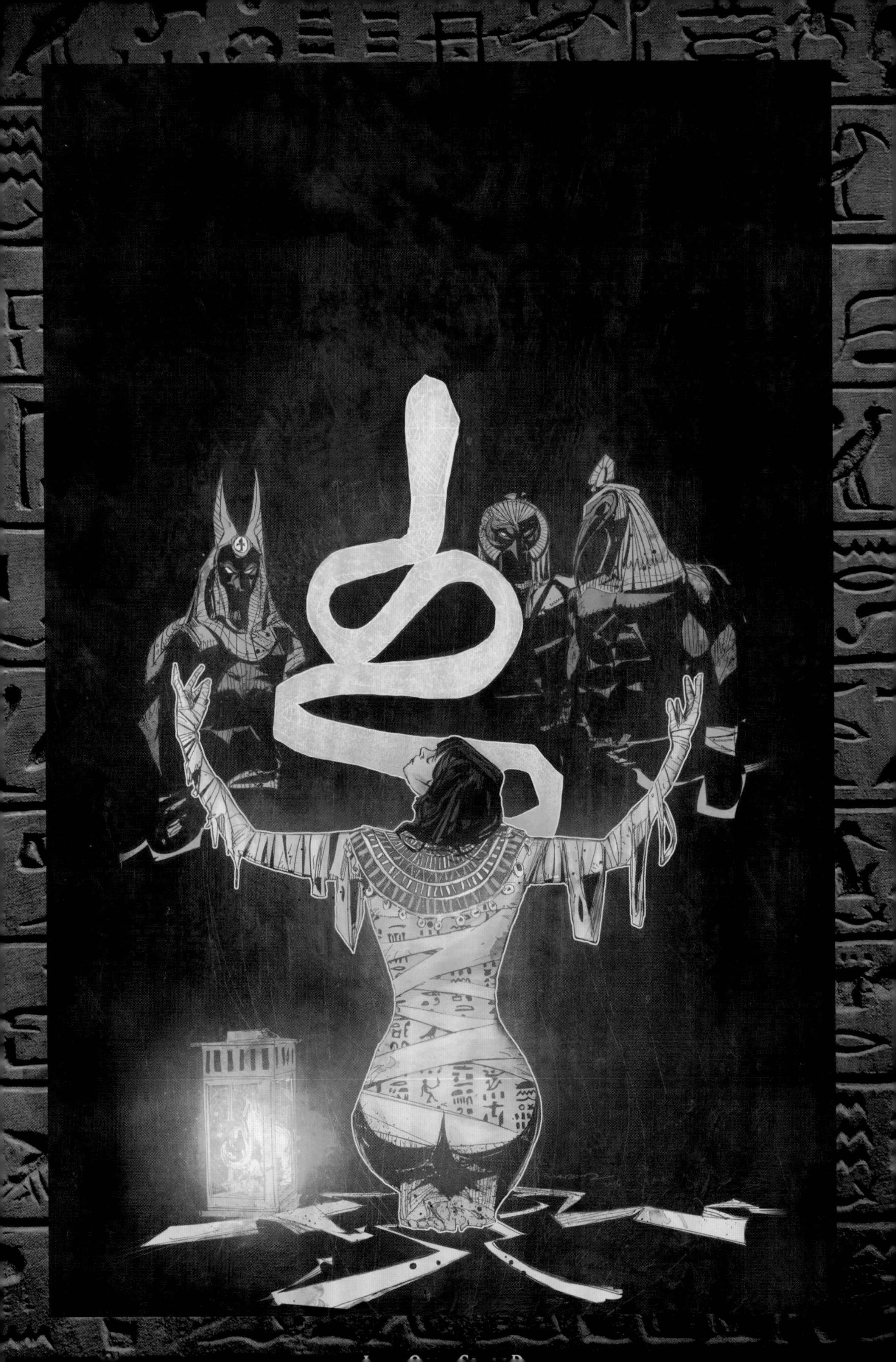

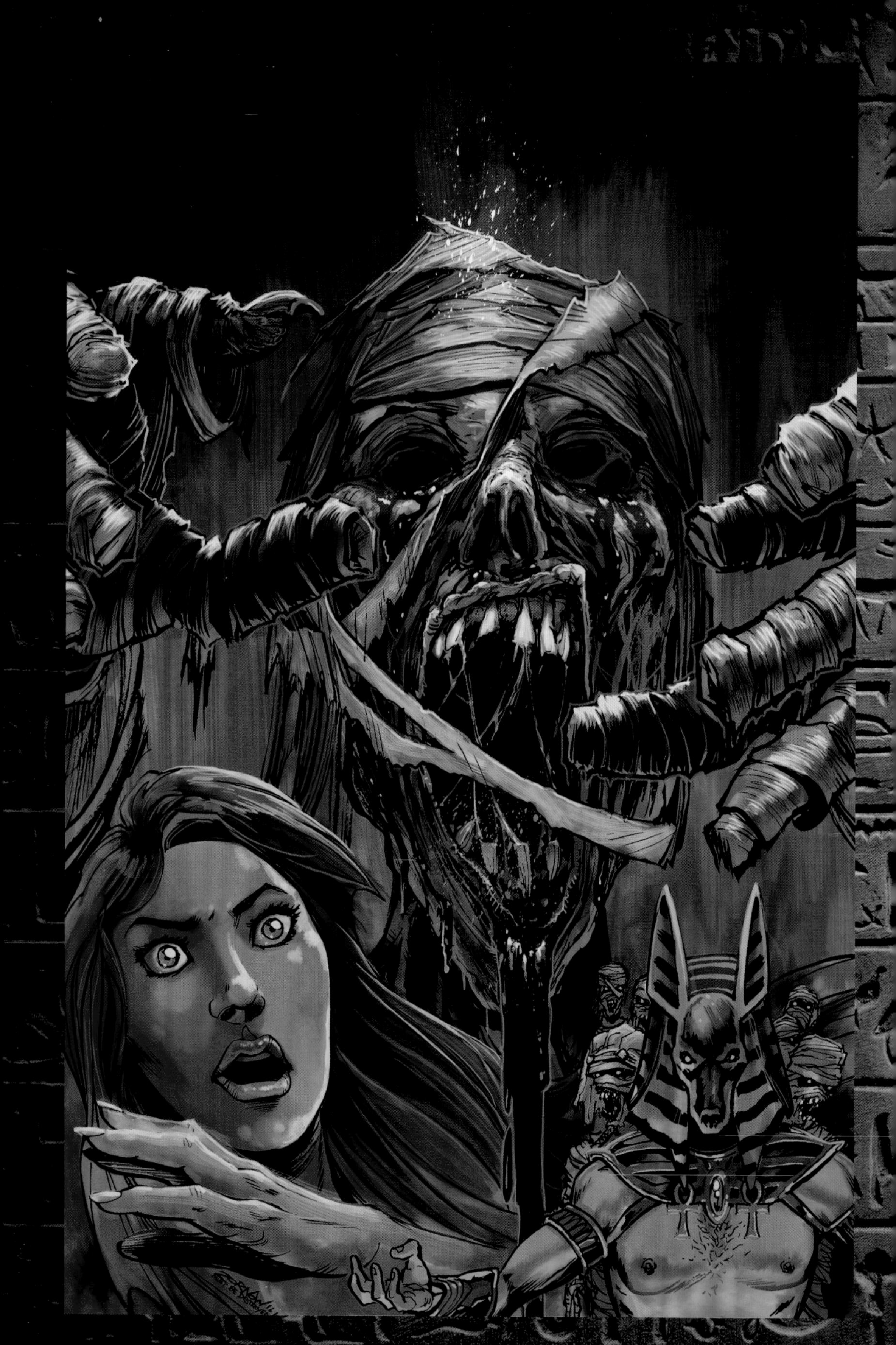

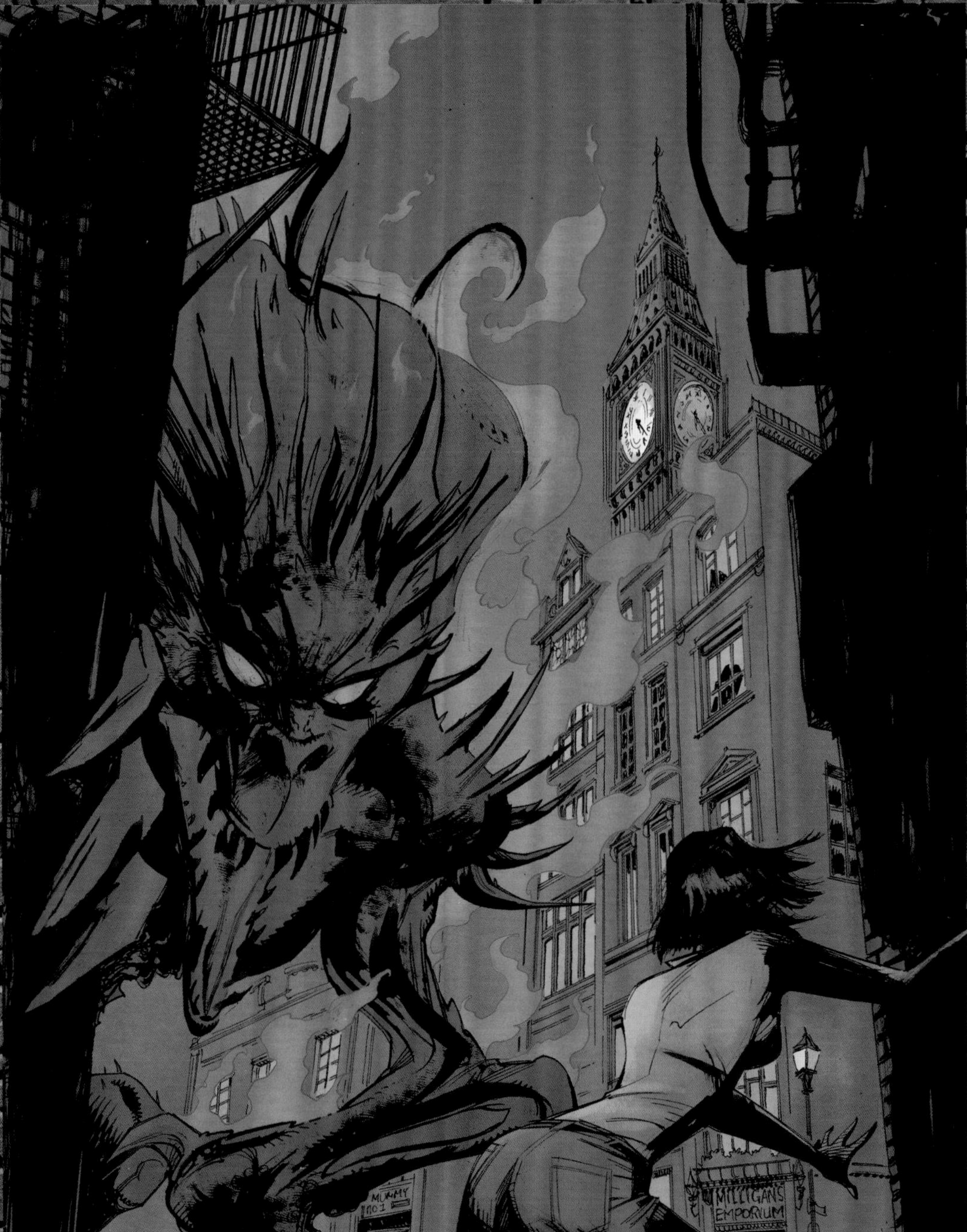
MILLIGAN'S
EMPORIUM

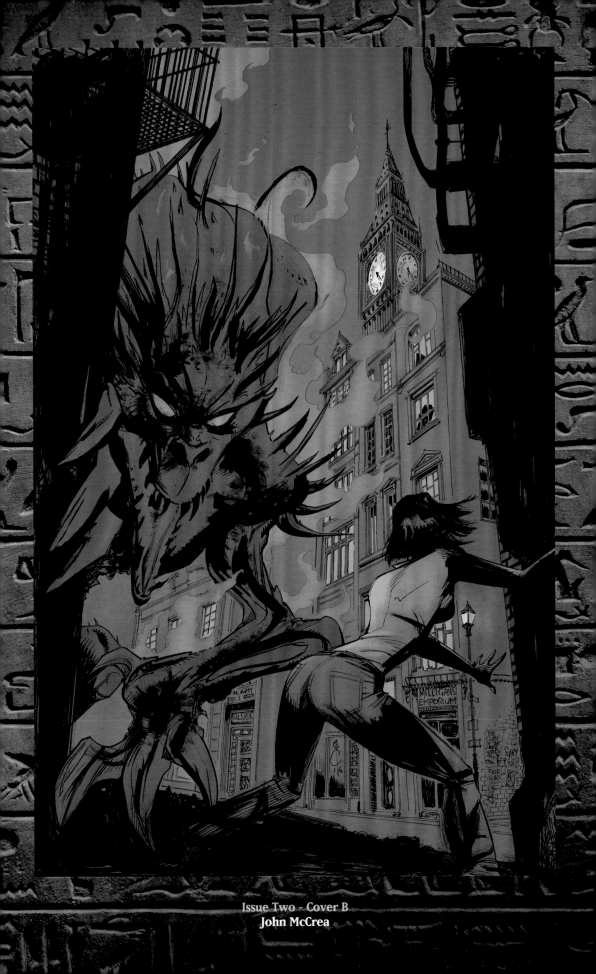

Issue Two - Cover B
John McCrea

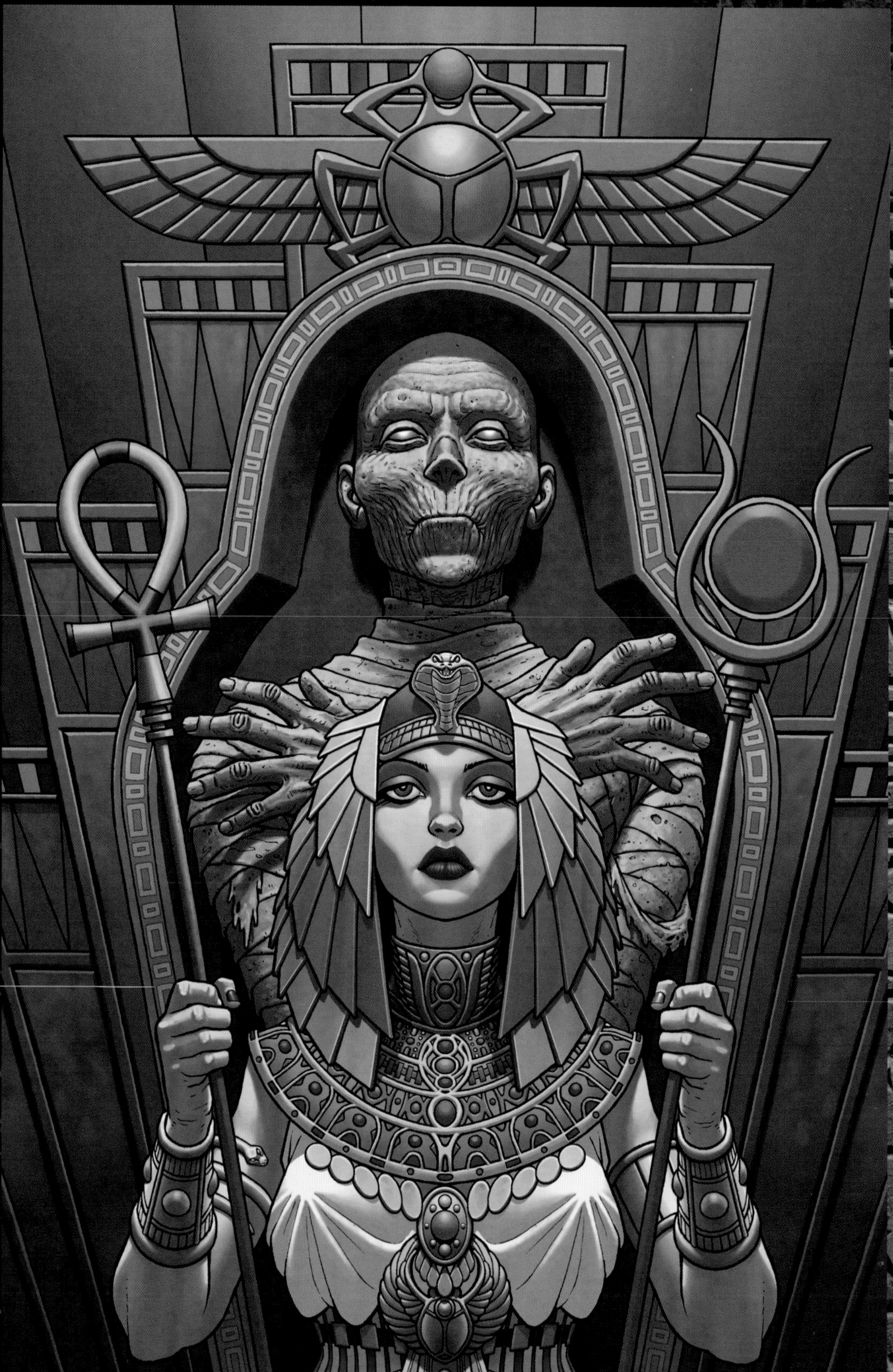

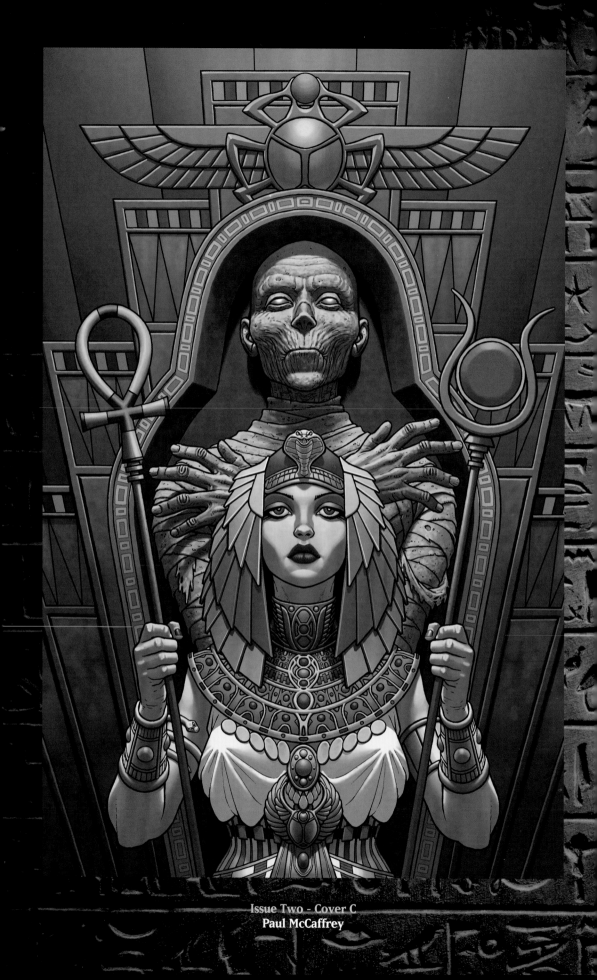

Issue Two - Cover C
Paul McCaffrey

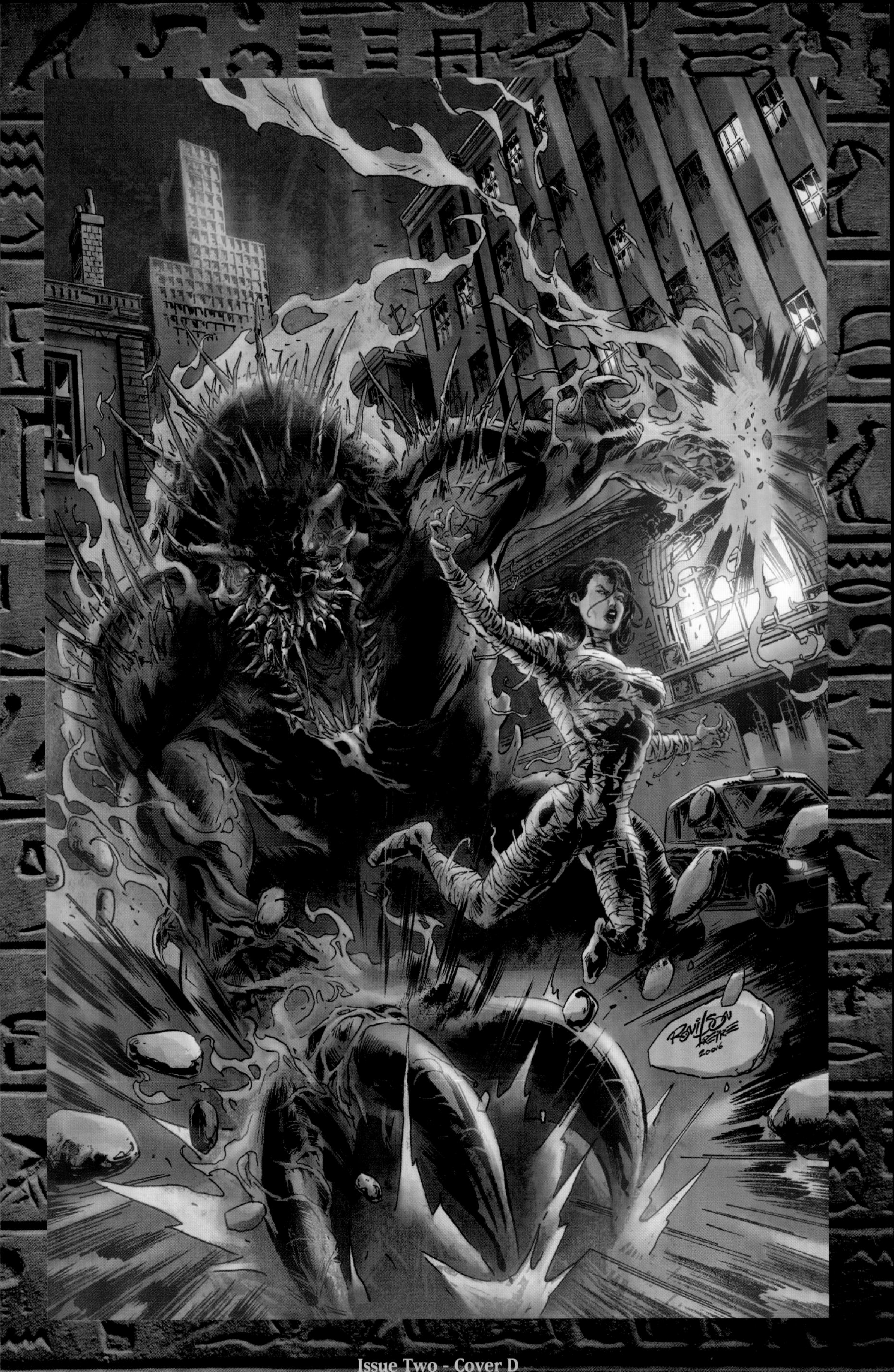
RONILSON FREIRE 2006

Issue Two - Cover D
Ronilson Freire

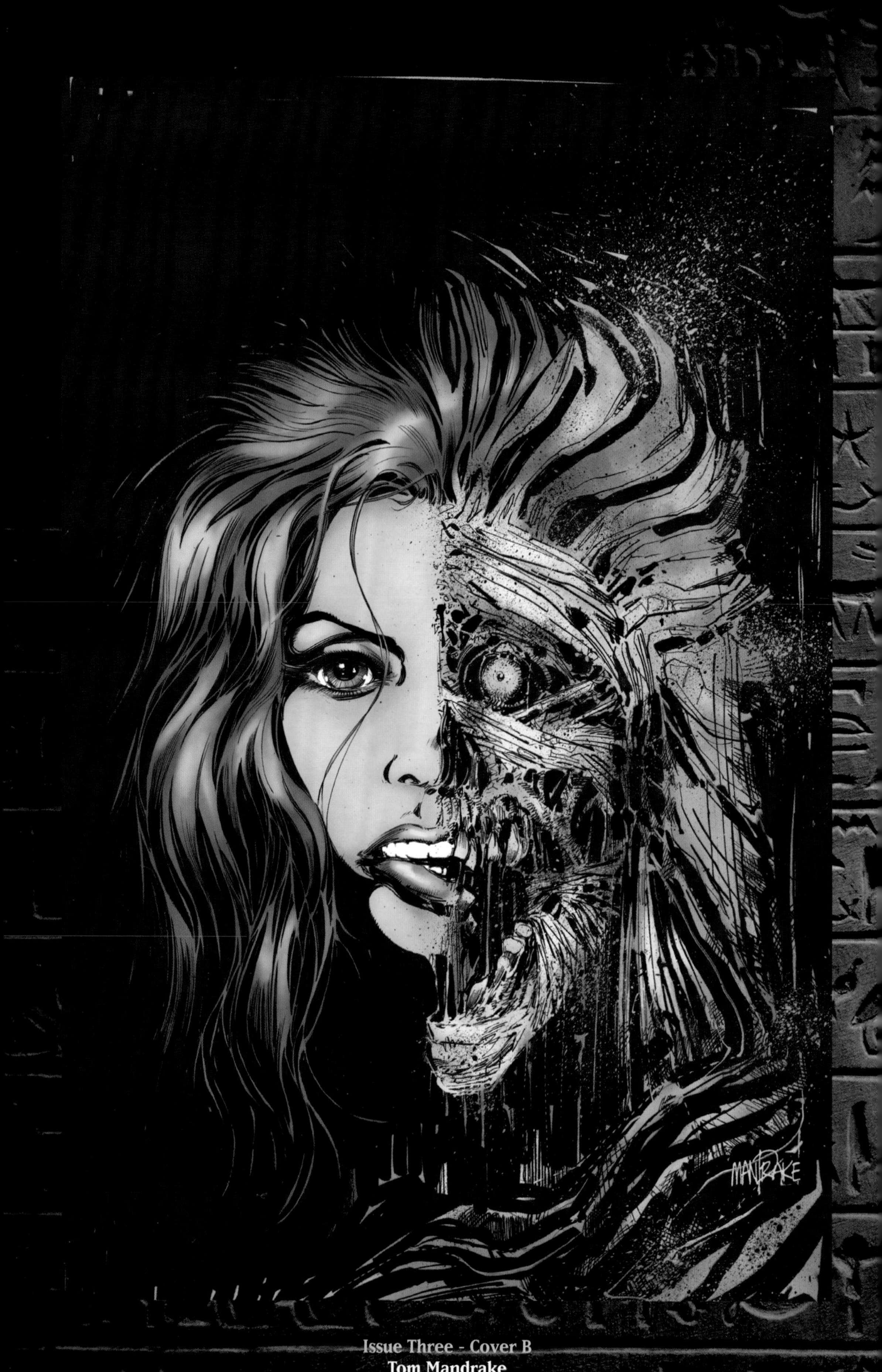
MANDRAKE

Issue Three - Cover B
Tom Mandrake

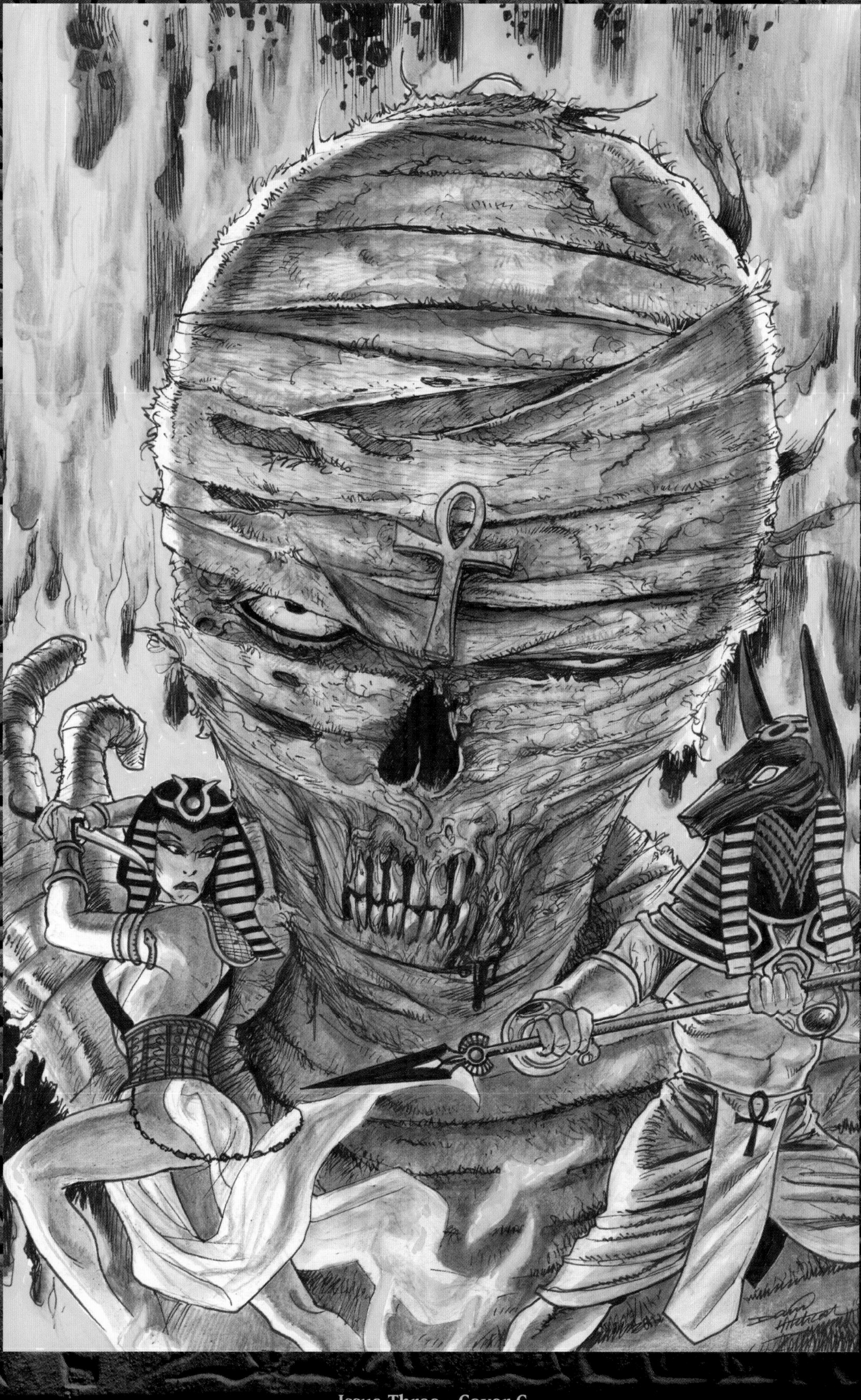

Issue Three - Cover C
DavId Hitchcock

Issue Four - Cover B
Nick Percival

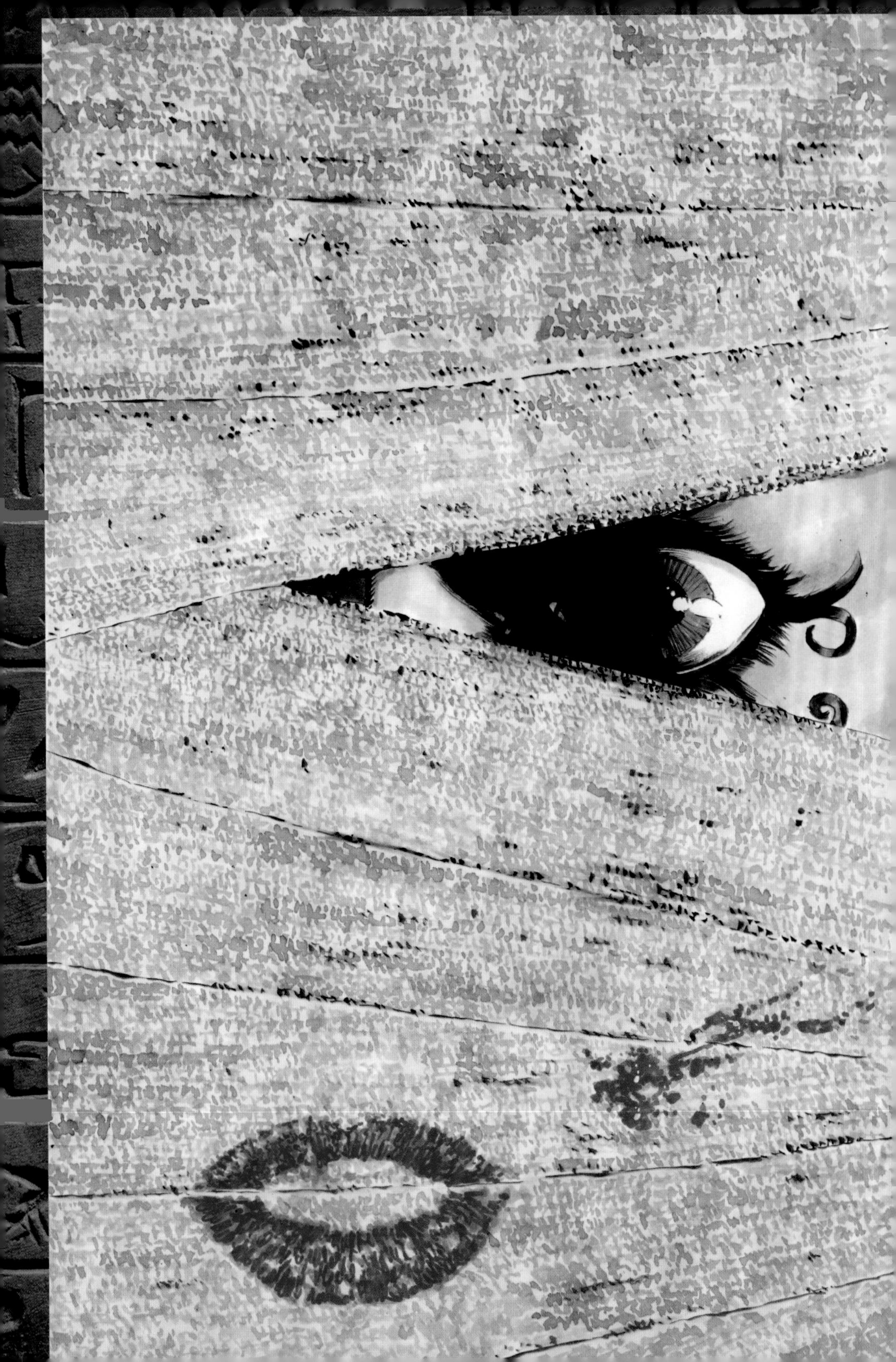

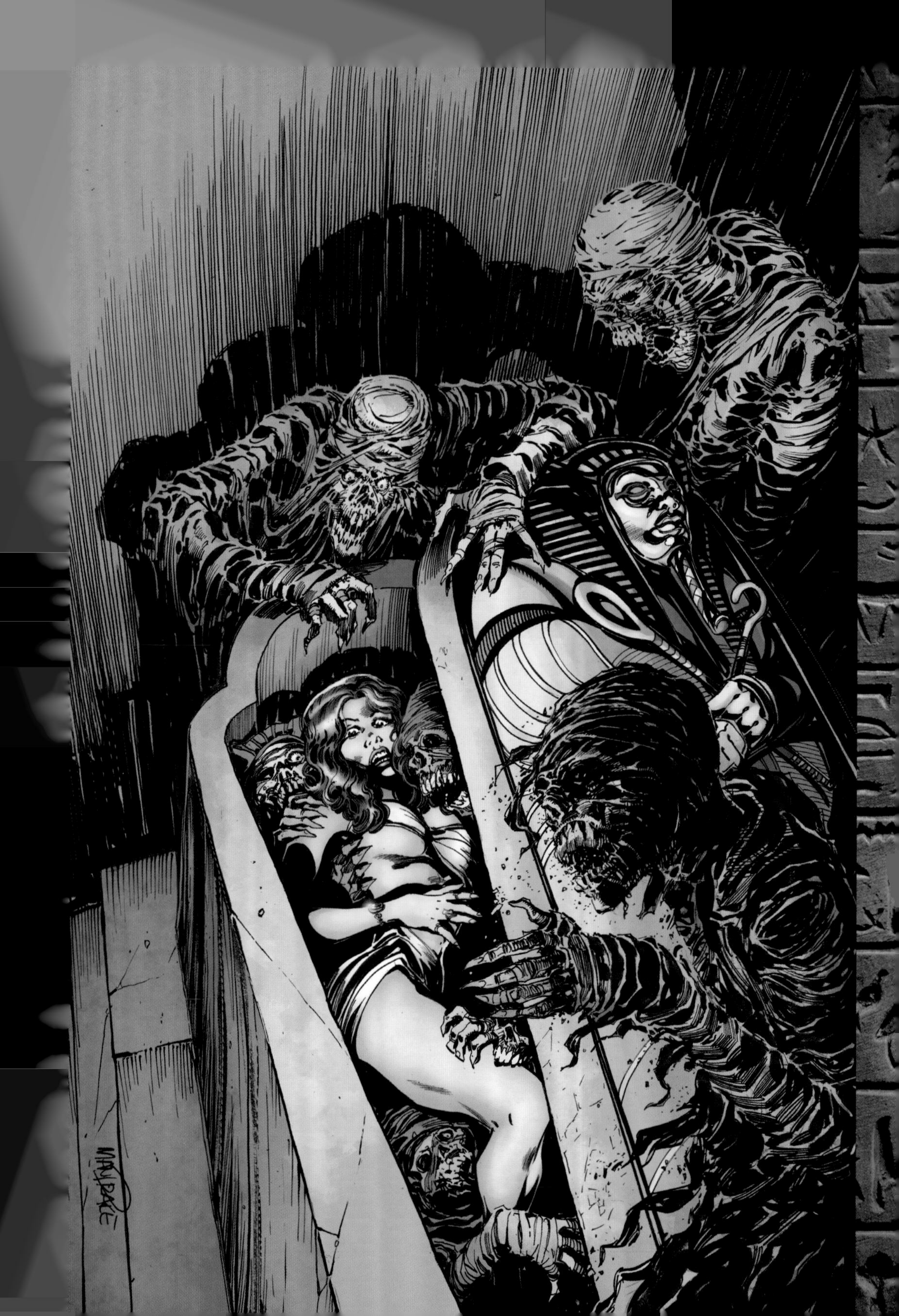

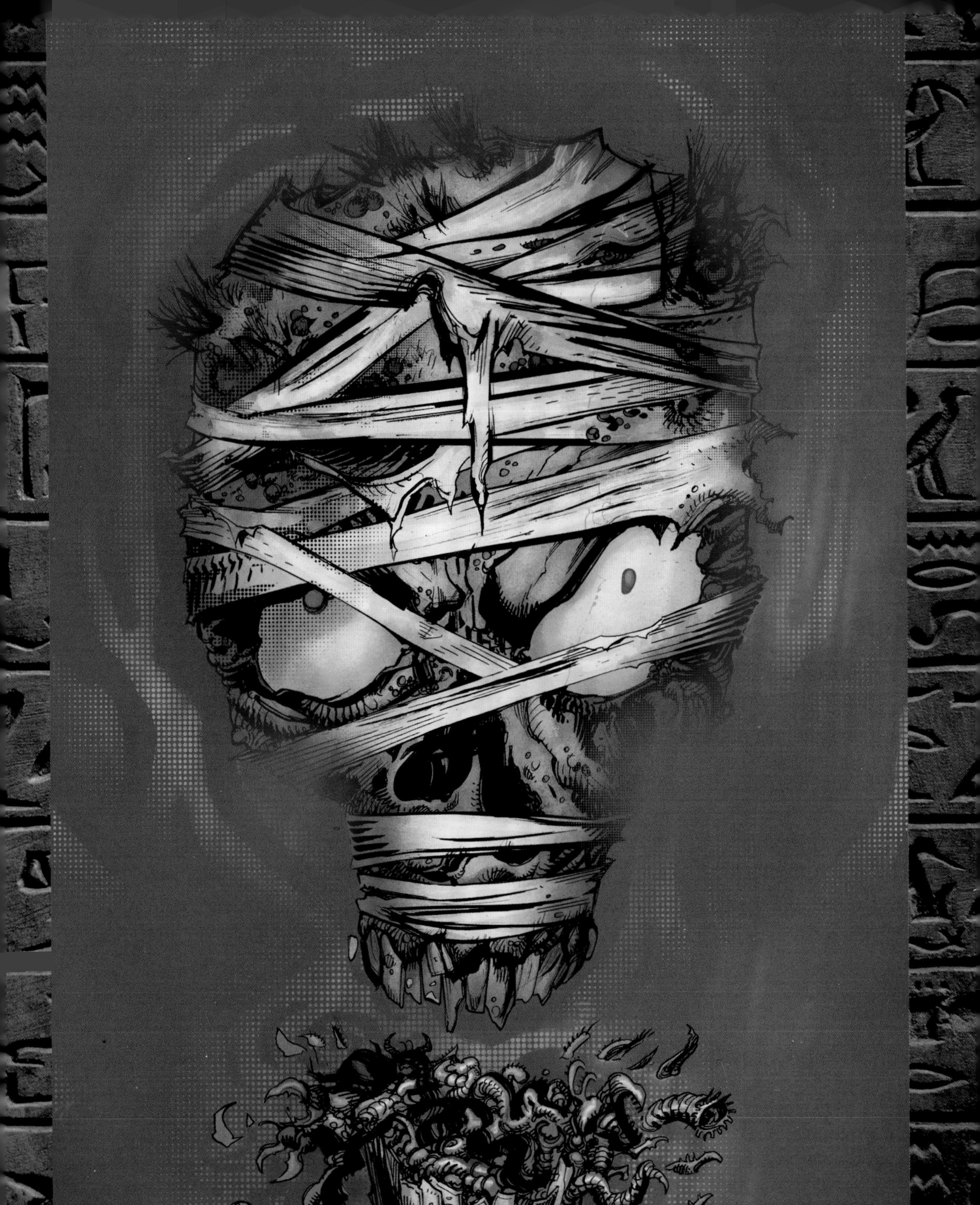

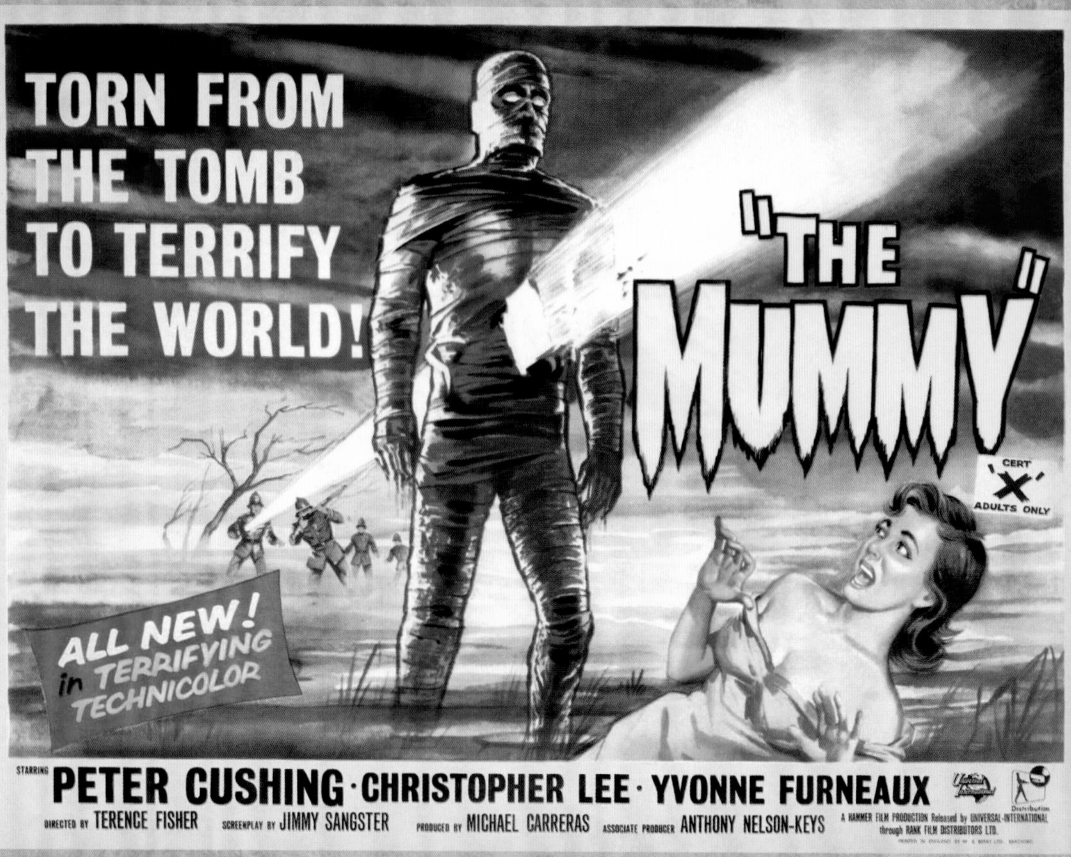
TORN FROM THE TOMB TO TERRIFY THE WORLD!
"THE MUMMY"
CERT 'X' ADULTS ONLY
ALL NEW! in TERRIFYING TECHNICOLOR
STARRING PETER CUSHING · CHRISTOPHER LEE · YVONNE FURNEAUX
DIRECTED BY TERENCE FISHER
SCREENPLAY BY JIMMY SANGSTER
PRODUCED BY MICHAEL CARRERAS
ASSOCIATE PRODUCER ANTHONY NELSON-KEYS
A HAMMER FILM PRODUCTION Released by UNIVERSAL-INTERNATIONAL through RANK FILM DISTRIBUTORS LTD.

THE MUMMY

Hammer Films' historian Marcus Hearn describes how the company's tomb-raiding producers reinvented a legend.

The 1959 film *The Mummy* is a cornerstone of Hammer horror.

Some critics maintain that Hammer built its formidable reputation by producing colour remakes of Universal's black-and-white classics. Although this is a lazy misrepresentation of the British company's unique style – which owed far more to Gainsborough's bodice rippers than Universal's monster movies – Hammer's *The Mummy* undoubtedly owes a significant debt to its American forebears.

Hammer's *Dracula* was a huge success when Universal distributed the film across America in 1958. Universal executive Al Daff invited the film's stars, Peter Cushing and Christopher Lee, along with members of Hammer's board, to a meeting in his New York office, where he told them that Dracula had saved his company from bankruptcy. The story seems highly unlikely, but Daff's gratitude was genuine – Hammer was offered a new distribution partnership, with permission to adapt any of Universal's renowned horror subjects.

The public had become fascinated by Egyptology – and

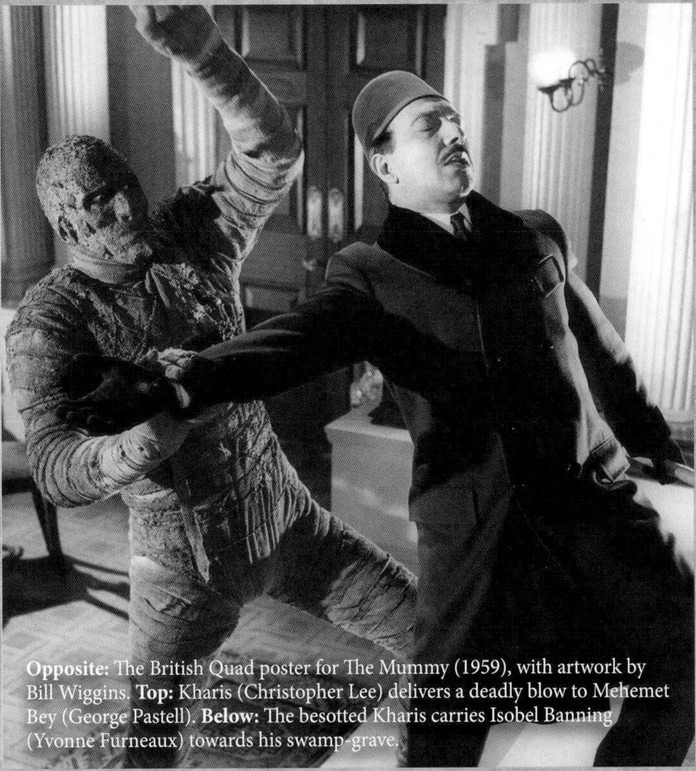

Opposite: The British Quad poster for The Mummy (1959), with artwork by Bill Wiggins. **Top:** Kharis (Christopher Lee) delivers a deadly blow to Mehemet Bey (George Pastell). **Below:** The besotted Kharis carries Isobel Banning (Yvonne Furneaux) towards his swamp-grave.

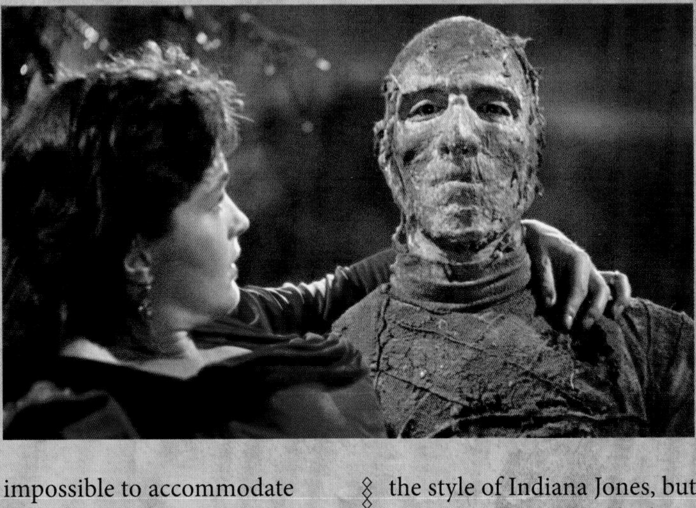

the curses that supposedly plagued its practitioners – following Howard Carter's sensational discovery of Tutankhamun's tomb in 1922. This fascination was most prominently exploited by Universal, who began its Mummy series with Boris Karloff in the title role. For its initial film Hammer would not only plunder *The Mummy* (1932), but take additional inspiration from three subsequent Universal pictures: *The Mummy's Hand* (1940), *The Mummy's Ghost* (1944) and *The Mummy's Curse* (1944).

In the late 1950s creative control of Hammer fell to just two executive producers, Anthony Hinds and Michael Carreras. Hinds had overseen *The Curse of Frankenstein* (1957) and *Dracula*, the films where the company had perfected its controversial 'sex and death' formula, elevating Cushing and Lee to the status of international stars. Now steeped in literary Gothic, Hinds had less enthusiasm for Universal's more recent cinematic traditions.

The job of producing *The Mummy* therefore went to Carreras, who saw it as an opportunity to broaden the potentially restrictive parameters of Hammer horror. Under Carreras' guidance, screenwriter Jimmy Sangster, director Terence Fisher, production designer Bernard Robinson and cinematographer Jack Asher evoked Hollywood's biblical epics wherever the budget would allow. Composer Franz Reizenstein employed a choir to heighten the drama of his score, and the opening tomb sequence was filmed at Shepperton when it proved impossible to accommodate the pyrotechnic effects needed at Hammer's relatively modest Bray Studios.

Despite his ambitions to diversify, Carreras never lost sight of the fact that *The Mummy* was aimed squarely at the audience for X-rated Hammer horror. Hollywood now regards the Mummy as a vehicle for archaeological adventures in the style of Indiana Jones, but Hammer's film presents the undead Kharis as a ruthless, neck-breaking serial killer. Lee referred to the character as a "bandaged juggernaut", but was equally adept at conveying Kharis' underlying tragedy using little more than his eyes.

A spent force at Universal, the Mummy had found new life at Hammer.

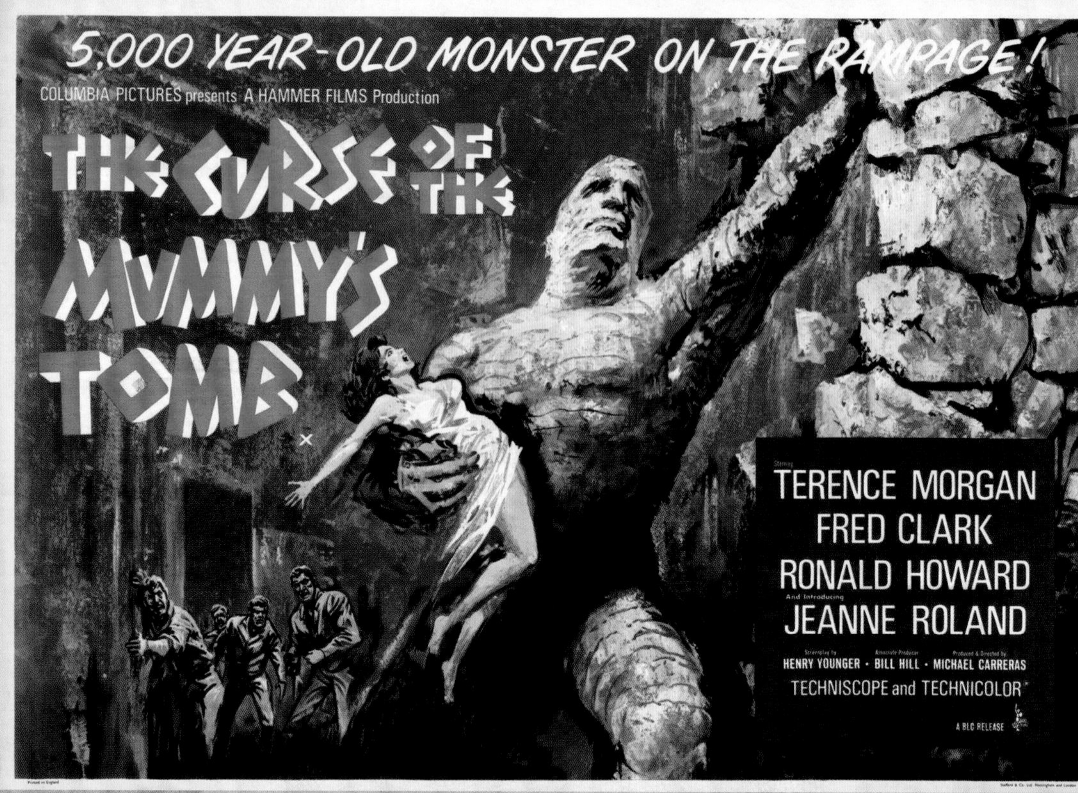
5,000 YEAR-OLD MONSTER ON THE RAMPAGE!
COLUMBIA PICTURES presents A HAMMER FILMS Production
THE CURSE OF THE MUMMY'S TOMB
TERENCE MORGAN
FRED CLARK
RONALD HOWARD
And Introducing
JEANNE ROLAND
HENRY YOUNGER · BILL HILL · MICHAEL CARRERAS
TECHNISCOPE and TECHNICOLOR
A BLC RELEASE

THE CURSE OF THE MUMMY'S TOMB

Hammer's historian Marcus Hearn goes behind the scenes on the gruesome 1964 follow-up to *The Mummy*.

Although renowned as one of Britain's greatest independent production companies, from the mid-1950s to the late 1960s Hammer was totally reliant on distribution from major American studios. *The Mummy*, released in 1959, had been made in partnership with Universal. The film's belated follow-up was offered to the same distributor in 1963, but *The Curse of the Mummy's Tomb* would eventually be produced for Columbia the following year.

Since overseeing *The Mummy*, producer Michael Carreras had left Hammer, disillusioned by the company's increasing reliance on horror films. He was lured back by the opportunity to direct a mummy film, as this was the only part of Hammer's traditional Gothic canon that held any allure for him. Carreras wrote the script for *The Curse of the Mummy's Tomb* as well, working alongside television director Alvin Rakoff under the pseudonym 'Henry Younger' – a joke at the expense of Hammer's executive producer Anthony Hinds, who frequently adopted the on-screen credit 'John Elder'.

Carreras and Rakoff unashamedly reprised the vengeful, serial-killing scenario of the previous film and the Universal classics, packing in so much sadistic violence that the British Board of Film Censors ordered a long list of cuts to the script before a single frame had been shot. The Board was particularly alarmed by the story's preoccupation with dismemberment, and changes would be made to numerous scenes featuring severed hands. Towards the end of the screenplay, the Board observed that, "Adam wrenches the remains of his crushed arm from the crack and falls backwards screaming into the whirling waters of the sewers... we really do not want to see hands coming off, bleeding stumps, etc."

It was in Hammer's interests to comply with the BBFC, as it was more economical to censor a film at this stage than to waste expensive footage on scenes that would only be cut later. *The Curse of the Mummy's Tomb* relied on its murder sequences, however, and Carreras was able to retain at least some of his original intentions when he shot the film in Techniscope widescreen at Elstree Studios from February to March 1964.

The Curse of the Mummy's Tomb was budgeted at little over £100,000 and lacked star names, but its solid cast included Terence Morgan (as Adam Beauchamp) and American comedy actor Fred Clark (as Alexander King). Hammer favorites George Pastell and Michael Ripper were retained from *The Mummy*, albeit in different parts. The little-known Dickie Owen played the

Opposite: Hammer's original pitch to Universal included a rampaging 20-foot mummy, but this idea only survived in the film's uncredited poster artwork. **Top:** Archaeologist Dubois (Bernard Rebel) is captured in the (Elstree Studios) desert. **Below:** Producer, director and co-writer Michael Carreras (right) with the film's technical adviser, Egyptologist Andrew Low.

Photos © Hammer Film Productions/Columbia Pictures.

mummy, Ra-Antef, Christopher Lee having long since eschewed such heavily disguised roles.

Despite its relatively modest ambitions, *The Curse of the Mummy's Tomb* was a sizeable hit when released as the lower half of a double-bill with *The Gorgon* in October 1964. Hammer wouldn't leave it quite so long before visiting the tombs of Egypt for a third time.

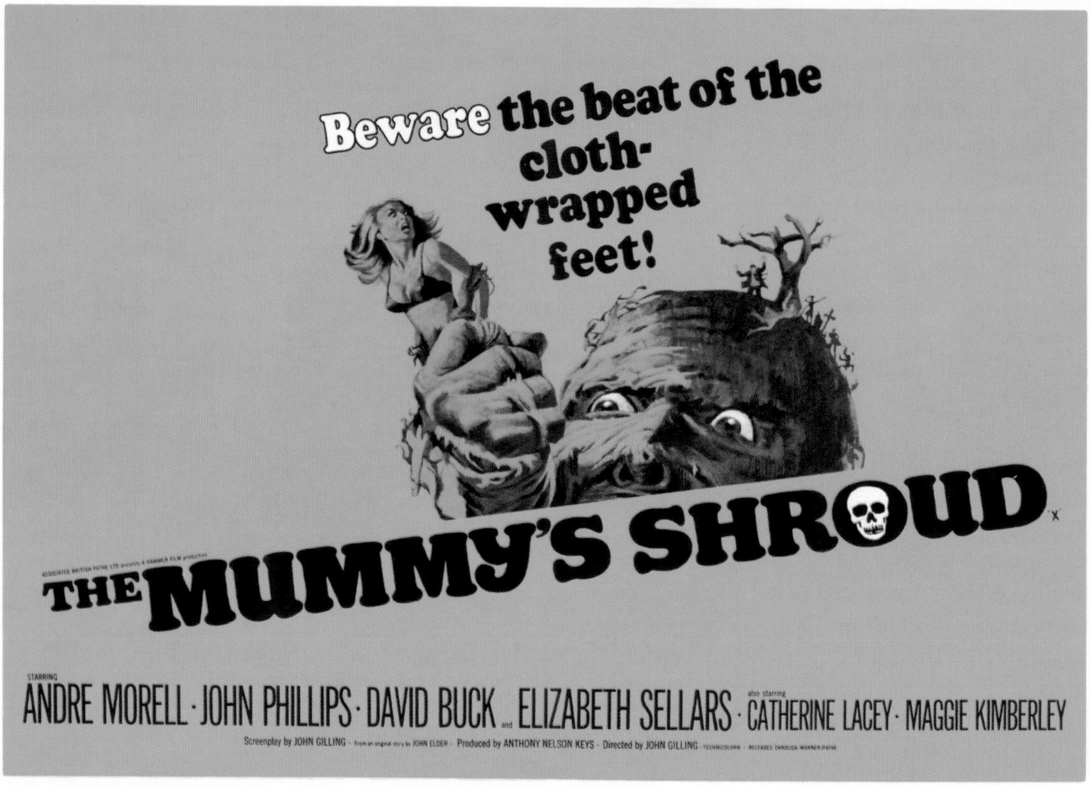
Beware the beat of the cloth-wrapped feet!
THE MUMMY'S SHROUD
'X'
STARRING
ANDRE MORELL · JOHN PHILLIPS · DAVID BUCK and ELIZABETH SELLARS · also starring CATHERINE LACEY · MAGGIE KIMBERLEY
Screenplay by JOHN GILLING · Produced by ANTHONY NELSON KEYS · Directed by JOHN GILLING

THE MUMMY'S SHROUD

Hammer historian Marcus Hearn describes how production of the company's third mummy film marked the end of an era.

In 1966, Hammer's executive producer Anthony Hinds devised the story of *The Mummy's Shroud* before handing the project over to John Gilling. Although unpopular with Hammer executives and certain actors, the abrasive Gilling was an inventive writer/director who had already delivered some of the company's finest films of the decade, including *The Pirates of Blood River* (1962) and *The Plague of the Zombies* (1966).

Gilling assembled a fine ensemble cast led by *Plague*'s André Morell as ill-fated archaeologist Sir Basil Walden. Prem, the devoted slave of boy Pharaoh Kah-to-Bey, was portrayed by two actors. Dickie Owen, who had been the mummy in *The Curse of the Mummy's Tomb* (1964), played Prem in the film's lengthy flashback, while Eddie Powell – who had doubled for Christopher Lee in *The Mummy* (1959) – was cast as Prem in his mummified form.

The Mummy's Shroud is notable for giving Michael Ripper, Hammer's most prolific actor, one of his most prominent

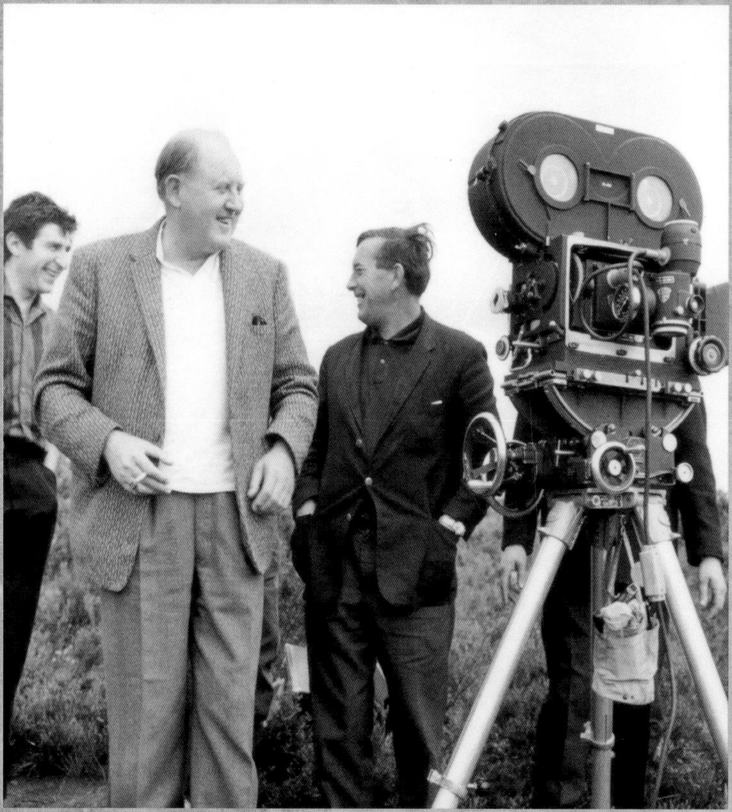

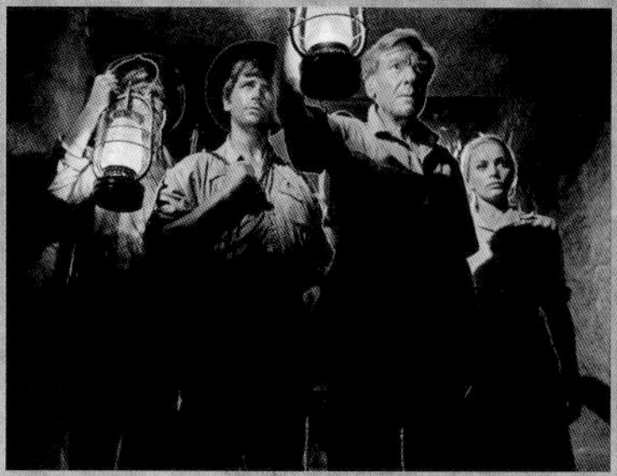

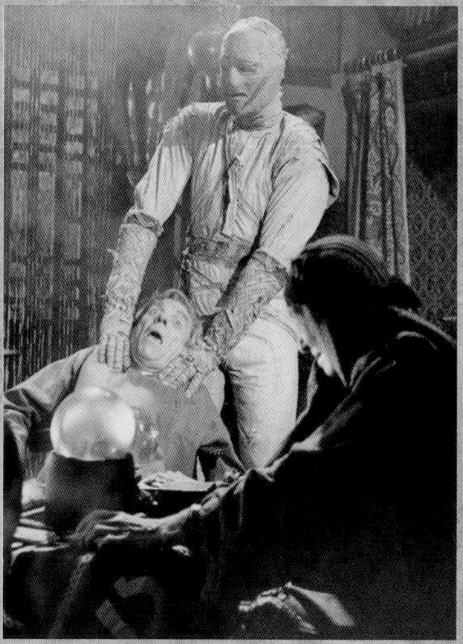

Opposite: UK Quad poster for *The Mummy's Shroud*. **Above left:** Writer/director John Gilling (center), pictured in 1965. **Top Right:** Harry (Tim Barrett), Paul Preston (David Buck), Sir Basil Walden (André Morell) and Claire de Sangre (Maggie Kimberley) explore the tomb. **Above right:** Sir Basil becomes the first, but not last of Prem's victims.

roles. Ripper had played a poacher in *The Mummy* and a nightwatchman in *The Curse of the Mummy's Tomb*, but he emerged from the ranks of Hammer's bit-part players to portray the downtrodden Longbarrow. Ripper's sympathetic portrayal of the myopic press officer makes the character's demise – defenestrated by the pitiless mummy – all the more affecting.

At the end of the film, linguist Claire de Sangre (Maggie Kimberley) recites the "words of death" that prompt the mummy to claw at its face until it disintegrates into a pile of dust, bone and bandages. Filmed at the Slough studio of special effects designer Les Bowie, this is one of the few Hammer sequences that can rival the climax of *Dracula* (1958) for its technical accomplishment.

The Mummy's Shroud would prove to be Gilling's final film for Hammer, ending a long association that began when he served as an assistant director on *The Mystery of the Mary Celeste* in 1935. This was also the last film that Hammer completed at Bray Studios, the legendary Thameside facility that had been its production base for 15 years. By a strange coincidence, actress Elizabeth Sellars (who played Barbara Preston) had only previously worked for Hammer in the first film shot at Bray Studios, 1951's *Cloudburst*.

Shooting on *The Mummy's Shroud* came to an end on 21 October 1966, after which Hammer largely relocated to Elstree Studios in Borehamwood. Many fans and critics believe that when Hammer left Bray, its films lost a quality that would prove irreplaceable.

The Mummy's Shroud was released as the support feature to *Frankenstein Created Woman* in May 1967. The double-bill's protagonists may have been familiar, but Hammer's marketing moved with the times by referencing what was then known as 'beat music' in the poster's memorable tagline.

In later years, Gilling expressed satisfaction with Michael Ripper's contribution, but felt that the "worn-out" theme of mummy films compromised much of the picture. Hammer's fourth, and to date final, exploitation of that theme would ring the changes.

BLOOD FROM THE MUMMY'S TOMB

Hammer's fourth, and to date final, Egyptian film was beset by tragedy, as Marcus Hearn describes...

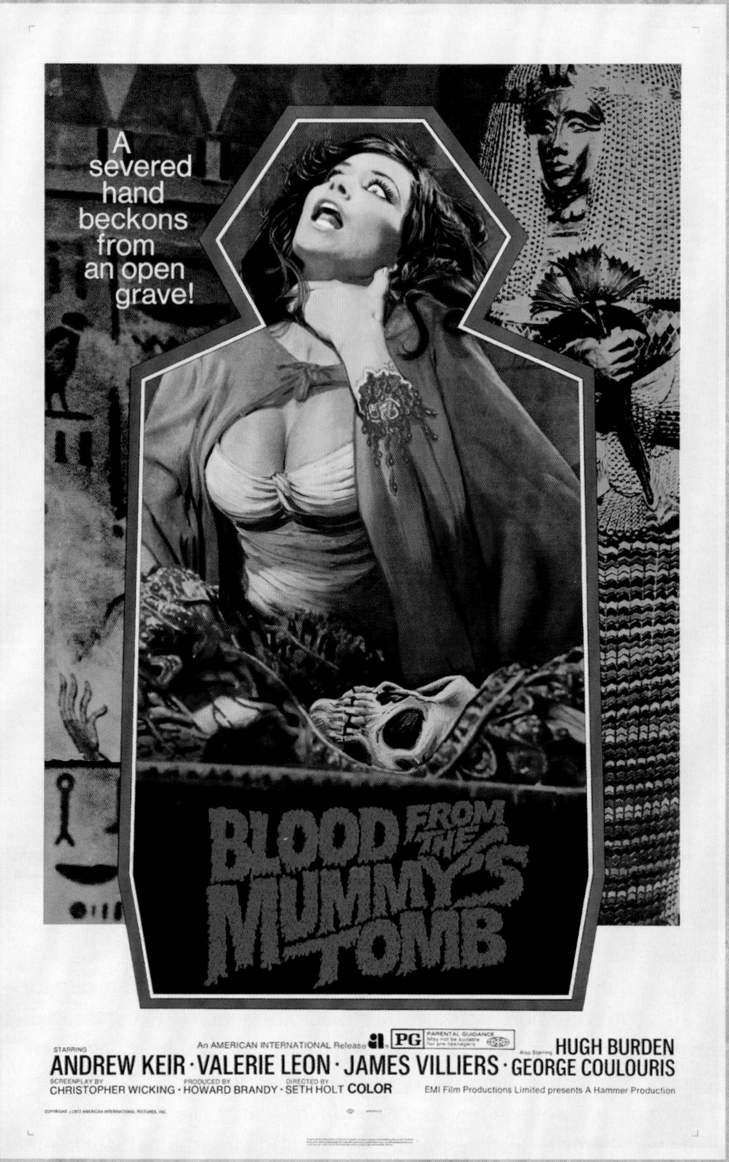
A severed hand beckons from an open grave!
BLOOD FROM THE MUMMY'S TOMB
An AMERICAN INTERNATIONAL Release
PG PARENTAL GUIDANCE May not be suitable for pre-teenagers
STARRING
ANDREW KEIR · VALERIE LEON · JAMES VILLIERS · GEORGE COULOURIS
Also Starring HUGH BURDEN
SCREENPLAY BY CHRISTOPHER WICKING · PRODUCED BY HOWARD BRANDY · DIRECTED BY SETH HOLT COLOR
EMI Film Productions Limited presents A Hammer Production

Michael Carreras, the executive producer who had been responsible for Hammer's first two mummy films, returned to the fold at the beginning of 1971 as the company's new managing director. The first ongoing project he inherited was *Blood From the Mummy's Tomb*, which entered production at Elstree Studios on 11 January. Produced by American publicist Howard Brandy and written by Christopher Wicking, the film was an adaptation of Bram Stoker's 1903 novel *The Jewel of Seven Stars*. *Blood From the Mummy's Tomb* is unusual for not actually featuring a lumbering mummy as its protagonist, but remains chiefly notable for being the most troubled film in Hammer's long history.

Things got off to a difficult start when a dispute between Wicking and Brandy led to the writer being banned from the set. In order to continue work on the screenplay, Wicking was forced to meet the director, Seth Holt, in the evenings after shooting. Holt had been an acclaimed editor at Ealing Studios in the 1950s before embarking on a sporadic career as a director. His black-and-white films *Taste of Fear* (1961) and *The Nanny* (1965) are widely regarded as two of the best thrillers Hammer made, but other companies seemed wary of Holt's reputation as an alcoholic. By the time he was commissioned to direct *Blood From the Mummy's Tomb* in 1970, Holt hadn't completed a picture for nearly three years.

Hammer stalwart Peter Cushing led the cast as Professor Julian Fuchs, the scheming archaeologist whose daughter Margaret (Valerie Leon) is haunted by Tera, an ancient Egyptian sorceress she uncannily resembles.

Cushing had only completed

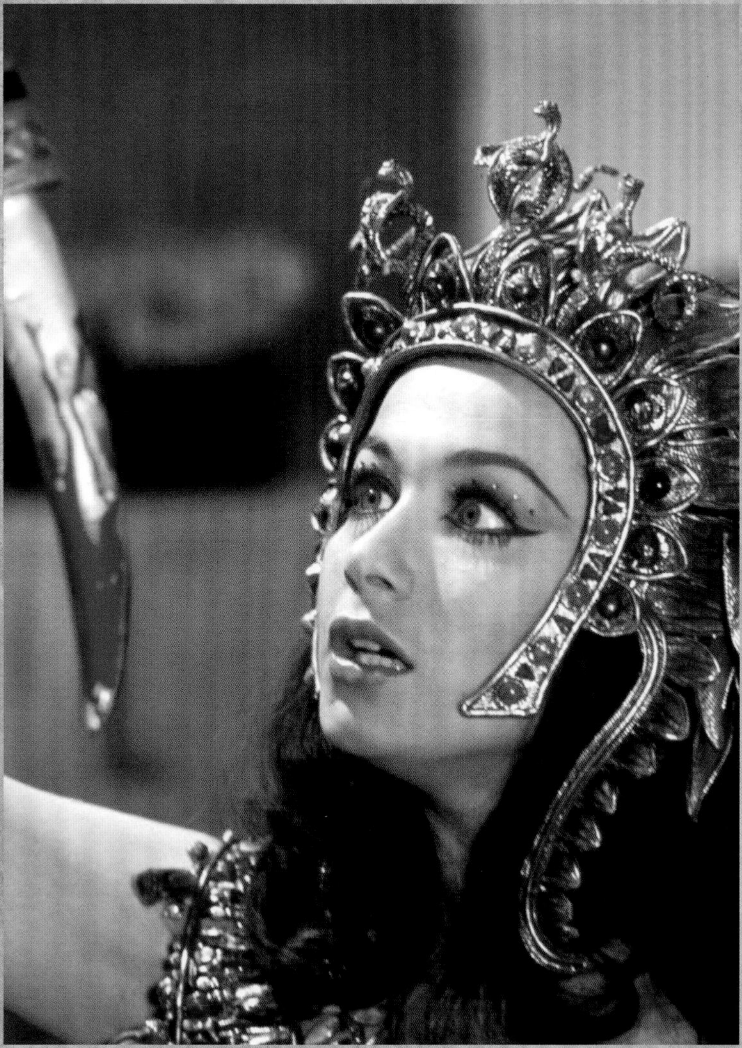

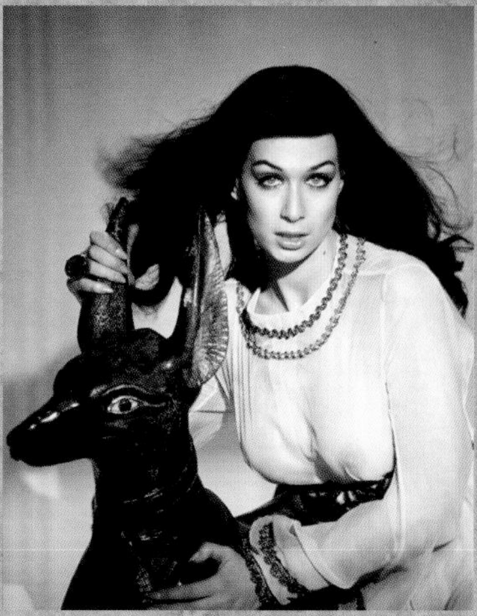

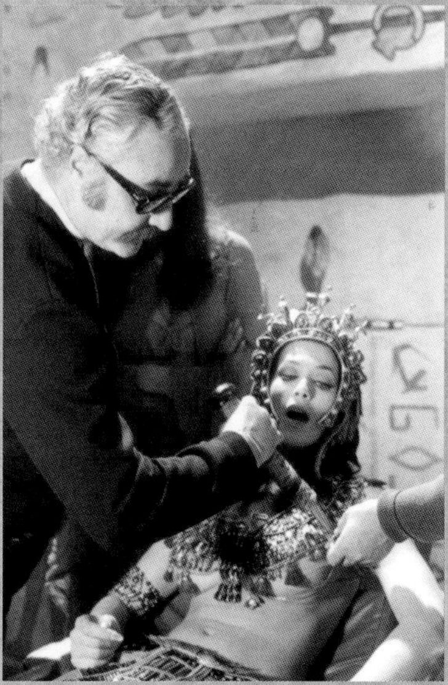

Opposite: The film's US one-sheet poster. **Above left:** Valerie Leon in *Blood From the Mummy's Tomb*. **Top Right:** A publicity shot of Valerie Leon, in her first starring role as Margaret/Tera. **Above right:** Michael Carreras took over as director following Seth Holt's sudden death.

one day's filming when his wife was taken to hospital, suffering from emphysema. He immediately left the production, and was with Helen when she died on 14 January. He never recovered from the loss. Cushing's footage was abandoned and Andrew Keir, who had previously starred in Hammer's *Quatermass and the Pit* (1967), assumed the role at very short notice.

Keir was also taken to hospital when he suffered an accident on set during his first day, and Leon was subsequently given time off because she fell ill. Soon after, a member of the art department was killed in a motorbike accident, but this wasn't the last of the film's tragedies. Around four weeks into shooting it became noticeable to the cast and crew that Seth Holt had developed a chronic bout of hiccups. This continued until the evening of Saturday 14 February, when Holt suffered a heart attack and died. He was 47.

Faced with another crisis, Michael Carreras had no alternative but to complete the picture himself. He arrived at Elstree on Monday morning, at times struggling to discern Holt's intentions from the remaining script pages and fragmented rushes he had left behind.

Blood From the Mummy's Tomb premiered at the National Film Theatre on 7 October 1971. Recognised at the time as an unconventional Hammer horror, it challenged both a traditional formula and what some have described as its very own curse.

TO LIVE AGAIN: THE MUMMY AS CULTURAL ICON

Egyptologist John J. Johnston considers the literary history of Egypt's ancient dead across more than 2,000 years...

Somewhat unexpectedly, the first 'living' mummy in fiction hails from ancient Egypt. Papyrus Cairo 30646, dating from the Egypt's Ptolemaic period (332 – 31 BC), recounts the tale of Setne Khaemwase, a real figure who had lived several centuries earlier. In his fictional search for a book of spells, Khaemwase enters the ancient tomb of the sorcerer-prince, Na-nefer-ka-

Ptah. Unhappy at this intrusion, the deceased man challenges Khaemwase to play a potentially lethal version of the ancient boardgame, Senet. In keeping with Egyptian religious beliefs, the dead man is not a bandaged, desiccated corpse but a vigorous immortal, possessed of enormous power.

With Napoleon Bonaparte's 1798 campaign, Egypt and her archaeological splendors began to

be revealed to the West, sparking a fascination with Egyptian art and culture throughout Europe and America. Mummy unrollings, frequently presided over by eminent surgeons, became popular entertainments, both in public lecture halls and at more sophisticated, high-society gatherings.

Consequently, the idea that these ancient mummies might

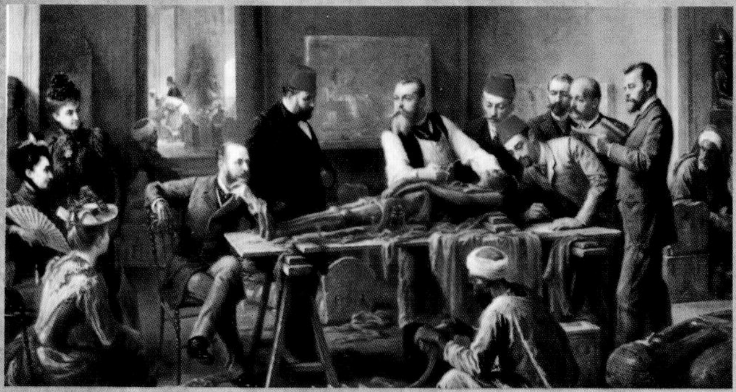

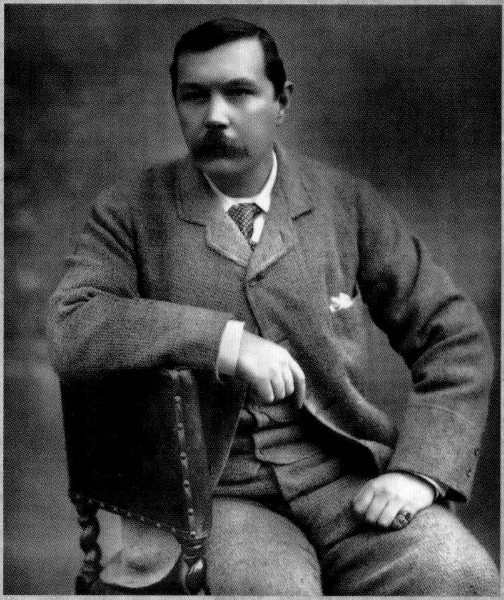

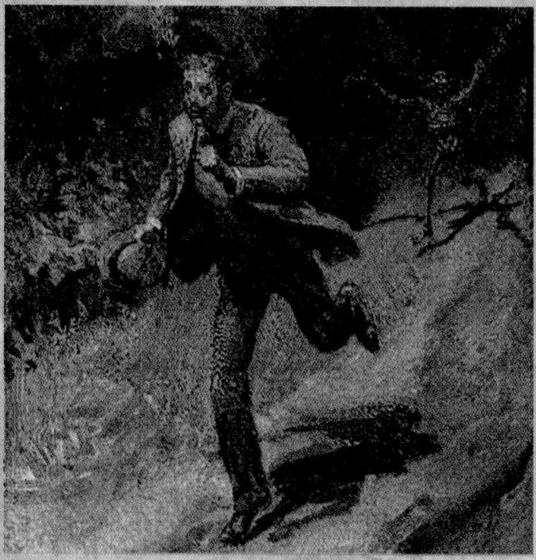

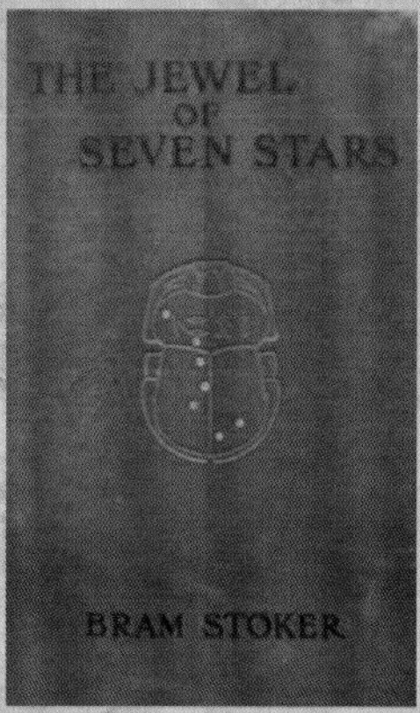
THE JEWEL OF SEVEN STARS
BRAM STOKER

Opposite: Sandstone conglomerate statue of Prince Khaemwase now on display in the British Museum (c. 1260 BC). **Above left:** *Examination of a Mummy - The Priestess of Amun* by Paul Dominique Philippoteaux (c.1895). **Above right:** Arthur Conan Doyle by Herbert Rose Barraud (1893). **Far left:** Illustration from *Lot No. 249* by William Thomas Smedley (September 1892). **Left:** First UK edition of *The Jewel of Seven Stars* (1903).

live again began to grip the imaginations of writers and, in 1827, Jane Webb published her lengthy science fiction satire, *The Mummy!: Or a Tale of the Twenty-Second Century*, in which Cheops, builder of the Great Pyramid, is resurrected at the height of an electrical storm, inspired, no doubt, by Mary Shelley's *Frankenstein*, published only nine years before. However, Cheops, as befitting a king, is no brutal monster but a noble figure, interested in the politics and culture of the 21st Century.

A number of similarly whimsical tales, including Edgar Allen Poe's *Some Words with a Mummy* (1845), were published thereafter, but it was not until 1869 that the first 'cursed' mummy was to appear, in the short story, *Lost in a Pyramid*, written by Louisa May Alcott, renowned as the author of *Little Women* (1868).

Sherlock Holmes' creator Arthur Conan Doyle published two short stories utilising the atmosphere of mystical Egypt: *The Ring of Thoth* in 1890 and *Lot No. 249* in 1892. It is the latter which first presents the mummy as a killer of colossal height and tremendous strength, wrapped in trailing bandages, and revived by a vengeful Egyptologist, adept in ancient magic. The passages detailing the cadaver crashing, tirelessly, through twilit Oxfordshire in pursuit of victims, would provide potent inspiration for later cinematic depictions, most notably Christopher Lee's chilling nocturnal perambulations in Hammer Films' 1959 classic, *The Mummy*.

In 1903, Bram Stoker's novel, *The Jewel of Seven Stars*, presents the beautiful, perfectly preserved sorceress, Tera, who is confined to her coffin and manipulating events to effect her own resurrection. The eerily claustrophobic novel has provided effective inspiration to writers and filmmakers for more than a century.

It was, however, the series of events surrounding Howard Carter's discovery of Tutankhamun's tomb in 1922, which were to fully fire the public imagination. Outside the tomb in the Valley of the Kings, journalist and erstwhile Egyptologist Arthur Weigall concocted the curse tale, which would flourish in the popular press following the unfortunate death, in 1923, of the expedition's patron, Lord Carnarvon. Weigall's companion in the press enclave was John L Balderston, who would go on to write the screenplay for Universal's ground-breaking *The Mummy* (1932), starring Boris Karloff, which in turn would ultimately propel the mummy into the recognizable legendary horror icon it is today.

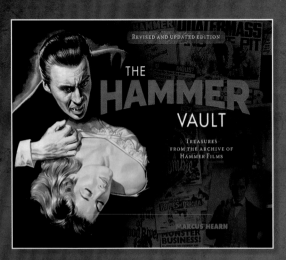

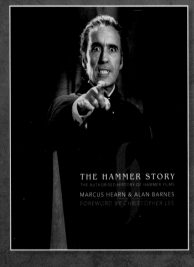